Therapeutic Culture

Jonathan B. Imber
editor

Therapeutic Culture

Triumph and Defeat

Transaction Publishers
New Brunswick (U.S.A.) and London (U.K.)

This book is printed on acid-free paper that meets the American National Standard for Permanence of Paper for Printed Library Materials.

Library of Congress Catalog Number: 2004051649
ISBN: 0-7658-0592-8
Printed in the United States of America

Library of Congress Cataloging-in-Publication Data

Therapeutic culture : triumph and defeat / Jonathan B. Imber, editor
    p. cm.
  "Essays in this volume grew out of a conference held at Boston University in April of 2001 under the auspices of the Institute for the Study of Economic Culture (now the Institute on Culture, Religion, and World Affairs)"—Introd.
  Includes bibliographical references and index.
  ISBN 0-7658-0592-8 (alk. paper)
    1. Social psychology—Congresses. 2. Civilization, Western—Psychological aspects—Congresses. 3. Social institutions—Psychological aspects—Congresses. 4. Psychoanalysis and culture—Congresses. I. Imber, Jonathan B., 1952-
HM1033.T44   2004
302'.17—dc22   2004051649

Contents

Part 3: Therapeutic Culture in Contemporary Life

For Philip Rieff, in gratitude

"Whatever else students do or do not get they will always get your attitudes—as open-minded or dogmatic, adventurous or conventional, confident or suspicious, self-absorbed or appreciative of their personalities. For the last they are always grateful."

—Charles Horton Cooley, *Life and the Student*

Introduction

One Culture, After All

Jonathan B. Imber

The essays in this volume grew out of a conference held at Boston University in April of 2001 under the auspices of the Institute for the Study of Economic Culture (now the Institute on Culture, Religion and World Affairs), along with the generous support of the Lynde and Harry Bradley Foundation. I am personally grateful to Peter Berger for supporting the idea of the conference and to Irving Louis Horowitz for assuring tangible results in the form of essays that first appeared in *Society* (in different form) and now in this volume.

The authors here owe a great deal to the emergence of an idea that can be traced to the writings of several influential thinkers, including Christopher Lasch, Philip Rieff, and Thomas Szasz, among others. That idea, "therapeutic culture" has taken on a life of its own well beyond such formulations as "the culture of narcissism," "the triumph of the therapeutic," "the therapeutic state," or even the more technically sociological "medicalization." Yet empirical illustrations of something called "therapeutic culture" can also be elusive, since the phenomenon has worked its way through far more visible systems and major institutions, such as family, school, law, and state, which have endured for millennia. These essays provide fresh material that documents this elusive transformation within these systems and institutions. They describe a theoretical problem in the process of its own formulation. They illuminate the idea of the "therapeutic" in its relation to the problem of culture. In what follows here, I examine how the concept of culture has been used as an explanatory idea in ways that have linked culture with politics, and politics with self. I rely first on insights from the work of Philip Rieff and then delineate those forces of thinking and feeling that commend both the triumph and defeat of the therapeutic ethos. A constructive social science devoted to exposing that triumph is also a key to its defeat. In a coda, I offer further reflections on a theory of culture, through reminiscences of Philip Rieff as a teacher and sociologist.

Doubting Culture Wars

Among intellectuals, journalists, and politicians, the theme of "culture wars" has become symbolic of titanic struggles within and among major institutions.[1] When James Davison Hunter published his widely cited book, *Culture Wars: The Struggle to Define America* more than a decade ago, it was hardly difficult to identify the problem of the excluded middle in his provocative thesis about the struggle between the "progressivists" and "orthodox" over then many politically volatile issues. (One that has emerged of late, besides "partial-birth abortion," is "same-sex" marriage.) Yet the major incentive for pursuing further empirical research about this volatility was due to his conceptual boldness and the originality of his thesis, which Rhys H. Williams and his collaborators examined in *Cultural Wars in American Politics: Critical Reviews of a Popular Myth* in 1997.[2] Hunter's important work was, in the spirit of open inquiry, criticized, and as Williams noted in his introduction to *Cultural Wars in American Politics*, the range of response to Hunter's general thesis had already resulted in various attempts to explain these struggles in other terms. For example, traditionalists were said to be at odds with "new class" knowledge workers; egotism was said to be drowning out all expressions of altruism, indicating the underlying impetus for such works as *Bowling Alone* by Robert Putnam; and identity politics, particularly sexual and racial, were fragmenting the older and presumably more united left-wing coalitions.

Hunter's thesis, deriving in large part from his earlier and innovative work on religion in American life, was criticized for giving too much credence to media attention of elites and not enough to the larger sources of consensus already established in the modern welfare state among the mass of citizens. The once highly charged debate over abortion "rights" illustrates the elite *kulturkampf*, while public opinion has remained largely opposed but also largely open to exceptions. And it is important to recognize that murdering physicians who perform abortions cannot be debated with disinterest. That is to say, whatever the motivation or rationale for such vigilantism may be, arguments against abortion may not, without losing their moral force among a broader public, appeal to any means possible for stopping it. Opposition to and support for abortion rights can nevertheless be civil. The slander against abortion opponents by calling them complicit in the murder of physicians is no more persuasive than trading on the Holocaust to condemn abortion itself. Indeed, the willingness to disagree civilly while seeking ways to persuade, short of violence, is part of what the present civil consensus about abortion appears to mean.

The pursuit of consensus in the social sciences is important to revisit regularly in what appears now to be a waning of the larger and more publicized cultural struggles that Hunter and others identified. Even the urgency about "political correctness" has dissipated, but it should not be assumed that with a decline in symptoms that certain underlying problems do not exist related to cultural struggle. Whether we bowl alone or just get along better because we bowl alone only provides a surface description of personal and public boundaries about our lives together. Our present optimists of ameliorative practices of "live and let live" may have to consider a modified version of Ambrose Bierce's definition of peace: "In international affairs, a period of cheating between two periods of fighting." In a time of reduced cultural struggle, conflicting worldviews appear like ships passing in the night, but only because we say so.

I will lay out a brief argument about two ways to think about culture sociologically in an effort to define the enduring nature of cultural struggle beyond the present optimism about moral pluralism. The first way is taken from my long-standing interest in the writings of Philip Rieff whose development and analysis of the idea of culture has deeply enriched subsequent debates about the idea of culture conflict. In 1968, Rieff published an essay entitled "Cooley and Culture," using the occasion of celebrating the life and work of Charles Horton Cooley to formulate a rudimentary distinction in a theory of culture.[3] He wrote, "Every culture system organizes the tension of two types of thought-worlds, one type *technological* and the other *religious*. There are two ways to mend a canoe, to keep it afloat, rendering existence on the water both possible and ordinary; all this is a part of technology. There must also be ways to 'mend' what is directly not yet mendable—death, for example. To do so is obviously the task of religion."[4]

Rieff proposed to call everything that falls within some technological thought-world, "minimal culture" and everything that falls within some religious thought-world "maximal culture". He attributed to the ideas of Auguste Comte and Herbert Spencer, among others, the advocacy of an increasingly powerful and influential minimal culture, leading to his observation that "Our civilization is rapidly producing what is in effect a cultural lumpen proletariat of unsophisticated therapeutic types, intensely demanding beneficiaries of the sheer plenitude, material and otherwise, promised by the folklore, the *popular* thought-world of technology."[5] At the same time, these same theorists acknowledged what Emile Durkheim and others regarded as the social functions of religion, which could be identified and applied strategically to the maintenance of social order. Rieff remarked, "Maximal culture has finally become what some sociological theorists in the nineteenth century conceived it to be: a means for the maintenance of social order, not the level from which that order can be judged and reordered."[6] And he concluded, in 1968, with the following observation on the fate of maximal culture: "In the culture of the therapeutic, inherited criteria of good and bad, right and wrong, are dissolved into the new criteria of well and ill, interesting and uninteresting; there is psychology where there used to be religion, morality, and custom."[7]

The Cognitive Right and Left

The distinction between minimal and maximal culture holds to the present moment, perhaps more so than in 1968, before all politics became local and before utopian ambition defined by existential choice became personal ambition defined by career path. Within the realm of minimal culture, the explanatory powers of how things work grind on, turning the human genome, for example, into a fantastic and ongoing press release, unrelenting in its reshaping of expectations about human destiny. Such insights make little use of unwieldy claims from maximal culture about such destiny, there being no "meaning to it all" necessary to understand genetic fate. Culture, in the maximal sense, is thus epiphenomenal to explanations of human motivation, action, and, finally, social order. At the other end of the continuum are those who consider a functional, maximal culture *the* reigning explanatory model in all that is human.

The aims of minimal and maximal culture are informed by explanatory powers that I will call the cognitive right and the cognitive left. I mean to use these terms heuristically, as a way of discovering more about culture conflict, and my aim is to delineate two broad tendencies in how those politically inclined to the left or the right think about general causation on many matters, though, certainly not all the same way on all matters. The cognitive right examines a presumed range of controls on human action that are determined by biological and thus evolutionary features that are said to be common in some ways to all living things. In Rieff's terms, the cognitive right, insofar as it directs the popular understanding of human action, represents the triumph of minimal culture. At the same time, broader explanations of human behavior (e.g., group behavior) that move from "how" to "why" illuminate a functional, maximal culture. For many reasons, some like to refer to evolutionary explanations as having little or nothing to do with human culture at all, but the hostility is largely to certain types of religious explanation, that is, a maximal culture, of the critical as distinct from functional kind.

On the other hand, the cognitive left upholds what Durkheim termed the ineffable *sui generis*, that is, that aspect of the social which acts upon the social and which is said to be greater than the sum of its parts. For many reasons, some like to refer to this as having much, if not everything, to do with culture, and they mean it in both the functional and critical, maximal senses. Minimal culture, from the cognitive left, is what capitalism is conceived to be, that is the mindless pursuit of more without maximal reasons for why more is better, except for those who have more. The cognitive left draws its energy from a powerful envy that it would eliminate, while the cognitive right sees that envy as constitutive of and constructive to social order itself.

It is now a well-worn fact of our academic silliness that the staid, demographic categories of class, race, and sex serve as ideological hammers and nails in the periodic crucifixions of dissenters from the pieties of the allegedly horrible realities of class inequality, racism, and sexism. I need not deny the existence of such realities to remain at least skeptical about what can be generalized from their empirical representations. An exemplary, paranoid generalization that admits nothing in the way of empirical skepticism can be found in Donald M. Lowe's *The Body in Late-Capitalist USA*, published by the most advanced cognitive left publisher in the world, Duke University Press: "Racism is not a single, discrete, isolatable item, nor is it the result of a conspiracy. It is always, already present everywhere in the Social" (p.111).[8] The stylists of such pronouncements add the further sight gag of capitalizing the "s" in social, so as to give it that *sui generis* ineffability already mentioned. The phrase, "always, al-

xiv   Therapeutic Culture

ready present everywhere," is also a piety of anti-positivism. The effacement of the particular precludes any possibility for consensus about what counts as evidence, much less what might follow from it. There is considerable seepage of this kind of piety into the kangaroo courts that have been held in many colleges and universities over the last two decades. This was illustrated in Richard Bernstein's important 1994 book, *Dictatorship of Virtue: Multiculturalism and the Battle for America's Future.*

The sociologist Joan Moore wrote in 1990 that "Any academic who is not white, male, and middle-aged knows that the moment he or she stands in front of a class, a portion of the class expects something that will illuminate their place in the social structure. This is a constituency. It is not a public. The woman or minority sociologist feels instant pressure to act as a social critic...I cannot say this strongly enough. It is not possible for a woman or minority sociologist to walk into a classroom in modern America and not face instantly and squarely the twin issues of equality and poverty, which I submit, cover many of the issues that public intellectuals purport to address" (229).[9] Such phrases as "instant pressure" and "face instantly and squarely" speak to a decided loss of disinterest in the purposes of teaching and learning. Yet there is something poignant about this, about the *sui generis* reality of one's racial, ethnic, or sexual status in relation to one's motives and actions and others' expectations about them.

These two examples may be taken as simple illustrations of the vagaries of political correctness. The problem with political correctness as an analytical idea is that those who condemn it most also use it regularly for accusatory and adversarial purposes rather than to clarify what is going on. Social scientists should be thinking more about and examining theoretically and empirically what is going on. Lowe and Moore are poster people of the cognitive left. They lay special claim on the essential nature of their own cultural determinations. The cognitive-left analysis stipulates the ascribed status of such things as race and sex, but these are not biological categories in the older sociological renderings of ascribed status. They are instead first and foremost experiential categories of identity. What is more, if you have not had the experience that Moore describes, you are not yet fully awake. In this way, the idea of false consciousness returns not as an instrument to challenge the "white, male and middle-aged" self-concept (that, apparently, is a hopeless endeavor) but rather to re-educate, at best, those with identities that have been designated as oppressed. Marx contended that the proletariat was already converted to be revolutionary by virtue of its station and that the bourgeoisie could not be because class consciousness defined identity as well as action. Marx's alleged determinism did provide the generational trapdoor that would allow the children of the bourgeoisie to become revolutionary in some manner. Yet cognitive-left sentimentalists of cultural essentialism do not take it for granted that those who belong in their thought-world, by ascribed status, have by that criterion been converted. They are post-colonial missionaries.

Cultural essentialism imposes on each particular self a group consciousness that is always, already present everywhere. It is a form of determinism so powerful today that it seems likely we will have to wait for sometime before its logical inconsistencies are recognized, popularized, and resisted. The principal inconsistency is free will, something that even Marx allowed in his limited choice of types of consciousness. False consciousness, after all, could be overcome. Social orders in which free will has been deeply suppressed are not unknown, but we have been accustomed since the rise of totalitarianism to assume that these suppressions are political and that they require a police state, with its uses of force and terror, to maintain. What would it mean to say such suppressions can also be cultural, as Orwell understood when he noted the political effectiveness of manipulating the meaning of words? The political totalitarian had all the means of power, including violence, at his disposal. The cultural totalitarian operates from the experience of frustration at the status quo, taking the struggle directly to the schools and the media. The producers of popular culture rail against the regulators of culture, with the First Amendment serving as the fig leaf to an otherwise naked ambition to smash what are taken to be the false idols of maximal culture: religion, morality, and custom.

The problem with smashing idols is that they must be replaced with some way of explaining why the world is the way it is. It is this replacement that, in every culture, is always struggling to be born. That is to say, the process by which cultural authority establishes itself is never set once and for all, but the shifting contents or directives that define what is or is not permitted are communicated more or less effectively. Public media and popular culture in democratic societies inevitably proceed from the assumption that market share *translates* as "effective" communication, in the minimalist sense. But one of the problems with any short-term strategy about achieving such market share is how long it can be maintained and at what cost to the culture. One of the virtues of the cognitive left is its wholesale endorsement of strategies and programs that inevitably keep the wheels of commerce turning—there are literally hundreds of associations, professional and therapeutic, whose *raison d'être* is to tinker with nearly everything but common sense. Often those who act out most capriciously or least attractively—who claim to be leaders—find themselves eventually hanging out on various limbs, casting blame at everything and everyone for their failure to be noticed and rewarded. Imagining themselves as charismatic, they are in fact paranoid, as Philip Rieff defined the pathological side of charisma.[10] This pathology advanced by illiterate and politically naïve leaders in higher education and the media has reaped what it has sown, so much so that students and media audiences have begun to catch on to the scam, leading protest after protest about their littlest problems and testifying endlessly about how they have been cheated, abused, and generally unappreciated. Cognitive-left thinking, which forbids the blaming of the victim, opens upon a landscape of frenetic positioning for position, each according to his need for attention.

At the other end of the continuum, the cognitive right occupies a much smaller, but much more controversial, place in academic and public life. Evolutionary psychology, formerly sociobiology, has developed a larger public reputation, partly off-setting the momentum of endless grievance that has come to define so much of the cognitive left. Blaming the victim is cleverly avoided by attributing the cause of currently defined "problems" not to cultural or historical circumstances, usually only a few generations in duration, but to the longer frame of "species-time." A particularly controversial example of this kind of reasoning appeared with the MIT publication in 2000 of *A Natural History of Rape: Biological Bases of Sexual Coercion* by Randy Thornhill and Craig Palmer. Reviewed in the *New Republic*,[11] the book was strongly criticized for the *absence* of any mention of culture in the kinds of generalization that conclude that women's post-rape trauma is an adaptive function that enables them to cope with their loss of control of their own evolved ability to choose the best mate or to retain the trust of their present mate, or that rape increases reproduction, giving the most aggressive males the chance to continue their line. The reviewer, Jerry A. Coyne, of the Department of Ecology and Evolution at the University Chicago, argued against the coherence of such claims rather than appealing to audience sensitivity. On culture, Coyne predicted: "Flies and ducks do not create, and live in, a culture, as humans do; and human culture guarantees that there will be many meaningless parallels between the behavior of humans and of other species" (p. 30).

Coyne seemed to argue that the parallels drawn between the way animals and humans behave can be of only limited use in understanding the pervasive nature and function of human culture. There is something to be said for this insofar as it is a statement about causality, whether we generalize from saccharin in mice or genes in ducks. But it is possible that Coyne also shares much in common with his renegade colleagues over this idea about the function of culture, seeing how much it represents a kind of repository of infinite meanings, some linked to biological understanding but most not. To have to *deny* that flies and ducks do not create and live in a culture as humans do could be taken as evidence that biologists, and now their counterparts in evolutionary psychology, assume that human culture offers mostly meaningless "data" so far as scientific generalization goes. Whereas the cognitive left has made subjectivity an abyss, the cognitive right does everything it can to eliminate what in effect is the bias of human consciousness and its creations, those aspects of human existence that are often remarked as most unique to it.

Some would call this reductionism. It is also a fundamental attribute of the cognitive right. Reductionism is a way of defining the origins of more determinative forces in what motivates and thereby guides human beings. The old instinct theorists along with Freud should all be assigned to the cognitive right. From this end of the continuum, culture may be present, but it is not omnipresent and certainly not *sui generis*. The anthropology of Margaret Mead and Ruth Benedict, which brought the recognition of cultural differences to several generations of social science, stood tenuously on the borderline between the cognitive left and right. The clearer emergence of what came to be called "cultural relativism" acquired political uses far beyond the distinctive anthropological insights about the "relatively" autonomous and indigenous dynamics of societies that had yet to be transformed by contact. "Contact" now remains only interesting with imaginary meetings between humans and aliens, that is, literally off-earth life forms that possess intelligence, gentle or destructive, depending on whether one entertains the upside of the end of scarcity or the downside of our becoming the staple of someone else's diet. The fate of cultural relativism is something akin to fission, where, finally, each individual is culturally relative to every other individual, forbidding biological explanations for personality disorder at precisely the same time that medication for depression and other mental ailments is most endemic.

Following the fission brought on by a thorough politicizing of cognitive left thinking and by the efforts at fusion led by cognitive right thinking, one culture, after all, is at stake. It is the culture through which these struggles over explanatory hegemony take shape. That culture, in its deepest meanings, belongs to no particular group and cannot be imagined to belong to any group exclusively without elimination of other groups. The sociological idea was born at that moment no single group, no empire, no historical period could name itself as a form of finality, except on terms of those who claimed to belong to them. All the nineteenth-century historical determinists implicitly recognized the failure of their certainty about being most in the present—and thus most certain about the future—leaving a legacy of social science that was required to negotiate the given with what was demanded beyond the given, for whatever reason. The cost of enlightenment means no faith can be, by its nature, a guarantee for all. And those who would claim otherwise, and pursue their claims by non-democratic means, have become, whether from the left or the right, the most dangerous figures of all.

"The Darwinization of Everything"

The cognitive right maintains a certain and useful indifference to individual outcome. But lately the entire reasoning behind group outcome has also come under intense scrutiny. The admixture of identity politics and individual grievance has produced two versions of response to how and why people end up where they do. From the cognitive left, a strong alliance of identity with the group has inspired all egalitarian demands about future outcome, while from the cognitive right an equally strong alliance of identity with the group has been used to justify present social conditions. It is no coincidence, in this regard, that it is now nearly impossible to talk about human nature on the cognitive left, a subject of considerable social-scientific investigation historically, because it tends to produce status quo assessments of conflict (e.g., the inevitability of war) and cooperation (e.g., rational choice). At the same time, the psychometricians, with their battery of comparative assessments, conceal a deep admiration for the status quo while disclaiming pretensions to influence public policy.

On the cognitive right, a principal formulator of evolutionary psychology and sociobiology, E.O. Wilson, has felt the full gale of reactions to such ideas over the years. Jerry Coyne in the previously referred to review in the *New Republic* claims that the larger goal of such works on rape is "the engulfment of social science and social policy by the great whale of evolutionary psychology." He goes on, "This attempted takeover is not new. It was first suggested in 1978 in E.O. Wilson's *On Human Nature*, and more recently in his *Consilience*, Wilson extended the program to nearly every area of human thought, including aesthetics and ethics. We are witnessing a new campaign for the Darwinization of Everything" (p. 33).

The Darwinization of Everything resonates with "Racism is always, already present everywhere in the Social." The progress of original sin may very well be its bifurcation into two modes of explanation at a time when maximal culture exclusively achieves functional, if not critical, purposes. In criticizing E.O. Wilson's effort to resolve this bifurcation in explanatory powers, Coyne directs us to consider Wilson's strategy more specifically.

The word consilience was coined in 1840 by the English natural philosopher, William Whewell, (1794-1866). Whewell was a contemporary of far better remembered figures today, such as T.H. Huxley, John Tyndall, Herbert Spencer, and Michael Faraday. Consilience is defined as "concurrence or accordance in inferential results." In other words, generalizations from different disciplines and fields are found to be related from widely differing inductions. All particulars lead to the same whole. There is a long philosophical tradition that has examined this, from Aristotle, to Francis Bacon, to John Stuart Mill. What is important to keep in mind is that Wilson is a consummate inductivist.

In 1867, Edward Livingston Youmans edited a book, *The Culture Demanded by Modern Life*, in which Whewell, along with his contemporaries just mentioned contributed essays. Whewell's posthumous contribution, entitled "On the Influence of the History of Science upon Intellectual Education," in title alone, acknowledged that there were then, as remains the case today, two types of education: one from below and the other from above. The one from below, the school of hard knocks, is not unknown to Wilson whose many bio-graphical sound bites, include mention of his fabulous climb up the intellectual and status ladders of American life, toward inclusion in that rarest and most publicly self-conscious of pantheons of highest education, Harvard University. But when it comes to academic suc-cess, the survival of the fittest does not entirely explain where we hungry souls end up in life. Other forces that have been personified along with nature, such as good and bad luck, agreeable and dis-agreeable character, helpful and unhelpful mentors, go some dis-tance in providing answers of sorts, too.

In Wilson's account of his Southern Baptist upbringing in Ala-bama, "laid backward under the water on the sturdy arm of a pas-tor," the religious impulse itself is recreated in the image of Science, which becomes for the evolutionist "religion liberated and writ large" (p. 6).[12] Like Freud and Durkheim, Wilson has found a "purpose" for religion, which is not the same as finding a purpose in life and measuring oneself against it. Unlike Freud, Wilson preaches a kinder and gentler end to human uncertainty and anxiety, something that the sociologist Howard Kaye has remarked upon in decisive ways over the past twenty years.[13] Wilson leaves the old fundamentalists, those inheritors of critical, maximal culture, standing more or less helplessly all along their watchtowers. In their place, from his ivory tower, he appears to find alliances with the post-religious funda-mentalists who are environmentalists, postmodernists, feminists, and others inhabiting a disproportionate quantity of guilt-tripping space in higher education today. (Wilson's efforts to curry favor among the avant garde of intellectual trendiness are worth comparing to a similar effort made more than a decade ago by Stephen Toulmin in his work *Cosmopolis*.[14])

Education from above now dictates the virtues of "spirituality" over and against "religiosity" in the elite academy, and for good reason: no inspired religious leadership has led the most prestigious schools for several generations, but the adolescent biological reality of who regularly inhabits the schools in the greatest numbers has remained virtually unchanged for two thousand years. Like Wilson's epiphany about evolution, which arrived during adolescence, so the epiphanies of legions of student generations have been about doubt-ing everything and about revolting against nearly everything, but only up to a point.

Because he takes evolution as his guide, Wilson joins forces with all those who enjoy the excitement of change. The only problem with his particular excitement is that as a relative naïf who exploded upon the world with his (then) incendiary accounts of sociobiology, he was traumatized (I do not think this is too strong a term) by the reaction, especially among some of the more politically hostile social scientists, who interpreted his efforts only politically.[15] They did not want to argue with him, they wanted to shut his thought-world down, and still would if they could. And to this extent, they are not alone on their side, seeing how accounts about evolutionary psychology in conservative periodicals such as *Commentary* and the *Weekly Standard* have voiced strong reservations about this worldview as well.

The broaching of sociobiology in the 1970s became a public relations disaster, leading to Wilson's ostracism in certain circles. He joined the National Association of Scholars. Everything about the book *Consilience* (including the title itself which probably denotes "conciliation" in the minds of many who will not look it up in an unabridged dictionary) speaks to his unconscious hope to be redeemed precisely in the minds of those whose cognitive-left suspicions cast doubts about his ultimate "intentions". He is tough on postmodernism, but it is the cliché version of that idea. If it were only a matter of intentions, one could state them, like an oath, and be done with the suspicions. But suspicions run more deeply, because what we doubt in others is as much a matter of what they think as with whom they associate. The key, finally, is association. The sociologist, for example, who takes up the subject of sociobiology, is a pariah among the vast majority of his colleagues. The biologist who takes up the same subject is doing her job, although, making behavioral observations that are supposed to substitute *for* sociology is still mostly beyond the pale.

Yet the cognitive right is on its way to establishing more than a beachhead in the battle with cultural essentialists. It is altogether a different kind of culture war, not one that engages the religious against the post-religious, and not one that is deadened by the legal doping of millions of people whose therapeutic thought-world controls all but their suicidal tendencies. Rather the culture war in academic precincts especially concerns the fate of generalization about the meaning of culture itself. If we adopt the thought-world of the cognitive left, we give up a great deal in our effort to understand the failure of social policy that has been guided by ideological illusions of equality that no advance in prosperity will ever achieve. On the other hand, if we adopt the thought-world of the cognitive right, we admit certain inevitabilities that make us mostly concerned with the incidence of such failure rather than with what it means to live largely indifferent to some acceptable and expected level of it. The cognitive right attracts the specialists without spirit and the cognitive left attracts the sensualists without heart.

Maximal culture, which is supposed to attend to that which cannot be fixed by human intervention alone—death, for example—contains elements of both the cognitive left and cognitive right. On the left are utopian strategies, on the right adaptive ones. Those who live for the long term behave differently than those who do not, or so we are told by the legions of public health experts who derive such wisdom from what has rapidly become a medicalized view of right and wrong. The cognitive left has appropriated much of the vernacular of a functional, maximal culture, dictating continuous memoranda on the rightful and wrongful ways of living a long, if not what used to be called a moral, life.

The gap between gene and behavior is no longer a theoretical imponderable, only a technical challenge to those who subscribe to the ascendancy of ambition of the cognitive right. The cognitive right's version of revelation, read scientifically as "breakthrough," heralds the triumph of a minimal culture with only a functional, maximal cultural mode of explanation upon which to rely. The gradual and fateful disappearance of what Rieff described as a maximal culture "from which order can be judged and reordered" rather than maintained, manipulated, and managed, is difficult to pinpoint because judgment is what we now seek for our grievances rather for our own good. The cognitive left once defended the eugenics of political murder in the era of political totalitarianism. In our era of competing, cultural, totalistic thought-worlds, the consensus may very well be that pressure from both sides of the cognitive divide will remain with us as the cost of enlightenment in a world where moral judgment is at best expedient and at worst absent. Doubting culture wars, even as they may recede from media attention, will only lessen the scrutiny of the fateful ways in which moral sensibility has changed.

Coda: For Philip Rieff

Philip Rieff traces his use of the term therapeutic, by inversion, back to Philo, who wrote on the *Therapeutae*, whose discipline is remarkable for its abstinence.[16] The emergence of a therapeutic character type, Rieff's "psychological man" of *Freud: The Mind of the Moralist*, finds only the cause of health to be a rationale for abstinence. This is the abstinence of a narcissistic culture, where self-improvement, even spiritual self-improvement, has all the earmarks of a suspect ambition. No motive is without cultural predicates, and Rieff was not alone in asking his colleagues to consider what was at stake in their vocation as teachers and scholars in a culture motivated by therapeutic ideals. Robert Nisbet approached the matter with similar insights about what was happening in the academy in *The Degradation of the Academic Dogma: the University in America 1945-1970*. It is striking still how clearly Nisbet and Rieff identified the emerging therapeutic ethos of the modern university.[17]

This emerging ethos has had lasting consequences for the nature of professional authority. Rieff has consistently argued that all relations in authority require assent. It is this assent that is the foundation of trust, and without this foundation, as Marx and Nietzsche observed in their fatal ways, all is power and all is mistaken for power. The therapeutic ethos of higher education has also led to a diminution of the place of reason among those allegedly most entrusted first with its application. Even if the "faith in reason" grows from what reason provides, as Rieff once wrote, "reason itself depends upon motives that are not themselves rational, thus limiting its strength severely at the very point of origin."[18] Most of what is true precedes intellect, which is forever in search of what it cannot itself be, or guarantee. Insofar as we are resigned to this enduring problem, we have schools. For those more hopeful about it, we have always had the school of hard knocks. Everyone used to know the difference but it was a sign of upward mobility to stay in the former as long as possible and the latter as briefly as possible. Now, of course, everyone is in school, including murderers.

Schools are the elite embodiment of what Rieff has always meant by "theory". In his classroom, the moral dissections, which we performed regularly in our graduate study with him, left some of my fellow students without any idea about what on earth the "unpacking" of texts had to do with theory. After all, theory is supposed to

establish a scientific form of explanation, the core of which provides an account of causality. Rieff often remarked about moral causation, arguing that such distinctions as is/ought and fact/value, provided an illusory distance between life and action. He would say, "I
ought not because I cannot," turning on its head the customary form
of philosophical reasoning about moral action, thus rooting in who
we are what we should be rather than deriving from whatever pre-
established forms of moral reasoning what we can be. This simple
reversal of expectation was also a challenge to ideology in relation
to social science. Marx always has something to teach, Marxists rarely.
Freud saw further into realities that acolytes and followers would
test against nothing more permanent than their ambitions to do so.

A rule observed in Rieff's classroom was that we had to assent to
the texts we read. Not only were we supposed to be the only living
Nietzsche, or Paul, or Kafka, but we were also to trust that what each
wrote was true in the most important sense of truth, a vision of the
highest that is revealed and known to the human mind. Such truth is
not scientific, nor is it exclusively found in any one or another tradition of revelation. It is this distinct aspect of Rieff's idea of sociological theory against which both ideologues on the left and right
might lodge the criticism of relativism (more about which I will say
below).[19] The texts themselves were the midwives to such truths
that could be unpacked in the texts themselves. And when that moment of insight arrived that brought the text to life in relation to what
we were able to observe with the power of our own minds and
senses—what Rieff called text-analogues—then we were doing
theory.

This sense of theory is peculiar in several ways. Theories in the
vernacular of social science are not done, they are built, constructed,
propounded—I do not recall engaging the idea of theorizing with
Philip Rieff in this manner in his teaching. This is not to say that he
has not theorized in this manner. Anyone familiar with his writings
on culture will recognize this constructive aspect of his approach to
theory. But "doing theory" was largely interpreting others' works
rather than building theories of our own. Another peculiarity was
how the canon of works was selected. This may be of even more
concern to the disciplinary idea of each of the social sciences than
the pedagogic practices considered effective in teaching theory. This
is an intellectual rather than didactic difficulty.

Facts Rising

There is today a profound disagreement among self-identified social theorists about the nature of their enterprise. There is a lot at stake in being a theorist. Being ignored is not a happy circumstance in such business. It is also the case that being "a theorist," even in sociology, is something more like an occupation than it was a century ago. The ASA has a section. Although ASA members who are theorists do not speak for the ASA, say, in the same way that Cardinal Ratzinger speaks for the Catholic Church and its dogma, the sociological similarity I would call attention to is between church and professional association. In my view of ASA tactics over the years, I have seen far more of the dogmatic than the theoretical as Rieff would have it. My purpose is not to take this issue on directly here about how a theory becomes an institution but rather to suggest that there are interesting and illuminative lines to be drawn among vocation, profession, association, institution (or school in this case), and the larger public. I am certain that one of Rieff's enduring contributions has been to illuminate those lines in ways that provide troubling questions to bureaucrats and revolutionaries alike.

On the several occasions when Rieff described a process in which facts rise to meet theories rather than theories arising from facts themselves, he was challenging a conventional view of theory that is attributed to the practice of "normal" science. An hypothesis is proposed, a method to test it is designed, a study is performed, results obtained, and findings presented. This entire process requires little in the way of elaboration. Without it, there could be nothing like natural and social science as we know them. I subscribe without reservation to the practice of so-called "normal" science as among the more constructive human activities that exist. Rieff's question may appear to represent a challenge to this kind of activity, but I would contend it is very much the opposite. Most researchers in social science already find themselves, as it were, within a theory, or as Rieff has called it, a thought-world, even, and perhaps especially, when they are not fully aware that this is the case. What they observe as scientists are facts that are already rising to meet the theory, however consciously or unconsciously it may be present to them.

It is the fact/theory distinction that conceals a truth about facts: there is no such thing as a fact without a theory (i.e., thought-world) that gives it meaning. Theory in this way always precedes the facts

that illuminate it. Max Weber advanced such a view in his assessment of the subjective meaning that actors ascribe to actions. Such
subjective meaning connotes a theory of understanding which the
facts of action illuminate. Cutting a tree down may be, subjectively
speaking, a traditional, affective, goal-directed, or value-related type
of action. In other words the same "fact" of a particular action takes
on a different meaning depending upon how it is understood to begin with by actor and observer. When we say that facts do not exist
without theories, we do not mean to make a statement about existence but about meaning. And in Rieff's account of theory, the mere
existence of things is outside all theoretical thought-worlds. It may
be that the well-informed sociological theorist knows this to be true,
but such sophistication shows little practical result in the consistent need
to help students in particular distinguish between context and meaning
without giving into an utterly relativistic notion of meaning.

Surely the confusion over fact and theory is partly attributable to
more recent philosophical schools that question the nature of existence as if it had any meaning outside a particular theoretical thought-
world. The conceit of all modern "theory" in this respect is that it
has a human author. But Rieff has always been more than just skeptical about such a conceit, because we are all quite literally born into
a theoretical thought-world, a world that can no more be wished for
than wished away. The artistry of escape from a theoretical thought-
world is, in Rieff's theory of culture, the basis for distinguishing
between conformative and transformative theoretical traditions.

In those traditions defined as conformative, escape has been named
in many ways. Christian tradition has had much to say about such
escape along the lines of sexual abstinence and temptation, each
requiring the other to provide sufficient tension to produce judgment about how each is defined. In our time, such definition and
judgment have become procedural and ideological, so that, for example, sexual harassment is both a definition of disapproved interaction and a judgment that derives from subjectively experienced
interaction. In this way, given the right ideological conditions, adultery with an intern can be far less consequential to a reputation than
suffering the accusation of having once remarked about pubic hair
on a coke can. In Rieff's sociological insights about interdicts, remissions, and transgressions, the inversion of judgment, where alleged accusation can be more damaging than confirmed action, takes
place in a theoretical thought-world where the procedural and ideo-

logical no longer subserve, as Rieff puts it, the interdicts. Conformative traditions have always been subject to procedural and ideological uses, but their powerful abuses should be kept theoretically separate from their authoritative uses.

In traditions that may be called transformative, even the formerly powerful strictures of the procedural and ideological may lose their force. The erotic and sexual, far from being subject to conformative pressures defined by temptation or by pseudo-conformative pressures defined by accusation and self-accounts, are viewed within our therapeutic thought-world, as escapes from boredom. Consider the title of a book whose author's approach is a kind of chatty, clinical disposition to do right by the harried well-off: *The Great Sex Weekend: A 48-Hour Guide to Rekindling Sparks for Bold, Busy, or Bored Lovers: Includes 24-Hour Plans for the Really Busy.* That such a book was written by a sociologist confirms how advanced sociologists regularly are in those transformative tactics that no longer name Puritanism as the enemy of the people but rather boredom and busy-ness, apparently two sides of the same therapeutic coin. Transformative traditions test all convictions that invoke modesty and moderation and that spurn indecency and inconsiderateness. The moral valence of the four qualities of character just mentioned has shifted sufficiently that constructive examples of their presence and practice in everyday life are considered exceptional rather expected.

Rieff's ideas about the "moral" have been central to his observations about social change, sometimes leading to confusion about whether he simply substitutes moral opinion for social observation. Again, the idea that there is a separation between the two follows from a view of theory, which imagines the "objective" to be something outside a particular thought-world. But moral opinion, like all theory, exerts what Rieff has often called a "pressure". In the age of the therapeutic, moral opinion is arbitrary, if not completely weightless. How else do we explain why so many who sympathize with animal rights reject the "rights" of the living yet unborn child? Rieff wondered about this long ago, as he did about the advance of the techno-cannibalism of organ transplantation. That demand for human organs, and now more recently human fetal tissue, may create flesh markets which are the result of the globalization of therapeutic culture seems naturally of little consequence to those on the demand side.[20]

It makes perfect sense to me after so many years to appreciate (very much in fact) how Rieff's own presiding presence exerted a certain pressure on his students, not to conform or submit, but to be directed to his insights about so many objects of contemporary sociological attention. During the 1990s he may finally have been assigned the designation of "conservative," but this is an ideological label that does not begin to do justice to his intellectual challenges to the reigning pieties of therapeutic comfort. *Fellow Teachers* had that kind of direction and insight, even though, compared, say, to Allan Bloom's *The Closing of the American Mind*, Rieff's polemical intentions were less the motivation for, than the inevitable result of, addressing spiritually and publicly controversial matters. Long before the loud charges of political correctness, Rieff was patiently taking inventory of the transformations that were leading to the outbreaks of cultural struggles that describe so consistently the confrontations within higher education.

Neither Therapist nor Theologian

Rieff's complexity, if that is an appropriate way to characterize it, arises, in the important quality of disinterest that follows from his observation that "Education is precisely the freedom and capacity to speculate that aristocracy or monarchy or totalitarianism may possibly be better than democracy. Otherwise, neither democratic values nor any others can ever by clarified."[21] This approach to education is not the same as a defense of scientific detachment or objectivity, about which Rieff has provided an extraordinary insight:

> No ideal has been more misleading than that of scientific detachment. The cult of neutrality that dogs the rationalist and scientific traditions was no original part of those traditions, but developed much later—when rationalism no longer had to contend seriously with its great enemy, dogmatic theology. For rationalism, and the sciences of which it is composed, arose first as a negative instrument, to penetrate the spurious logic of dogma. When dogma failed, rationalism lost its object and became, in lieu of an object of attack, objective.[22]

At the same time, in apparent contrast to his characterization of rationalism, Rieff decried the merging of the "freedom and capacity to speculate" with the aims of social movements:

> Now is always the wrong time in which academics can make up their minds, without the tension of historical memory, which, rightly exercised, is likely to leave us always refusing to announce the ardors of the moment. We cannot be advertising men for any movement. Herald nothing.[23]

The objectivity Rieff defends is not the positivist but the historical. The historical is to be understood as distinct from the ideological, and it is a tribute to Rieff's vocation that he recognized long
before more recent controversies that the fate of the Jews is inseparable from the fate of the authority of the past.[24] That so much irra-
tionality attends to such spectacles as Holocaust denial, the vandal-
ism of Jewish sacred places in the aftermath of September 11, and
the murder of Jews, including beheadings, first and foremost because they are Jews, cannot be explained by the instruments of positivist social science alone.

If all histories are equally inventible, and measured against nothing other than the interpreter, then what basis is there, even in education, to argue for a moral authority that is not simply power dis-
guised? In a remarkably hopeful passage about the future of sociology, Rieff observed, "As scientists of the present, sociologists can
only know what they are doing in terms that derive from the authority of the past. Perhaps sociology can do, in our academy, what literature has failed to do: teach in an acutely historical yet normative
way—as a science that is defensive."[25] What is most remarkable to
me about this observation is Rieff's acknowledgment that sociology, perhaps among the humanities and all the other social sciences,
has the greatest obligation, even more so than the discipline of history which is charged with composing narratives, to illuminate the
living thought-worlds that give meaning to the present moment by
virtue of their pressure on that moment.

If I understand Rieff's criticism of literature, and perhaps take it
one step further, it is that what may have begun, nearly a century
ago, as an opportunity to reveal moral insight in literary description
ended up in our time as a version of ideological social science, for
example, seeing class, race, and gender in every gesture and interaction. Why this contraction of insight has occurred might, finally,
have more to do with the multiple hostilities that inhabit academic
life than with some alleged decline in intelligence and ability among
those who are more recent to the enterprise. If the invocation of the
authority of the past is simply read as a form of nostalgia, then, of
course, the sharpest minds are quite likely to flee to the open fields
in which the necessity of knowing what is going on in your discipline means keeping up with no more than five years worth of past
journal articles.

The necessity of learning deeply about historical context and historical argument in the social sciences is no longer of significant concern in a range of social science theories whose approaches require nothing of that older humanistic historical context. Evolutionary psychology, game-theory in economics, rational-choice theory in political science, all have become urgent in the application of their fascinating ideas to almost everything under the sun. Rape is a species moment; every winning bid is actually one increment of cost too high; and everything can be explained by self-interest, if not rightly understood in that old Tocquevillian sense, then understood in some way that implicates the power of human choice. Social science surely imagines itself in the process of mapping the social genome, a configuration of human inheritance and human choice that does not rely on even conventional historical understanding. Economics has to its credit now an Oscar, in addition to a Nobel Prize. Psychology has long since passed into a struggle between its clinical and positivist vanguards, while the clinical wing asserts its jurisdictional power over medicine proper. All of this takes place in an evermore transparent environment of activity and communication.

Yet for the authority of the past to be something other than nostalgia, the achievement of sociological insight must derive from more than ideological wishful thinking. Rieff once remarked that he was neither a theologian nor a therapist. And this is quite true and to the point. As a teacher, he has taken to heart the responsibility that theorizing means connecting what is already given with what comes before us whether we are awake or not. This provides neither proof of revelation nor resolution of our inner struggles. It is much less than either and much more than what now passes for teaching in the classroom. Rieff's early and sustained objection to what has come to be called "advocacy teaching" is that it comes to replace the more difficult and fragile efforts of learning whereby the suspension of, rather than devotion to, belief is the purpose of schooling in which moral clarity about many matters is already given and known. What the age of the therapeutic ushered in, on the far side of revelation, is a view of schooling in which that moral clarity is no longer recognizable, least of all to teachers.

And so recent successes in the publicity wars about certain theories of human nature or certain approaches to human action, are but confirmations that the urgency of cultural struggles in relation to teaching, particularly in the humanities and social sciences, is not so great at the moment, or so it appears. But such urgency may renew itself in certain circumstances, and this more modest ambition of the teacher is central to Rieff's teaching vocation. I know that my fellow students, in those few cohort years when we studied together with Philip Rieff at the University of Pennsylvania, sensed and responded to that urgency, even as we eventually would go our separate ways. I imagine regularly the reappearance of such a commitment to the task rather than to the outcome of teaching each time I walk into the classroom. Disappointment is not what I feel when nothing happens, only exhilaration when something does.

Philip Rieff was eighty years old on December 15, 2002. This volume is testimony to his enduring influence on a generation of scholars devoted to advancing insights that owe much to him and to his writings.

Notes

1.   Parts of this introduction are based on my previous essay, "Doubting Culture Wars," in *Society*, Vol. 38, No. 6, September/October, 2001; and on remarks made at a session of the American Sociological Association devoted to Philip Rieff's work in August, 2002.
2.   Rhys H. Williams, *Cultural Wars in American Politics: Critical Reviews of a Popular Myth* (New York: Aldine de Gruyter, 1997). See also James L. Nolan, Jr., ed., *The American Culture Wars: Current Contests and Future Prospects* (Charlottesville: University of Virginia Press, 1996).
3.   Philip Rieff, "Cooley and Culture," in *The Feeling Intellect: Selected Writings*, ed., Jonathan B. Imber (Chicago: University of Chicago Press, 1990), pp. 310-321.
4.   Ibid., p. 313.
5.   Ibid., pp. 317-318.
6.   Ibid., p. 319.
7.   Ibid., p. 320.
8.   Donald M. Lowe, *The Body in Late-Capitalist USA* (Durham, NC: Duke University Press, 1995).
9.   Joan Moore, "Social Criticism and Sociological Elitism." Pp. 227-230 in *Sociology in America*. Ed. Herbert J. Gans. (Newbury Park, CA: Sage Publications, 1990).
10.   Philip Rieff, *Fellow Teachers/of Culture and Its Second Death* [1973] (Chicago: University of Chicago Press, 1985), p. 163n.
11.   Jerry A. Coyne, "Of Vice and Men: The Fairy Tales of Evolutionary Psychology." *New Republic*, April 3, 2000:27-34.
12.   Edward O. Wilson, *Consilience: The Unity of Knowledge* (New York: Alfred A. Knopf, 1998).
13.   Howard L. Kaye, *The Social Meaning of Modern Biology*, 2nd ed. (New Brunswick, NJ: Transaction Publishers, 1996). For an earlier and similarly powerful criticism of Wilson's sociobiology, which also anticipates the later arguments of *Consilience*, see A. Hunter Dupree, "'Sociobiology' and the Natural Selection of Scientific Disciplines," a review in *Minerva*, Vol. XV, No. 1, Spring 1977, pp. 94-101.
14.   Stephen Toulmin, *Cosmopolis: The Hidden Agenda of Modernity* [1990](Chicago: University of Chicago Press, 1992).

15. See Wilson's own account in "Science and Ideology," in *Academic Questions*, Vol. 8, No. 3, Summer, 1995. See also Ullica Segerstråle, *Defenders of the Truth: The Battle for Science in the Sociology Debate and Beyond* (New York: Oxford University Press, 2000).

16. Philip Rieff, *Fellow Teachers: On Culture and Its Second Death* [1973] (Chicago: University of Chicago Press, 1985), p. 159n105.

17. "If the university were to be conceived as entirely, as lastingly, dedicated to the cult of individuality, to ego needs, identity crises, and the like, it is hardly likely that it would retain the kind of prestige that today draws these students to it. The point is, no one wants to go to an asylum. But a great many will become interested in going to an asylum if it is called a university, has the accumulated luster of the university, and the historic freedom of movement within that goes with life in the university. Once however, it ceases to be possible to call the asylum a university, to bask, so to speak, in the glow of great learning, all the while not having to learn, the spell will be over. Community for its own sake has never proved to be of lasting interest in the history of human behavior. People come together, not to *be* together, but to *do* things that cannot be done alone." — Robert A. Nisbet, *The Degradation of the Academic Dogma* [1971] (New Brunswick, NJ: Transaction Publishers, 1997), p. 195.

18. Philip Rieff, *The Feeling Intellect: Selected Writings* (Chicago: University of Chicago Press, 1990), p. 22.

19. The charge of relativism usually comes from the right; the left will typically make the same kind of charge but in the name of false consciousness.

20. See Ruth Richardson, *Death, Dissection and the Destitute*, 2nd ed. (Chicago: University of Chicago Press, 2000), "Afterword," pp. 409ff.

21. Philip Rieff, *The Feeling Intellect*, p. 233.

22. Philip Rieff, "Social Scientist Attacks 'Cult of Objectivity.'" Review of *Personal Knowledge—Towards a Post-Critical Philosophy*, by Michael Polanyi. *Unitarian Register*, 138, no. 8 (October, 1959), p. 15.

23. Philip Rieff, *Fellow Teachers*, p. 4n.

24. Consider the David Irving lawsuit against Deborah Lipstadt in Great Britain. See Richard J. Evans, *Lying about Hitler: History, Holocaust, and the David Irving Trial* (New York: Basic Books, 2001).

25. Philip Rieff, *Fellow Teachers* (Chicago: University of Chicago Press, 1985), p. 192n.

Part 1

The Emerging Therapeutic Culture

1

Liberation Therapeutics: From Moral Renewal to Consciousness-Raising

Elisabeth Lasch-Quinn

In 1968, two black psychiatrists published a best-selling book that captured the spirit of its times, particularly the turn toward a more militant posture in the civil rights movement, called *Black Rage*. The book argued that, among blacks, many signs of mental illness were actually understandable responses to continued white racism, which its authors believed was as virulent as ever, despite the revolutionary advances the civil rights movement had brought. Tracing the origins of contemporary psychiatric disorders—from neuroses to full-blown schizophrenia—as far back as slavery, William Grier and Price Cobbs delivered a mighty invective against the vestiges of white racism but in the process recast race relations—and indeed, the advancement of African Americans—as a therapeutic project. Although they believed that changing social conditions was the only way to address the personal problems that originated in racial discrimination and oppression, they prescribed not social or political activism but an activist psychiatry. Rather than turning to the outer world armed with the conviction that social reforms could help end needless individual suffering, the authors encouraged therapists to engage in a kind of reformist counseling, where new experts would help overcome racial discrimination.[1]

This project was part of a larger move away from the early civil rights movement's commitment to citizenship and political and social betterment to a therapeutic rendering of racial matters. This new approach not only spawned new forms of counseling, but influenced the content and forms of diversity training programs that came to the fore in the late 1980s and 1990s and the terms in which racial

3

issues increasingly got raised in public and academic forums. This tendency to deal with racial issues with terms and modes from psychiatry was part of the much larger cultural shift away from a religious and toward a psychological sensibility, as captured by the sociologist Philip Rieff in his book *The Triumph of the Therapeutic*. The coinciding of the social movements of the 1960s, and particularly the black movement, with the growing influence of psychiatry and the therapeutic sensibility yielded key features of late-twentieth and now early twenty-first century American life.

One of these features is the peculiar contemporary form of consciousness-raising. The notion that the civil rights movement of the 1950s and 1960s caused a majority of Americans, black and white, to become conscious of the nation's heinous treatment of its African American population is now part of the received wisdom or common knowledge about the age. Yet, this notion rests on an unexamined assumption about the content and method of such a coming-into-awareness or consciousness. It should go without saying that the civil rights movement was one of the most important mass democratic movements in the history of this country and the world, and that its moral and political assault on the fundamental injustice of black exclusion and mistreatment was an unmitigated good. However, the idea of consciousness-raising, one of the fundamental legacies of 1960s social reform still influential behind the scenes today, was not as unproblematic as this larger purpose of the movement. In fact, with hindsight it appears that consciousness-raising and the civil rights struggle, at least in its early phase, should be seen as quite distinct. If true, this means that many who believed in the 1960s and many who still believe that they carry the banner of the civil rights crusade have actually set out in a considerably different direction. While the civil rights movement has come under open and intense examination in its own time and since, this new departure has not, on the whole, been subjected to concerted public critique. This chapter seeks to raise a few exploratory questions about the content and form of consciousness-raising as a mode of purveying knowledge or bringing about change by pointing to some of its distinguishing characteristics, placing it in the therapeutic tradition, and considering some of its possible ramifications.

As early as 1966 when *Triumph of the Therapeutic* was published, Philip Rieff thought that the shifting emphasis in the civil rights movement signaled the likelihood that African Americans would embrace the therapeutic framework of the dominant culture. The early civil rights movement, in his view, had resisted theapeutic imperatives, instead drawing on the longer-term religious tradition that Rieff thought directly countered them. The therapeutic culture, Rieff wrote, obliterated "distinctions between right and wrong," preached an "ethic of release," set as an ideal a "manipulatable sense of well-being," and preferred individual satisfaction over sacrifice in the interests of a morally viable community. The civil rights movement during the years of Martin Luther King's leadership was notable precisely for its clarity about moral authority and responsibility to the larger community. Rieff thought the movement had the capacity to reinvigorate the whole "moral demand system in the white American culture."[2] But instead, the fateful shift away from civil and moral concerns toward an emphasis on personal and cultural identity, cast as the most radical option by adherents, meshed well with the dominant ethos of the age.

Building on Rieff, the sociologist James L. Nolan, Jr., lays out three major traits of the therapeutic ethos. He agrees that it relies above all on the idea that the individual is and should be free of any external moral authority or pressure to deny impulse for a transcendent purpose: "Where once the self was to be surrendered, denied, sacrificed, and died to, now the self is to be esteemed, actualized, affirmed, and unfettered." Following the scholar Alasdair MacIntyre, Nolan argues that this self-obsession leads to an "ethic of emotivism," whereby personal feelings take center stage as the only possible source of truth. The result is a belief in the primacy of personal authenticity, now associated with emotional disclosure: "To fail to express is to be in denial or to be dishonest. In this sense, the very notion of honesty is redefined, because the basis for honesty becomes one's willingness to be in touch with and to express one's feelings." The third attribute of the therapeutic culture is its formal institutionalization in what Nolan calls "a new priestly class," the army of clinical psychologists, clinical social workers, psychiatrists, and other counselors and therapists that has mushroomed since the 1960s and now has the authority and role of helping "individuals make sense of life in the modern world" by using the terms and explanatory apparatus of the new ethos.[3]

These traits of the therapeutic culture fit the new direction of the black movement, led by those who took to heart the slogan "the personal is political," believing that strict boundaries between private or non-political realms and public or political ones threatened justice and democracy. The emphasis on individual identity, nearly always construed as a form of self-presentation, and the emotivist ethic appeared in ostensibly political writing that actually shared much in common with the emotional disclosure encouraged by the new therapies, creating a new codified form of identity quest qua racial harangue.

Rage, it goes without saying, was an intrinsic part of the African American experience from the start, given the exploitation and degradation of blacks during slavery and segregation. It had a strong presence in formal black political expression going at least as far back as David Walker's insurrectionist "Appeal" of 1829 and the abolitionist Henry Highland Garnet's "Call to Rebellion" speech at the National Negro Convention of 1844. Later, in Richard Wright's *Native Son* and James Baldwin's *The Fire Next Time* anger also figured prominently, though very differently. Each, though with varied meanings given the critical difference of the twenty years separating them, contained an implied threat to white society. But in the mid- to late-1960s, a new form of invective took a more explicit and pared-down form, with works such as Julius Lester's blatant *Look Out Whitey! Black Power's Gon' Get Your Mama!* (1968). Lester, once a field secretary of the Student Non-Violent Coordinating Committee (SNCC), recounted the now well-known and well-documented discrimination and violence against blacks and attempts of civil rights activists to stop them. This historical polemic was laced with the extremist black power language of the day—the simplistic, no-holds-barred rhetoric that neatly divided the black community into resisters or assimilationists and the whole population into revolutionaries or upholders of a vague, evil "system." The account of events offered in *Look Out Whitey!* ranged from what Lester painted as the hopeful, but naïve nonviolent resistance of the early sit-ins to the horrifying backlash against the movement such as the bombing of the 16th St. Baptist Church in Birmingham in 1963, which killed four young black girls, and the later turn toward black power militancy. What is interesting here is that in championing this turn, Lester spoke of it as a new "awareness" or "consciousness." Like other cultural nationalists of the time, he believed that African Americans had been deprived of their culture and dignity by what he called the "American lie of assimilation."[4]

Although Lester's views later bbecame much more nuanced, this early book perfectly illustrates the shift away from a concern with the public rights, responsibilities, and roles of blacks in society to an obsession with individual identity that was becoming so prevalent in the late 1960s. Thus, it helps us ferret out the traits of the new emphasis. First, this emphasis assumed the primacy of the psychological state of blacks, casting them as in a state of identity crisis. Lacking their own language and an unequivocal sense of their national or religious heritage, Lester wrote, blacks were caught between and denied connection to "two native lands: America and Africa":

> This denial of America and Africa has created the central psychological problem for the black American. Who am I? Many avoid their blackness as much as possible by trying to become assimilated. They remove all traces of blackness from their lives. Their gestures, speech, habits, cuisine, walk, everything they can consciously control, becomes as 'American Dream' as possible. . . A small minority avoid the crux of their blackness by going to another extreme. They identify completely with Africa. Some do so to the extent of wearing African clothes, celebrating African holidays, and speaking Swahili. They, however, are only unconsciously admitting that the white man is right when he says American blacks have nothing of their own.
>
> For other blacks the question of identity is only now being solved by the realization of those things that are theirs. Black people do have a language of their own. The words may be English, but the way a black person puts them together and the meaning that he gives them creates a new language. He has another language, too, and that language is rhythm. This has been recognized by black people for some time, and they call it "soul." In Africa they speak of negritude. The two are the same. It is the recognition of those things uniquely ours which separate us from the white man.[5]

Second, in this passage suggests, the solution to this identity crisis is recovery or invention of cultural traditions that revolve primarily around cultural expression or self-presentation, presume intragroup homogeneity and uniformity, and confuse cultural nationalism with the retrieval of cultural tradition.

Finally, the point of the psychological exercise is unclear: it is a coming-into-awareness *of or for what*? The result is that the act becomes a kind of end in itself. Lester wrote about how a heightened "consciousness had come about." He praised the leader of the Nation of Islam, Elijah Muhammad, and SNCC, but thought that "More than any other person, Malcolm X was responsible for the growing consciousness and new militancy of black people." Lester made only two points about how Malcolm X contributed to this new consciousness, neither getting very specific about its content. First, the militant leader stood for open expression of innermost feelings: "He said aloud those things which blacks had been saying among themselves. He even said those things we had been afraid to say to each other." Second, Lester quoted Ossie Davis on Malcolm X to show that the leader helped blacks discover their true identity: "Malcolm X did not hate white folks, nor did he love them. Most of all, he did not need them to tell him who he was."[6] Lester went on to praise the movement for "cultural awareness" and the "furtherance of black consciousness" in publications by intellectuals and in informal social circles where friends encouraged one another to "think black," wore their hair naturally instead of straightening it, and criticized others for "sounding too much like whitey." Perhaps ironically, Lester thought the white activist Anne Braden took this emphasis on awareness to a deeper level and showed its link to black power when she said that "Negroes need to reject the unconscious idea that what is white is better." "Black consciousness is an essential part of speaking and defining for ourselves," Lester concluded.[7]

It is no secret that Martin Luther King, Jr., and many other leaders of the early civil rights movement did not agree with this new approach. They warned of the dangers inherent in the turn toward black power such as what we now call reverse racism. King himself wrote extensively about his thoughts on black power in *Where Do We Go From Here: Chaos or Community?* in 1967, sympathizing with the new militants' desire to call "the Negro to a new sense of manhood" and "a new realization of his dignity and worth." King acknowledged the psychological aspect of the civil rights struggle when he spoke of the difficulties inherent in "the job of arousing manhood within a people that have been taught for so many centuries that they are nobody [sic]." He understood that "Black Power is a psychological reaction to the psychological indoctrination that led to the creation of the perfect slave." King also saw the renunciation of nonviolence as, in part, an understandable reaction to the frustrations of civil rights organizing itself, with not only the resistance of government and law enforcement officials but the outright violence the movement had endured. More enthusiastically, he pointed to those advocates of black power who believed in the need to strengthen social and economic institutions within the black community through mutual cooperation.[8]

Despite his understanding of the reasons behind black power sentiments, King called it a "nihilistic philosophy" that "carries the seeds of its own doom." King thought its separatist emphasis unrealistic, impractical, and undesirable. He emphasized the multi-racial nature of the United States, the vital contributions to the black struggle coming from outside the black community, and the interdependence of all groups of Americans. The black power movement, resigned as it was to failure rather than paving the way for hope, wasted time and energy on "romantic illusions and empty philosophical debates." Its openness to the use of violence was, of course, anathema to King, who questioned its claims of newness, instead seeing it as "the inseparable twin of materialism" in modern civilization, "the sin-sick world," which needed to be redeemed.[9]

Yet, it is even more revealing to contrast Lester's version of the black movement as an act of consciousness-raising to a book King published before the achievements and tumultuous events of the 1960s. *Stride Toward Freedom* chronicles the Montgomery Bus Boycott of 1955 and 1956 and King's own emergence as a leader in the boycott. For our purposes, it offers an ideal opportunity to examine what King thought led to the successful mobilization of the blacks and its white sympathizers. While the 224-page book would seem to lend itself to a discussion of the mass mobilization as a mass act of consciousness-raising, King's terms are differ markedly from those employed by Lester. Briefly, King saw the boycott as a way of "withdrawing our cooperation from an evil system" and traced the origins of his own commitment to the boycott to two factors: a childhood in which he was, from a very early age, fully aware of the wrongs of discrimination against blacks; and his intellectual trajectory in college and graduate school, that is, his well-known immersion in the ideas of Walter Rauschenbusch, Henry David Thoreau, Karl Marx, Mahatma Gandhi, Reinhold Niebuhr, Georg W. F. Hegel and others. As for the black population in Montgomery, he described the origins of its mobilization as a problem of overcoming three obstacles in the black community itself: "factionalism among the leaders, indifference in the educated group, and passivity in the uneducated." In laying out the reasons these problems were ultimately surmounted, King said that "it was the culminating of a slowly developing process." While the arrest of Rosa Parks sparked the boycott, the underlying cause "lay deep in the record of similar injustices," thus in the long history of oppression itself: "Almost everybody could point to an unfortunate episode that he himself had experienced or seen." What happened in Montgomery was that "there comes a time when people get tired of being trampled by oppression" and "plunged into the abyss of exploitation and nagging injustice."[10]

King's only explanation for the change—the preexisting knowledge of the daily injustices of Jim Crow, the boiling point people had reached, the triggering arrest of Parks, the assistance of new leadership—did not satisfy him. Why, when other black communities suffered from poor treatment, was it Montgomery that witnessed this successful and inspiring act of mass resistance? King found the answer not in some mass awakening or awareness, but in divine intervention. However we might choose to think about it, to him what drove the boycott was not purely rational and individual, but some kind of "extra-human force" that "labors to create a harmony out of the discords of the universe," a kind of "creative power that works to pull down mountains of evil and level hilltops of injustice." "It seems as though God had decided to use Montgomery as the proving ground for the struggle and triumph of freedom and justice in America," he concluded.[11]

As is well known, this belief in the moral content of the civil rights crusade pervaded King's writings. Here he spoke of the spirit of faith, perseverance, and forgiveness in the mass meetings among blacks. There he spoke of nonviolent resistance as "merely a means to awaken a sense of moral shame in the opponent." His famous invocation of *agape*, a "love seeking to preserve and create community" through "understanding, redeeming good will for all men, a source of "cosmic companionship" essential to any struggle for justice and community, further established his point that it was a moral and spiritual impulse that led both to the protests and to their goal: moral and spiritual community that was their goal. This was a far cry from Lester's notion of individual identity as an end in itself and his vagueness about the purpose of awareness. King too spoke of the increasing self-respect of American blacks, but quite differently conceived of the point of the "new consciousness" as the black individual's discovery that he or she "is an equal element in a larger social compound and accordingly should be given rights and privileges commensurate with his or her new responsibilities." King was clear that attendant on blacks' achievement of self-respect was an "awakening of moral consciousness on the part of millions of white Americans concerning segregation."[12]

It was not King's notion of growing moral insight—for blacks, a heightening of their sense of dignity and moral agency, and for whites, a heightening of moral conscience—but Lester's stress on a

consciousness of oppression and separate identity that came to pre-
vail. The costs of this particular version of consciousness have not been
fully explored. It is the remaining task of this paper to raise some of
the questions that need to be raised if we wish to begin to do so.

A troubling passage stands out in one of the most well-known
black power invectives from the time, Eldridge Cleaver's *Soul on
Ice*, which was published in 1968. The book of essays includes an
account of how Cleaver, later minister of information for the Black
Panthers, had embarked upon a career as a rapist and later came to
understand and repent his crimes. The book, an eclectic mixture of
diatribe and intelligent commentary, scans the contemporary scene,
covering everything from the civil rights and student movements to
the writings of James Baldwin and Norman Mailer. It recounts
Cleaver's prison experiences, including his infatuation with his white,
female lawyer, and his growing belief that the racial situation would
only be improved when blacks dealt with the psychological legacy
of inferiority by overcoming their crisis of identity. For black men,
that meant not only recovering their self-respect, but also embracing relations—especially sexual ones—with black women, holding
them up as a standard of beauty and strength rather thanviewing white
women as the ideal.[13]

Delving into the past of racial wrongs while also tracing his own
personal trajectory toward rape and incarceration, Cleaver walked a
very thin line between genuine remorse and moral awareness, on the
one hand, and excuse, on the other. While he stated outright that he
fully realized his moral waywardness and culpability, the juxtaposi-
tion of the fiery invective against white America and his personal
story left some room for a reader's uneasiness about the crimes to which
Cleaver admits. But for our purposes, what is of particular relevance is
the way he describes an initial act of attaining consciousness.

In Cleaver's telling, before he was jailed for possession of mari-
juana in 1954 at age eighteen, he had never reflected deeply on the
situation of American blacks and, like them, passively "accepted
indignities and the mechanics of the apparatus of oppression" as if
under "novocain." But because of the heated debate over racial discrimination triggered by the Brown versus Board of Education decision and the segregationist resistance to it, he became consumed
with "horror, disgust and outrage" against the United States. Cleaver
described his trajectory in prison as he associated with other young
black men who "were in vociferous rebellion" against "everything

American," and said he came to the realization that he should "go for myself." He could gain power and freedom if he took "the initiative: instead of simply *reacting* I could *act*."[14]

First this meant indulging in "tirades of criticism and denunciation" against "all forms of piety, loyalty, and sentiment." Then Cleaver became fixated on the question of why so many of his fellow black inmates, himself included, had a preference for white women as sexual partners. Cleaver became embroiled in conversations on the matter with an inmate named Butterfly, later a black Muslim, who said this preference resulted from being "indoctrinated with the white race's standard of beauty." When the horrific lynching of Emmett Till for flirting with a white woman occurred in 1955, Cleaver "flew into a rage at myself, at America, at white women, at the history that had placed those tensions of lust and desire in my chest." He had a nervous breakdown and was put first in solitary confinement and then in psychiatric treatment. Despite all of his efforts to steer the therapy sessions toward his hatred of whites, Cleaver wrote, his psychiatrist refused to pursue the issue and inquired instead into his childhood. Cleaver returned to his cell and read widely, from Marx to Machiavelli, using Marx as support for the "hatred and contempt" he felt for American capitalism and Machiavelli and others as guides for "tactics of ruthlessness" he increasingly sought to use "in my dealings with everyone with whom I came into contact." As a result, he said, "I began to look at white America through these new eyes." He particularly came to believe that "it was of paramount importance for me to have an antagonistic, ruthless attitude toward white women." When released from prison, he deemed himself an "outlaw," a "law unto myself—my own legislature, my own supreme court, my own executive." Once out of jail, he wrote, "I became a rapist," first "practicing on black girls in the ghetto," and then turning to white women:

> Rape was an insurrectionary act. It delighted me that I was defying and trampling upon the white man's law, upon his system of values, and that I was defiling his women. . . I felt I was getting revenge.[15]

What does this sequence of events tell us? At the very least, it points to the seemingly obvious fact that not all forms of coming-into-awareness are benign. Once apprehended for rape, Cleaver went on to say, he "took a long look at myself and, for the first time in my life, admitted that I was wrong." "Even though I had some insight into my own motivations, I did not feel justified. I lost my self-respect. My pride as a man dissolved and my whole fragile moral structure seemed to collapse, completely shattered." While the reader cannot help but appreciate hearing that Cleaver "did not feel justified," that the remainder of the book is much more a litany of the nation's racial wrongs than his own brings out the tension between a moral inquiry and a quest for personal identity.[16] That the book was lauded as "extraordinary," "remarkable," and "brilliant and revealing"hints at the extent to which the search for identity, with its new mode of therapeutic disclosure, had replaced traditional moral self-analysis.[17]

Returning to Grier and Cobbs's *Black Rage*, the association we find between consciousness-raising and therapeutic disclosure is similar, but more literal. Now that we have seen the self-referentiality and emotivist ethic at play in the rise of the therapeutic understanding of race, we come to the third part of James Nolan's triad: the "new priestly class," in this case, the new authorities on race. First published in 1968, the best-seller was reprinted in 1980 and again in 1992. In the introduction to the 1980 edition, the authors wrote that "The most important aspect of therapy with blacks, we are convinced, is that racist mistreatment must be echoed and underlined as a fact." While it seemed obvious, given the cultural milieu when the book initially came out, that the effects of racial discrimination would crop up in therapy, that the authors still held focused so much on racism in all therapy with blacks fourteen years later helps point to the single-mindedness of their vision.[18]

In the book, these psychiatrists described the problems of a number of their patients in detail, concluding in case after case that these problems originated not only in ongoing white racism but in slavery itself. Grier and Cobbs seemed to presume a kind of collective unconscious when they wrote: "Because there has been so little change in attitudes, the children of bondage continue to suffer the effects of slavery. There is a timeless quality to the unconsciousness which transforms yesterday into today."[19]

With excursions into history, simplified drastically for the purposes of the book, Grier and Cobbs reiterated the then common interpretation of black men as emasculated as a result of slavery and of black women as suffering from inferiority at the hands of the white female standard of beauty. The authors began with cameos of three patients, all of whose maladies they traced to racism. In the first cameo, a man named Roy had worked on high scaffolds to paint tall buildings, hoping one day to use his savings to pursue a second career as a golfer. Previously in great physical shape, he fell one day at his job and was hospitalized for various pains. While his doctor subsequently told him he could resume work, he found that he had become impotent. Since the doctor found no physical basis for this condition, he sent Roy for psychiatric counseling. The authors then explained that his peripatetic, con-artist father and domestic mother both beat Roy when he was a child and early life for him had been "squalid and humiliating." He became extremely ambitious, working hard and saving his money in order to escape the ghetto. Before the fall, his marriage had been rewarding and his sexual relations with his wife "vigorous," but afterward he became so dependent on his wife for emotional support and so consumed with his impotence that she left him. In typical fashion for them, Grier and Cobbs concluded that he was programmed to fail because "for three hundred years his 'place' in America had been shaped by powerful forces" and he had come to believe that "the proper place in life for him was as an ineffectual, defenseless, castrated man." Many subsequent diagnoses exhibited this same tendency to contort the evidence into a rigid formula in which racism is the root of all problems. At one point, the authors wrote that some of their clients showed a "determination not to see" that "their difficulties are a consequence of the prejudice of whites." *Black Rage* made it clear that therapy with blacks needed to involve tracing blacks' problems to white racism.[20]

While there seems to be no doubt that racial discrimination played a role in the individual and shared psychological experience of blacks, it is far less clear that it is best understood as a universal factor. Looking at American life through warnings about its psychological ramifications for blacks constitutes a persuasive polemic and social critique, but when applied to therapy with individuals, *Black Rage* at the very least raises questions about the possibilities for misreading individual cases.

Besides getting people to become aware of the nation's wrongs against blacks, which, by the publication of *Black Rage* were widely known, the goal of the book, and of the therapy laid out in it, seems to be emotional catharsis. Blindness to the influence of white racism in blacks' lives was blamed for constricting expression of feeling and individuality, as was religion. "Religion plays a role in the cancer of black self-depreciation and the exaltation of whites," the authors wrote, since "All religions urge their adherents to look beyond the problems of the day to some major guiding principle or to the will of some superior being or to follow certain rules that will assure happiness in an after life." Worse yet, "Religion teaches that one should in general be kind, be fair, be modest, restrain impulses and love everyone." Grier and Cobbs argued against religion's tendency "to evoke guilt" and to invoke the premise that humans "are inherently wicked and can gain pardon and find a welcome into the house of God only by some extraordinary act of faith." They wrote that this guilt was "lethal to black men," who have always been taught they are "wicked and base." Any religion with a concept of sin would thus only reinforce the negative messages blacks had always received; such a religion works in concert with white supremacy. Likewise, the goal of integration reinforced a sense of white superiority by making it seem desirable for blacks to seek acceptance into the majority group.[21]

After *Black Rage*, Price Cobbs went on to be a management consultant and diversity trainer, instituting a kind of interracial encounter group style of therapy called "ethnotherapy." Since the 1960s, he has led diversity workshops for every type of institution from police departments to businesses. He is just one member of the field of diversity training which has mushroomed since the late 1980s in response to litigation and concerns about diversity in the workplace. So many individuals have chosen to ride this wave, and workshops and training materials have proliferated so exponentially that one observer easily substantiated his claim that a veritable "diversity machine" had come into existence. Sociologist Frederick Lynch has written a searching analysis of this movement. He traces it to a variety of influences, from identity politics to new management trends and the human potential movement.[22]

The approaches and materials used in this movement are varied, but many reveal that the movement has more in common with the projects fashioned by Lester, Cleaver, and Grier and Cobbs than that of King. Using materials like training videos that drastically simplify the nation's racial past and present in the interest of the limited time allotted for workshops, diversity trainers frequently cast their work as consciousness-raising. For black participants, this means a coming-into-awareness of their status as victims of ongoing oppression. For whites, this means grasping their complicity in the oppression of blacks and other groups. One guide for counselors by Woodrow Parker, called *Consciousness-Raising: A Primer for Multicultural Counseling* drew on the human potential movement's gurus Abraham Maslow and Carol Rogers to state goals for counseling such as self-actualization and self-awareness. In works like this, designed to instruct therapists in dealing with clients of other cultural backgrounds, there is no hint of moral inquiry, community or national improvement, or moral self-improvement. Instead the desired process that is "the internal growth process," which proponents define as self-fulfillment. Further, the movement trains scores of new workers to lead others on this path of "becoming aware through group experience."[23]

It is difficult, perhaps, to see what could possibly be wrong with a movement based on such seemingly innocuous and banal pieties. Only when we look further to the content of the awareness that is being taught do we find a strong dose of racial identity theory, which exhibits the growing preoccupation with identity sketched above. Racial identity theory appears in works like D.W. Sue's *Counseling the Culturally Different* and Beverly Daniel Tatum's *"Why Are All the Black Kids Sitting Together in the Cafeteria?" And Other Conversations about Race.*[24] These and other writers state that there is a set of fixed developmental stages which blacks experience as they develop a sense of identity. What stands out in these theories is an odd parallel between individual development and the course of the civil rights movement from integrationism to identity politics. That such a basic parallel can be seriously posited hints at the simplistic nature of these writings.

Varying slightly from author to author, the story line of such works is that a black individual begins in the "conformity stage," adhering to the tenets of the dominant culture and believing unconsciously in white superiority. Some event triggers a state of "confusion and conflict" over race and this leads to the "dissonance stage" in which the individual begins to question the dominant culture. The "resistance and immersion stage" finds the individual forsaking the dominant culture and finding out as much as possible about his or her own "ethnic history, traditions, foods, language, etc." In the ensuing "introspection stage," the individual questions the rejection of the dominant culture and "struggle for self-awareness." Finally, in the "synergetic articulation and awareness stage," according to Parker, the individual achieves "a sense of fulfillment regarding cultural identity," a tolerant attitude toward other cultural groups, and a desire to work against oppression. Other authors write that a similar developmental process takes place among whites, who must embrace their white identity as well.[25]

A review of these and other materials from the diversity training and multicultural counseling movement raises questions about when the mode and content of consciousness-raising is no longer innocuous or benign. The diversity movement, after all, has become established largely behind the scenes, without subjection to open debate and discussion by the public. Participants truly act like Nolan's "new priestly class," wielding authority over how citizens will think about everything from race relations to social life more broadly. The methods most often employed place a premium on emotional expression and individual identity formation through the development of self-awareness. While ostensibly a neutral term, this awareness bears much cultural baggage—that of the therapeutic rendering of race that replaced, in the mid- to late-1960s the much more promising path of the early moral crusade for civil rights, with its goal of revitalizing democratic civic culture. Rather than renewing our entire "moral demand system," as Rieff put it, this therapeutic turn threatens to replace our notion of individual and collective moral development with a "manipulatable sense of well being." Judging by the content of the awareness promulgated by the diversity movement of the 1980s and 1990s, the very notion of a moral demand system, and its role in maintaining community, might already have receded into the long-forgotten past.

Notes

1.   William H. Grier and Price M. Cobbs, *Black Rage* (New York: Basic Books, 1968), 180, for example, on unabated racism; 154-58 on the role of therapists; and 177-79 and 206 on what the authors call the "Black Norm." According to this concept, therapists must become familiar with psychological dysfunction among blacks as a legitimate and appropriate adaptive response to white oppression: "to find the amount of sickness a black man has, one must first total all that appears to represent illness and then subtract the Black Norm. What remains is illness and a proper subject for therapeutic endeavor" (179).

2.   Philip Rieff, *The Triumph of the Therapeutic: The Uses of Faith after Freud* (New York: Harper and Row, 1966), 3-4, 12-17, 63n. See also Philip Rieff, *The Feeling Intellect: Selected Writings*, edited by Jonathan B. Imber (Chicago: University of Chicago Press, 1990), 222-231, for Rieff's later thoughts along these same lines.

3.   James L. Nolan, *The Therapeutic State: Justifying Government at Century's End* (New York: New York University Press, 1988), 3-8; Ellen Herman, *The Romance of American Psychology: Political Culture in the Age of Experts* (Berkeley: University of California Press, 1995).

4.   Julius Lester, *Look Out Whitey! Black Power's Gon' Get Your Mama!* (New York: Grove Press, 1968), 90.

5.   Lester, *Look Out Whitey!*, 90-91.

6.   Ossie Davis quoted in Lester, 92. Lester, in turn, found this quote in Lerone Bennett, Jr., "What's In a Name?" *Ebony* (November 1967).

7.   Lester, 93; the Anne Braden quote is from her "The SNCC Trends: Challenge to White America," *Southern Patriot* (May 1966), quoted in Lester, 93.

8.   Martin Luther King, Jr., *Where Do We Go From Here: Chaos or Community?* (Boston: Beacon Press, 1967), 40-41, 34-38.

9.   King, *Where Do We Go From Here*, 44-66.

10.   Martin Luther King, Jr., *Stride Toward Freedom* (Rpt. 1958; San Francisco, CA: HarperCollins, 1986), 51, 90-101, 37, 69.

11.   King, *Stride Toward Freedom*, 69-70.

12.   King, *Stride Toward Freedom*, 88, 102, 104-106, 190.

13.   Eldridge Cleaver, *Soul on Ice* (rpt. 1999, New York: Delta, 1968).

14.   Cleaver, *Soul on Ice,* 21-24.

15.   Cleaver, *Soul on Ice*, 24-33.

16.   Cleaver, *Soul on Ice*, 34.

17.   Cleaver, *Soul on Ice*, back cover of paperback edition.

18.   William H. Grier and Price M. Cobbs, *Black Rage* (Rpt. 1968, New York: Basic Books, 1992), xiii.

19.   Grier and Cobbs, *Black Rage*, 5-8.

20.   Grier and Cobbs, *Black Rage*, 5-8.

21.   Grier and Cobbs, *Black Rage*, 196-198.

22.   Frederick R. Lynch, *The Diversity Machine: The Drive to Change the "White Male Workplace"* (New York: Free Press, 1997). See also Elisabeth Lasch-Quinn, *Race Experts: How Racial Etiquette, Sensitivity Training, and New Age Therapy Hijacked the Civil Rights Revolution* (New York: W. W. Norton, 2001).

23.   Woodrow M. Parker, *Consciousness-Raising: A Primer for Multicultural Counseling* (Springfield, IL: Charles C. Thomas, 1988), 17-18.

24.   D. W. Sue, *Counseling the Culturally Different* (New York: John Wiley, 1981); Beverly Daniel Tatum, *"Why Are All the Black Kids Sitting Together in the Cafeteria?" And Other Conversations About Race* (1997; revised edition, New York, Basic Books, 1999). Tatum draws on William S. Hall, William E. Cross, Jr., and Roy Freedle, "Stages in the Development of Black Awareness: An Exploratory Investigation," in Reginald L. Jones, ed., *Black Psychology* (New York: Harper and Row, 1972), 156-165.

25.   Parker, *Consciousness-Raising*, 61-63; Janet Helms, "Toward a Model of White Identity Development" in Janet E. Helms, ed., *Black and White Racial Identity: Theory, Research and Practice* (Westport, CT, 1990), 49-66.

2

The Silent Ascendancy of Therapeutic Culture in Britain

Frank Furedi

After the unprecedented display of public emotionalism over the death of Princess Diana in 1997, it is difficult to sustain the myth that Britain is the land of the stiff upper lip. Although the role of the therapeutic ethos was rarely discussed before Diana's death, its influence on British culture has been significant for some time. Indeed, as we will argue, the therapeutic ethos has been systematically assimilated into British culture since the Second World War: moreover, during the 1980s it also acquired an important institutional dimension. The relative absence of any serious intellectual, cultural or theoretical debate over the import of this development is one the intriguing questions which this paper attempts to address.

Therapeutic Culture in Contemporary Britain

An exploration of the workings of contemporary therapeutic ethos inexorably leads to a consideration of the prevailing ideas about human subjectivity and personhood, that is British culture's ethnopsychology. "Every culture contains a set of ideas and beliefs about the nature of human beings, what motivates them to act, the way they perceive the world, how their minds work, and the emotions that are natural to them," writes Hewitt in his description of the concept of ethnopsychology.[1] Ideas about emotion, individual behavior and vulnerability are underpinned by the particular account that a culture offers about personhood and the human potential. As Derek Summerfield argues, such accounts embody questions as "how much or what kind of adversity a person can face and still be 'normal'; what is a reasonable risk; when fatalism is appropriate and when a sense of grievance is, what is acceptable behavior at a time of crisis including how distress should be expressed, how help should be sought, and whether restitution should be made."[2]

Until the eighties, the British cultural script regarding personhood invoked notions of "stoicism, understatement, the stiff upper lip and of fortitude (e.g., bulldog tenacity)" which popular memory associates with the nation's experience during the Second World War.[3] Although, as with all cultural constructs, the notion of British fortitude represented an idealized version of human behavior, it helped frame the interpretation of everyday life including the experience of adversity. Take the case of one of the most devastating industrial tragedies in post war Britain; the Aberfan disaster of 1966. Despite the horror of a village school engulfed by a coal-tip slide, nobody demanded compensation for their trauma or their psychological distress. The relatives of the 116 children and twenty-eight adults, who died during this tragedy, took the view that they did not want to pursue prosecution because that would be to "bow to vengeance." The surviving children resumed their education a fortnight after the tragedy "so that their minds may be taken off the disaster." A year after this disaster, Mary Essex, a family and child psychologist from the University of Wales, noted that the surviving children seemed normal and adjusted. The *Times* observed that "the villagers had done admirably in rehabilitating themselves with very little help."[4] Today, such a response to a major disaster would be unthinkable. There would be an automatic assumption that every survivor in the area was deeply traumatized and inevitably scarred for life. Sending young pupils back to school so soon after a tragedy would be scorned as bad practice. The very attempt by the community to cope through self-help would be denounced as misguided since such victims could not be expected to deal with such problems on their own.

A recently published book on Aberfan, is genuinely perturbed by the stoicism of the survivors of this strategy. It documents how people perceived offers of psychological help in negative terms and bemoans the fact that the local consultant psychiatrist found it difficult to get people realize they needed help. "The stigma of seeking psychological help was stronger in the 1960s than today," conclude the authors. The authors are delighted that since the subsequent invention of Post-Traumatic Stress Disorder, authorities are likely to respond to such a disaster with clearly focused therapeutic policies.[5]

Since the nineties the history of Aberfan is being rewritten in line with today's therapeutic ethos. Researchers are busy helping survivors to reinterpret their experiences through the language of trauma. A collection of recently conducted interviews of Aberfan survivors suggests that retrospectively people have discovered past traumas. A survivor who has authored a recollection of this disaster echoes this sentiment, when she remarked that "one crucial area where I feel we were badly let down in Aberfan was in the lack of proper counseling."[6] Such is the power of present day sensitivity to emotional injury that past events can only make sense through the language of trauma. Instead of exploring the resilience of this Welsh mining community, commentators are far more likely to treat the survivors as hidden victims whose emotional needs were ignored by a callous officialdom.

The stoic response to the tragedy at Aberfan was by no means exceptional. The public presentation of the 1953 flood disaster that led to death of 164 people provides a useful case study. The press coverage was mainly informational rather than emotional. Although the Queen "sent sympathy to relatives" there was none of the emoting that one associates with the media coverage of contemporary disasters.[7] Compare this response with the representation of the floods that wreaked havoc in Britain in 2001. Newspaper headlines proclaimed that Britain was in a state of crisis and facing a major natural disaster. Although the floods caused considerable damage and led to the indirect loss of four lives, it was a relatively minor disaster compared to previous experiences. Yet, the flood was experienced as a traumatic experience with far reaching consequences to people's emotional health.

Significantly, the health threat posed by the flood was often presented in psychological rather than physical terms. "The long term effects of flooding on psychological health may perhaps be even more important than illness or injury," warned an editorial in the *British Medical Journal*. It added that "for most people the emotional trauma continues long after the water has receded." It pointed out that "making repairs, cleaning up, and dealing with insurance claims can be stressful" and warned that "if there is a lack of support during the recovery process, stress levels may increase further."[8] This emphasis on the emotional vulnerability of flood victims is a recurrent theme in contemporary British culture. It is not only exceptional events like floods that are seen as the precursor to long-term emotional injury. Many experiences that have been hitherto interpreted as a normal part of life have been redefined as harmful and traumatic.

Stress is a clear example. It has become an everyday idiom that describes the state of people in virtually every conceivable setting, and stress is nearly always seen as "a bad thing" that should be prevented. Traditional means of assessing performance, such as examinations—have come under scrutiny for placing subjects under pressure—a bizarre criticism since this is precisely what the tests have been designed to do. Students facing exams are said to face exam panic attacks. Delegates at the 1999 conference of the British Professional Association of Teacher s denounced the examination system for the "sadistic" pressure it placed on children to perform well and called for its abolition on the grounds that it was little more than child abuse.[9] The discovery that the age-old system of school examination is actually dangerous to children's well being reflects the tendency to reinterpret difficult or challenging encounters as potentially damaging to the people concerned. It is not merely exams that have been given a health warning. Competition, particularly competitive sports have been attacked because they are said to strike a blow at children's self esteem. Pushy parents have been labeled as emotional abusers because they place "unacceptable" pressure on their children.

The complex emotional tensions that are integral to the process of growing up are now often defined as stressful events with which children cannot be expected to cope. Concern with children's stress has led some schools to train young students in "anger management" skills. A project in inner city Birmingham has been mounted to help secondary school pupils learn to deal with their emotions. This project offers an anger management course taught by a psychotherapist, who encourages secondary school pupils to release their aggression through role-play and exercises such as punching pillows.[10] And, it seems, it is never too early to start. One organization, Befrienders International, offers lessons to pupils, as young as six, on how to cope with the stresses of modern life. Chris Bale, the director of this initiative hopes that such lessons will help pupils in nursery and primary schools to deal with "crises later in life and, as result, reduce the suicide rate."[11] It appears that the therapeutic profession is determined to protect children's emotions from virtually any form of challenging experience. In September 2000, it was announced that telephone help-lines were being set up for children stressed by starting secondary school. These help-lines were complemented by numerous counseling schemes designed to help pupils to make the transition from primary to secondary education. The promoters of the helpline believe that "mental health work" should be integrated into teaching to help children cope with the pressure of secondary education.[12]

This pathologizing of children's emotion pales into insignificance when compared to the way in which the workplace has been transformed into a source of mental health problems. The notion that work makes you literally ill is regularly conveyed in surveys, newspaper reports and public discussion. So, according to one study published in July 1999, one in three people claimed that their health suffered because of their job. More than half of the respondents—55 percent—described themselves as "frequently" or "very frequently" stressed at work and a quarter associated their poor sex life with problems arising from their jobs.[13] In August 1999, a Joseph Rowntree Foundation report indicated that the drive to raise economic efficiency had created a British workforce that was characteristically insecure about its future, unhappy and, above all, ill. According to the Rowntree study, stress, ill health and strain on families are on the increase in both the public and private sectors.[14] Newspaper headlines like "Stressed? If you are an employee, you probably are" continually reinforce the message: work makes you ill.

The metaphor of stress has been extended to virtually every social setting. Since the turn of this century, the British public has been informed that one if five people "feel stressed or anxious about Christmas, that significant numbers of children as young as eight suffer stress over their 'love lives' and that British bosses are more stressed out than their counterparts in other countries."[15] Stress has become so normalized, that even children are sometimes encouraged to interpret their lives through this cultural metaphor. One academic, Stephen Palmer, who led the research team that discovered that children suffered stress over their love lives, claimed that "we were surprised by the problem." He observed that "if you had asked eight-year-olds about stress 20 years ago, they would have looked blank." However, "now they understand the concept and a significant number report experiencing it," he reported.[16] Of course, from a sociological point of view, what has happened is that children's perception of stress has fallen in line with their culture's expectations of their experiences. Individuals—young and old—tend to feel and interpret their feelings in accordance with prevailing expectations and cultural norms.

The normalization of stress constitutes part of a wider pattern of constructing a form of personhood whose defining feature is its vulnerability. Terms like depression, addiction and trauma are routinely designated to describe people's encounters with the problems of every day life. From this perspective, it follows that people find it difficult to cope and that they are therefore unlikely to be able to forge satisfactory relationship to one another and their communities. Hence the need for a therapeutic solution and intervention.[17]

Therapists have assumed the role of relationship experts and have succeeded in establishing a demand for their services in virtually every institutional setting. Since the eighties—when counseling became one of Britain's little growth industries—the number of people practicing talking cures has grown steadily.[18] Even sections of the counseling profession are concerned by the routinization of the demand for therapeutic intervention. The psychotherapist, Nick Totton has described counseling training as a "pyramid selling scheme," which has created a "huge increase in clients." "The only way to get therapy and counseling paid for...is to get the state and other institutions to pay for it," argues Totton.[19] Evidently, the counseling professions have proved successful in creating a thriving market for its services. It is now assumed that people facing an unusual event are likely to need or at least likely to benefit from counseling. Take the case of the disbanding of Cleveland county council in 1995. Although none of the employees faced redundancy —they were to be reassigned to a reorganized local authority—bereavement counseling was offered to council workers to help them overcome any sense of loss they might experience. The employees were warned that the experience could be like the death of a "friend or a loved one" Staff were told to expect symptoms, such as loss of libido, mood swings, eating disorders and panic attacks. The Council employed eighteen counselors to help employees identify signs of stress and to "tap into heir inner strengths."[20]

Therapeutic intervention is not simply confined to the relationship of the therapist and the client. Such interventions characterize all contemporary organizations and institutions in Britain. The assimilation of the therapeutic ethos and practices by a variety of pro-

fessions and institutions—teachers, lawyers, and social workers—
has been well documented. "The management of subjectivity has
become a central task for the modern organization" notes Nikolas
Rose in his comprehensive survey of the development of the institutionalization of therapeutic culture in Britain.[21]

The past two decades have seen a discernible expansion in the
influence of therapeutic activism in private business. The shake out
of British industry in the eighties, saw the acceptance of the idea
people who lost their jobs were likely to face trauma. Thus creating
a demand for redundancy counselors. Soon, these counselors were
not only managing those about to be made unemployed but were
also providing stress therapy to managers to help them handle making others redundant.[22] Since the eighties, counseling has become
incorporated into the normal routine of personnel management. A
growing group of British blue chip companies such as the leisure
group Whitbread and Cable and Wireless, have taken steps to provide therapy as part of the employee's contract. Such companies are
not merely buying in counseling services but are also training managers to use counseling skills as part of their work.[23] Within the field
of human resource management, the therapeutic approach has come
to inform a growing range of practices. The Institute of Personnel
and Development in London runs courses on emotional intelligence
for executives and actively crusades for the adoption of therapeutic
practices in business.[24]

The field of medicine has seen an important reconfiguration of
expert authority as psychological judgements have come to play an
increasing role in defining the concepts of health and illness. Clinical psychology is not simply concerned with mental health but also
with the mental health problems of people with bodily ailments. It is
now assumed that patients suffering from a physical disease are likely
to need counseling provisions for dealing with their mental distress.[25]
According to one account, doctors in general practice have expanded
their role to embrace the wider field of mental health and provide
treatment for a "range of personal problems not previously considered to fall within the sphere of medical practice."[26] Just over half of
all medical general practices now employ counselors and the National Health Service (NHS) has become the major employer of therapeutic professionals.[27]

The invasion of the therapeutic ethos into other professions and
forms of authority is particularly striking in relation to British reli-

gious institutions. Recently, the Archbishop of Canterbury has claimed that therapy was replacing Christianity in Western countries. According to Archbishop Carey "Christ the savior" is becoming "Christ the counselor."[28] Priests are increasingly encouraged to adopt counseling skills. Gradually, the theologian has assumed the role of a therapist. Organizations that have sought to harness therapeutic expertise for the work of the Church inevitably assume a secular orientation. For example the Westminster Pastoral Foundation, which was established by a Methodist minister in the early seventies in order to combine the insights offered by counseling, psychotherapy and Christianity has weakened its religious connection. Its director, Dr. Tim Woolmer states that, nevertheless they are still interested in "wider religious questions such as: why are we here and what's it all about."[29] This subordination of religious doctrine to concern with people's existential quest reflects a wider shift towards an orientation towards a preoccupation with the self.

The colonization of the sphere of religion by therapeutic authority is manifest in relation to the way British society engages with the phenomenon of death. Tony Walter's important exploration into this subject suggests that the experience of bereavement has changed away from the external mourning behavior of previous times towards a "grief process" played out within the bereaved inner psyche.[30] This displacement of the externally focused spiritual towards the psychological is highlighted by the example of CRUSE, the UK's leading bereavement agency. This organization, which was founded by Quakers in 1959, had become by the 1990s "an entirely secular organization in which counseling technique and a kind heart are seen as sufficient."[31]

It is evident that therapeutic culture has been internalized by a significant section of the clergy. It has become common for members of the clergy to complain about the emotional injury inflicted on them by an abusive church hierarchy. There is even an advocacy group "Bullied and Abused Lives in Ministry—A Christian Support Group for Damaged Ministers." Numerous reports have concluded that many priests find it difficult to deal with the stress and emotional demands associated with their vocation. According one recently published survey of members of the clergy, 38 percent of the respondents felt overwhelmed by "pastoral care demands" and 53 percent have considered leaving the ministry. This survey on pastoral needs shows that concern with stress (66 percent) comes top. Typically, the report concludes with a call for "more dialogues with secular counseling."[32]

In intellectual terms, the trends outlined above are expressed in the shift from a socio-economic to a therapeutic discourse. Consequently, the model of the individual as a rational calculating actor is gradually being displaced by a cultural framework that insists that human experience is best understood through the prism of emotion. The therapeutic imperative continues to alter the language of our times. Terms like stress, self-esteem and emotional literacy have acquired everyday usage and continually highlight the trauma of simply coping with everyday life. Explanations oriented towards the emotion are now used to make sense of problems that in the past were illuminated through socio-economic or philosophical analysis. Academics applying for financial support for their research are far more likely to gain funding for a project on "Unemployment and Mental Health" than for a proposal to study on "structural unemployment." When the *Guardian* published a major report on the crisis in Britain's education system, its emphasis was the emotional damage suffered by poor children, rather than on their social conditions or the failure of the system of education: "Poverty does its worst damage with the emotions of those who live with it."[33] It seems that society is far more comfortable in dealing with poverty as a mental health problem than as a social issue. This approach is driven by a widely held premise that adverse circumstances, even relatively banal ones are stress inducing and cause trauma and various forms of mental illness.

The influence of the therapeutic worldview is particularly striking in deliberations around old social problems such as racism. Whereas in the past critics of racism emphasized the salience of economic inequality, discrimination and violence, today there is a tendency to adopt the therapeutic language of victimization. A recent study conducted by the Joseph Rowntree Foundation focused on the "devastating stress" suffered by victims of racial harassment. The report self-consciously sought to win public sympathy for victims of racism by playing the therapeutic card. Its focus was on the "anger, stress, depression, sleepless nights" of the respondents to the survey.[34]

The Politicization of Emotion

The management of emotion and of personal relationships has become a key concern of the British State. Rose has noted that the "personal and subjective capacities of citizens have been incorporated into the scope and aspirations of public powers." The internal lives of British people "now enters into the calculations of political forces about the state of the nation and the problems facing the country about priorities and policies."[35] Since the eighties there has been a rapid acceleration of the assimilation of therapeutic objectives and practices by public authority. The current New Labor government is a robust and self-conscious promoter of this approach. As Arnar Arnason notes "it is telling that technologies similar to those employed by counseling have now become part and parcel of the way in which the current British government governs its people" Arnason believes that the government's obsession with focus groups and other instruments designed to gauge public opinion represents a quest to "gain unfettered access to people's subjectivity."[36]

The institutionalization of therapeutic policy making received a major boost in the eighties under the conservative Thatcher and Major regimes. But it was under the Blair government, that therapeutic politics came to exercise an important influence on the presentation of public policy. One of the principal underlying assumptions that inform New Labor policy making is the importance of connecting with people's emotional needs and to offer measures that can boost the electorate's self esteem. New Labor rhetoric is deeply embedded within the therapeutic discourse. Concepts like the Third Way, social inclusion and exclusion are directly wedded towards the objective of offering public recognition to the emotional needs of the British public. For example, according to Prime Minister Blair, the problem of social exclusion is not so much about material poverty as about destructive influences that are "damaging to self esteem."[37] Not surprisingly, almost every initiative promoted by the Blair government's Social Exclusion Unit is designed to raise people's self esteem.[38]

The language of therapy permeates the British government domestic policy initiatives. Officials and politicians regularly use expressions like "raising self-esteem" and promoting "emotional literacy." So a government initiative designed to tackle under achievement by girls promised to "boost girls' self-esteem."[39] Getting people to feel good about themselves influences government policy in education and health. Margaret Hodge, former under-secretary for education and employment remarked that "developing self confidence, self esteem and social skills is as vital as learning to hold a pencil and count to ten," when the government announced its plan to spend

£ 8 billion on an integrated early years and childcare strategy.[40] An integrated health care initiative launched in February 1999 was promoted on the grounds that the real health problem in many communities was "lack of self-esteem."[41]

Some of New Labor's most highly publicized initiatives—teenage pregnancy, employment schemes, parenting initiatives—prescribe the raising of self-esteem as its main objective. The June 2000 government sponsored "Body Image Summit" is paradigmatic in this respect. During the months preceding this event government ministers spoke out on the alleged danger that the pressure to be thin posed for young women's self-esteem. According to Tessa Jowell, the former minister for women, young women are "being held back from fulfilling their aspirations and reaching their potential because they lack confidence and self-esteem."[42] According to recent government statements, low self-esteem is a common factor associated with child prostitution, homelessness, teenage pregnancy, drug abuse and a variety of anti social and destructive behavior. Consequently social problems are increasingly presented as rooted in psychological pathologies that require therapeutic treatment. Even the hard-nosed Treasury has adopted this approach. One of its consultation documents, *Enterprise and Social Exclusion* argues that local development policies will be marginal unless they help foster "people's skills and self-esteem." Other consultation papers argue that people can be "removed from economic deprivation" through "raising poor self-esteem."[43]

Many of New Labor's distinctive policies target people's emotions and offer counseling, and therapy as part of its program. This approach has gained prominence in the field of education policy. There is now a manifest tendency for school pupil's socialization to take the form of emotional training. It is worth noting that a British Government Advisory Group on Education for Citizenship and the Teaching of Democracy in Schools considers self-esteem as an important core skill.[44] The Department of Education's guiding statement on "Sex and Relationship" education instructs schools to undertake the task of building pupil's self-esteem. Schools are advised to prepare young people to have "the confidence and self esteem to value themselves and others." A similar approach informs the pedagogic perspective of the Scottish Executive. Its national guidelines insist that if pupils lack self-esteem, they are "unlikely to make progress in classroom learning." Accordingly Scottish schools offer special focus programs which attempt to develop children's emotional skills. The most widely used technique is "circle time" in which "pupils sit in a circle and say something about their own feelings on a special issue." They may be asked to complete a sentence beginning "I feel happy when" or "I feel sad when." This technique is often linked to the realization of the objective of emotional intelligence, "that is the ability to understand and mange one's own emotion."[45]

Although, the development of emotional education within the national curriculum is still at an early stage, some local authorities have already adopted a self consciously therapeutic approach. In 1998, the Southampton Educational Authority took a decision to assign emotional intelligence the same level of importance as "ordinary" literacy. Southampton teachers are encouraged to "take time and stare" in order to understand their own emotions so that they can help develop the emotional literacy of their pupils.[46] A variety of government sponsored pilot projects aim to assess whether therapeutic techniques can be used effectively as teaching tools. One project, which involves four secondary and two primary schools in East London, presents itself as an experiment to see whether psychotherapeutic techniques can help children do better in class. The first phase of this project involves the carrying out of an "emotional literacy audit" in each school. Once problem areas have been identified, an action plan will be devised, leading to initiatives like anger management schemes and meditation sessions.[47] Another project, based in Lambeth—Supporting Parents on Kids Education—is run by Stephen Scott, a child psychiatrist. This three-year project aims to give children a good start by developing their self-esteem. The project also aims to involve the children's parents in a therapeutic relationship in order to show them how to parent.[48]

The role of therapy has acquired an important dimension in New Labor's social policy towards the unemployed. The practice of counseling the unemployed was adopted during the Thatcher era, albeit in a hesitant any unsystematic manner. Since, the election of the Blair government in 1997, this approach has become a key component of welfare policy. The Gateway program, which is designed to assist the government's project of modernizing the welfare state, offers guidance and counseling. In September 1998, it was reported that officials of the Department of Social Security were expected to switch their role from that of an officer to that of a counselor. "The ability of civil servants to switch from paper-bound administrators to flesh-and blood counselors is one of the New Deal's most crucial aspects," argued one analysis of this development.[49]

The government has encouraged the use of therapeutic techniques to manage the problems posed by homeless people. The government's "Rough Sleepers Unit" has adopted an outlook that defines the homeless as vulnerable people who require mental health services. In Scotland, Edinburgh City Council has adopted the policy of providing homeless women with lessons in aromatherapy and in using scented oils to combat stress.[50]

Therapeutic intervention in family life in order to alter parenting practices and to curb anti-social behavior has become one of the defining features of New Labor social policy. The management of inter- personal relationships by therapeutic experts appears as the government's answer to the problem of family life. Many public figures are still hesitant about pursuing policies that would in effect transform the citizen into a patient. "Governments have to be very careful in devising policies that affect our most intimate relation-ships," warns the government's consultation document *Supporting Families*. [51] Despite its rhetoric about exercising care, *Supporting Families* encroaches into areas that directly affect intimate aspects of family life. It outlines the intention of government to initiate a program for helping people to prepare for marriage and lays the foundation for the systematic management of family relations.[52] One key objective of this approach is to transform parents into clients of therapeutic experts. Jack Straw, the home secretary has stated that the culture of parenting needs to be changed so that "seeking advice and help is seen not as failure but the action of concerned and re-sponsible parents."[53]

Failed parents are the targets of "parenting orders," a new scheme enacted by the Blair government to deal with fathers and mothers whose children fail to turn up in school. The core requirement of a parenting order is that "the parent attends counseling or guidance sessions" as specified by the courts.[54] This approach has been an-ticipated by numerous local pilot projects that have experimented with the treatment model for dealing with anti-social families. For example the Dundee Family Project, launched in 1996, has sought to deal with anti-social tenants on local authority housing estates through the provision of family therapy. In order to avoid perma-nent eviction, problem families are sent to a residential unit, where they live for an average of nine months. These families have to agree to a "personally challenging supervisory regime," including three visits per day. During the course of their residence, the families are offered modules on domestic and anger management, addiction counseling and parent/child therapy.[55]

The application of the treatment model is most deeply entrenched within the British criminal justice system. Treatment programs for certain types of offenders (e.g., sex offenders) have been in place for some time. The Sex Offender Treatment Program, started in 1991 is based on getting a sex offender to publicly acknowledge his need to change. Such offenders are the offered 80 two-hour therapy sessions in which therapists use the cognitive-behavioral approach.[56] In recent years, the treatment approach has been extended and now assumes an important role within Jack Straw's plan to devise a policy of a "seamless sentence." The stated aim of Straw is to oblige more offenders leaving prison to be electronically tagged. Such offenders would also be forced to attend courses in anger management, drug and alcohol addiction or sex therapy.[57]

As will be evident from the discussion in the next section, the internalization of the therapeutic imperative by the British State has a long history.[58] However, the import of this trend was rarely acknowledged and was certainly not self-consciously promoted as an explicit political project. In recent years, however therapeutic policies have assumed considerable significance as part of the New Labor project of modernizing the Welfare State. The political approach associated with this project, particularly its emphasis on the concept of *social inclusion* is oriented towards establishing point contact with an individuated British public through the therapeutic management of social problems. One of the underlying features of this approach is the need for public authority to offer recognition and esteem to the individual self. Blair has defined his vision of a good society as one committed to the "belief in the equal worth of all." This recognition accorded to an individual's worth represents an important shift from the previous concept of social equality to that of equality of esteem based on the idea of "equality of esteem."[59] As a psychological/pseudo moral concept, equal worth has little in common with previous ideas about either equality of opportunity or equality of outcomes.

Although the concept of social inclusion is vague, and used to refer to a wide variety of problems, its central focus is to establish a series of linkages between formal institutions and the excluded. That is why policy statements across government departments continually adopt the rhetoric. In recent months there has been a systematic attempt to present policies in the sphere of sports, culture and arts from this perspective of inclusion. "Sport is an ideal vehicle for improving self-esteem and helping people feel better about themselves," states a Sports Scotland statement on social inclusion. The government is also promoting policies that can turn public libraries and museums into institutions that can help raise the esteem of the excluded.[60] The Northern Ireland Executive has also adopted this approach. One of its recent consultation papers affirmed the need to help "increase social inclusion and build self-esteem through participation in culture, arts and leisure activities."[61]

The importance that government policy makers attach to solving problems through raising people's self esteem is driven by the conviction that some of the key problems facing people are rooted in a private sphere that characteristically fosters emotional havoc and which produces emotionally illiterate individuals who are unable to sustain thriving relationships. In extreme cases, the casualties of the private sphere are seen as part of the army of the socially excluded who go on to inflict there anti social behavior on others. This commitment to a therapeutic outlook also contains an implicit cultural critique of an Old Britain. Old Britain is implicated with practices that make it difficult for people to acknowledge their emotion.

In an important study on the influence of liberation psychotherapy on American society, John Steadman Rice suggests that its impact is most noticeable in the realm of informal institutions. "The brunt of liberation therapy's anti-institutionalism has been borne by those largely informal institutions—such as friendship, courtship, intimate relations, family, community—that stand between and mediate the relationship between the individual and the abstract and exceedingly powerful structures of state and economy."[62] Therapeutic politics in Britain also targets the realm of informal relations for its criticism. It rarely confronts established formal institutions. Instead of attacking the police, it targets, what's often described as the police's "canteen culture," the informal banter and practices practiced by police officers. It does not attack Oxbridge as such but takes exception to this institution's informal "old boys" network. It does not explicitly question the family but is deeply suspicious of the informal relations practiced by its members. Recently, New Labor politicians have ex-

pressed concern about peer relations among children—again informal friendship networks—on the ground that "peer pressure" is responsible for teenage girls having babies.

Therapeutic politics' critique of informal institutions is understandable since its authority is based on its claim to possessing the expertise to manage relationships, most of which are still conducted through
informal means. However, the rise of therapeutic culture has encouraged activists to extend their critique of Old Britain beyond the
boundaries of the sphere of informal relations. Rice has argued that
because liberation therapy directs its critique "almost exclusively"
against informal institutions, it has remained "largely mute" about
wider political and economic ones.[63] This is no longer the case in
Britain. The politicization of emotion has emerged as an important
motif in contemporary British political life. This project also enjoys
the patronage of an influential section of Britain's new political elite.
A conference on the theme of the "The Politics of Attachment," organized at the Tavistock Clinic in March 1996, attracted leading Labor
politicians Marjorie Mowlam, Tessa Jowell, and Patricia Hewitt. The
aim of this conference was to use the "rich tradition of developmental psychology and attachment theory" to revitalize an "impoverished political debate."[64] Since 1997, both Mowlam and Jowell
played important roles as Ministers in the Blair administration. Patricia
Hewitt went on to be founder member of Antidote, a think-tank devoted to promoting the "politics of emotional literacy."

Antidote has close links with the Labor Party and its supporters
appear to have a privileged access to the departments of Education
and of Health. The aim of Antidote is integrate the insights of psychology into political life. It seeks to advocate policies that tend to
"foster emotional attitudes tending to support the development of
more cohesive societies."[65] One of its stated goals is the creation of
an Emotional and Social Index, which would gather information
about the emotional consequences of policies. Recently it has published a manifesto that touches on virtually every area of public
policy.[66] Associates of Antidote are intensely interested in promoting the institutionalization of the therapeutic ethos and in transforming the vocabulary of politics. A recently published book by Andrew Samuels, one of the founders of Antidote, explicitly argues for
this agenda. He contends that policy committees and government
commissions should have a "psychotherapist sitting on them as part
of a spectrum of experts." The book argues for a National Emo-

tional Audit and for the creation of a range of institutions, such as an Emotional and Spiritual Justice Commission "that would monitor the effects on psychological and spiritual health of all policy proposals."[67]

Antidote's psycho-politics is very much in the tradition of British Fabian social engineering. Its mission—to transform an emotionally illiterate British public into enlightened citizens—is motivated by its conviction that the expert knows best. Even some radical therapist recoil from the authoritarian implications of a system of government that is in the business of telling people how to feel. Nick Totton has criticized, Antidote spokeswoman, the therapist Susie Orbach for her advocacy of "government of all the experts" who undertake to manage the emotionally illiterate mob.[68]

Antidote's attempt to formulate a coherent program, notwithstanding, the politics of emotion lacks intellectual coherence. It is a diffuse movement that is not based on a distinct psychological perspective or worldview. Although some of its proponents are influenced by British attachment theory, the politics of emotion lacks a distinct theoretical foundation. Indeed, it often appears as a cultural critique that masquerades as a psychological one. The main intellectual influence on the politicization of emotion is the subjective turn taken by Western political ideologies. An important theme, stressed by theorists across the political spectrum is the central role of the individual self and its demand for recognition and respect. The struggle for recognition by the individual is conceptualized as a transcendent need that shapes social and political life by a variety of influential thinkers. Francis Fukuyama depicts the struggle for recognition as the driving force of history. Fukuyama is worried that the demand for universal recognition can lead to the trivializing of according respect to the individual. Others do not share Fukuyama's reservations about the automatic granting of esteem and respects to every individual. Charles Taylor contends that due recognition is a vital human need and that without the politics of equal recognition a democratic society is undermined. The German sociologist, Axel Honneth contends that the withholding of esteem "endangers the identity of human beings, just as infection with disease endangers their physical life."[69]

The political elites of Anglo-American societies have seized upon the demand for recognition—either by accommodating to identity politics or to therapeutic ones—in an attempt to forge a new bond with an otherwise socially disengaged and estranged public.[70] That is why the British political class and its institutions have been drawn towards the role of affirming claims for recognition and acceptance by individual members of the public. Back in the early seventies Peter Berger and his collaborators, anticipated this development in an interesting contribution "On the Obsolescence of the Concept of Honor." Berger claimed that the concept of honor had given way to that of dignity. He argued that whereas honor was linked to community, dignity related to the "self as such" divested of all "socially imposed roles and norms." This shift to dignity of the self implied an identity that is "essentially independent of institutional roles." Berger concluded that as a result of this shift the "identity-defining power of institutions has been greatly weakened."[71]

Berger's prognosis of the weakening of the "identity-defining power of institutions" has been vindicated by the subsequent rise of identity politics and the crisis of legitimacy experienced by the institutions of the Western State. However, it can be argued that the cultural preoccupation with individual dignity contains at least a provisional solution to the problem of legitimacy. Through refocusing the conduct of public affairs towards the objective of both managing and affirming individual subjectivity, the state has retained its power and authority to define identity. Although identity is now recast on an intensely individualized foundation, which inherently contradicts wider notions of community, the political class has found a new role for itself as managers of people's emotional anxieties. The colonization of the private world by public authority is the inexorable logic of the institutionalization of therapeutic politics. The lack of open debate or concern about this development indicates that it has become embedded in contemporary culture.

The Silent Ascent

The ascendancy of therapeutic culture in Britain has met with little resistance. There has been a distinct lack of intellectual engagement with this development. Even more striking is the relative absence of any influential critiques of this trend. Even to this day, it is often assumed that this development is culturally insignificant and that it impact is far less important than in the U.S. In an interesting contribution, Graham Richards, a leading scholar in the field of the intellectual history of British psychology, argues that "British psychology has never become so culturally central" as its American counterpart. Richards believes that psychology was relatively marginalized in Britain because its practitioners were "to some degree in opposition to moral authorities" whereas in America "where there were no such authorities, proto-psychologists were engaged in supplying the deficit."[72] There is little doubt that British psychology, as a formal discipline did not enjoy the cultural status of its American counterpart. However, the significance of the therapeutic ethos for culture is not directly determined by the status of the discipline of psychology. Indeed, it is adoption of psychological thinking and techniques by other disciplines and institutions that provide an indication of the cultural relevance of therapeutic culture. It is interesting to note that Richards' own work on the relationship between psychology and religion provides a vivid illustration of the influence of the therapeutic on key British cultural institutions. Richards' study shows that in the early part of the twentieth century, the Church sought to collaborate with psychology in order to use the discipline's insights for its own ends. This collaboration began to break down when the churches realized that religion's concessions to psychology "proved too high a price." As Richards notes "religious concessions to the New Psychology's expertise inevitably eroded religion's own territorial base."[73] This shift in the balance of influence towards psychology is itself significant. But probably, a far more important indication of cultural trajectory is the tendency for organized religion itself to come under influence of therapeutic authority.

There is considerable evidence that the therapeutic worldview gained increasing influence from the inter-war period onwards. The crusading spirit exhibited by the mental hygiene movement in the 1920s and 1930s met with a positive response from many British institutions. As Rose has noted, the institutionalization of therapeutic practices occurred under the stimulus provided by the experience of the Second World War. In this respect at least, the British experience parallels developments in the United States.[74] During this period, the influence of psychology on personnel management became discernible. The so-called caring professions, especially in the area of family life and parenting were amongst the first to assimilate therapeutic practices. The rise of the British Welfare State provided new opportunities for the development of therapeutic expertise.

In an early study of the institutionalization and professionalization of psychoanalysis, Berger claimed that what he called "the counseling and testing complex" extended into "large areas of the total institutional structure of the society, its heaviest sedimentation being in the areas of welfare organisation, both public and private, education, and personnel administrations."[75] It is worth noting that the systematic provision of these services was far more expansive in the UK than in the U.S. and that most of these provisions were provided through the public sector of the Welfare State. Not surprisingly, there was considerable scope for the development of therapeutic practices within the confines of the Welfare State. During the fifties and in subsequent decades the steady growth of influence of these practices was rarely acknowledged and studiously ignored. There were a few early figures, however, who noticed and commented on this trend.

Barbara Wooton's *Social Science and Social Pathology* (1959) represents one of the first attempts to explore the influence of the therapeutic ethos on the domain of public policy. Wooton claimed that the "psychiatrist along with his psychiatrically oriented satellites, has now usurped the place once occupied by the social reformer and the administrator, if not indeed the judge." She drew attention to the assimilation of terms like "diagnosis," "treatment" and "therapy" into the vocabulary of the social sciences and claimed that these terms "have already displaced the ethical formulae of an earlier age." According to Wooton, these linguistic trends reflected "changes in underlying attitudes, philosophies or unspoken assumptions." She concluded that this trend resulted in the "shifting of the boundary between medical and moral problems." Wooton was particularly struck by changing public attitudes towards social deviants and stated that mental illness had become an all-purpose explanation for forms of anti-social behavior.[76]

Paul Halmos's *The Faith of the Counselors* (1965) offers the first systematic attempt to investigate what today would be called therapeutic culture. Halmos uses the term counselor to describe "advice-giving," interventionist and directive professionals, who are characterized by a distinct moral stance or a faith. He argued that this layer of intellectuals could be found across a wide range of professions: "Psychotherapy and social casework have become avenues of betterment attracting ever larger numbers of socially concerned intellectuals to professional careers...The range of the so-called helping professions which demonstrably derive at least some of their working principles from the psychotherapeutic theories of healing is remarkably wide. Whether they work in a clinical or non-clinical setting, they have ingeniously contrived to professionalize their love for their fellow men and have cleverly invented institutions, in which they conceal the fact that they "prescribe themselves" by prescribing techniques."[77]

As evidence of the influence of the counselor, Halmos pointed to the weakening of the State's resistance towards mingling impersonal bureaucratic procedure with personal ones. He noted the impact of the counselor on the system of criminal justice, where the "statutes which provide for probation, for psychiatric treatment, for rehabilitation, and so on, assign more and more significance to unspecified and as yet unspecified personal services of professional workers, and less and less to fixed and definable material and institutional provisions and sanctions."[78]

Halmos indicated that the counseling trend was resisted by those "who regarded the psychotherapeutic ideology as subversive." But such resistance based on appeals "to go back to the general moral-political principles were no match for the point of view of the counselor." On the contrary, "the new statutes continue to give growing scope and discretionary initiative to the clinically trained Samaritans."[79] Halmos attempted to quantify the size of the counseling profession. He estimated that in 1960 they numbered 5,650 and after adjusting the figures for population levels, he claimed that there were three and a half as many professionals in the field in the US as in the UK. Halmos believed that the influence of this group of professionals extended way beyond their numbers because of their influence on the "ideological trends" of the period.[80]

Halmos's explanation of the growth of counseling was linked to the idea that the discrediting of political solutions had encouraged individual ones. He took the view that pragmatic reformers had retreated from their commitment to social change and sought refuge in a therapeutic position. Anticipating the development of the New Labor modernizer, Halmos noted that political reformists "mellow into first consenting to, and later positively sympathizing with, the extension of personal counseling activities as an essential part of the furthering of welfare in society." The marriage between counseling and the state represented a central theme in Halmos's analysis: "subsidized by state and local government, more and more of these counseling positions are being created for professionally specialized practitioners mainly in social work, social casework, clinical psychology and psychiatry."[81]

The concerns raised by Wooton and Halmos remained relatively underdeveloped in subsequent decades.[82] During the sixties the anti-psychiatry movement gained considerable intellectual authority. However, the target of its critique was psychiatry's coercive dimension and the problems posed by the professionalization of therapeutic power. This was a critique that sought to promote alternative therapeutic strategies rather than to question the authority of the therapeutic worldview. The seventies also saw the publication of critiques that focused on question of social control aspects of therapeutic authority but they seldom touched upon the wider question of therapeutic culture.[83] Since the eighties, most of the contributions on the subject tend to provide criticisms, which are internal to the psychiatric movement or alternatively, as is the case with Ernest Gellner (1985) offer a challenge to the scientific claims made by therapeutic authority.[84]

There is also an interesting literature produced by radical therapists and more critical thinkers within the therapeutic profession, who are concerned about the professionalization of counseling and its institutionalization. They are particularly worried about the "privatization of distress" and the individualistic orientation implied by the contemporary therapeutic worldview.[85] The psychologist Simon Wessely has published a series of articles that offer an eloquent counterpoint to the colonizing ambitions of the counseling profession.[86] However, these interesting contributions make no attempt to develop a sociology of therapeutic culture.

There are a number of factors that help explain why British therapeutic culture must still wait for its critics. The most significant restraint on the development of a tradition that is critical of therapeutic culture is the political and intellectual consensus enjoyed by the British Welfare State. The belief that the public provision of services is by definition progressive has meant that the state management of individual behavior and subjectivity is rarely questioned. Indeed the integration of the management of behavior into the welfare provisions and other public services means that therapeutic imperative is rarely identified as a distinct trend. Even the radical anti-psychiatry movement had little reservations about this role of the state. What this movement objected to were particular coercive strategies towards the management of mental health but not the integration of therapeutic authority into the social policy of the state.

One consequence of the statist outlook of British intellectuals is that they often regard the growth of therapeutic culture and the politicization of emotion as on balance a positive development. Leading British sociologist, Anthony Giddens, regards the growing importance of therapeutic culture as a symptom of the importance of an "in-depth understanding which allows one to feel 'all right' with one self." Therapeutic discourse, with its focus on the value of self-disclosure informs Giddens's axial concept of "the pure relationship."[87] Nikolas Rose, whose *Governing The Soul* provides the most comprehensive historical account of the subject, views the therapeutic ethos and its institutionalization in a relatively benign manner. Following Foucault, Rose is critical of social analysts like Christopher Lasch and Richard Sennett for adopting a "rather jaundiced view of the therapeutic culture of the self." "The paranoid visions of some social analysts, who see in the expansion of the therapeutic a kind of extension of state surveillance and regulation throughout the social body are profoundly misleading," he argues.[88] According to Rose the concern of the state with the management of subjectivity constitute "therapies of freedom." He argues: "These technologies for the government of the soul operate not through the crushing of subjectivity in the interests of control and profit, but by seeking to align political, social, and institutional goals with individual pleasures and desires, and with the happiness and fulfillment of the self. Their power lies in their capacity to offer means by which the regulation of selves—by others and by ourselves—can be made consonant with contemporary political principles, moral ideas and constitutional exigencies."[89]

The representation of state intervention in the internal world of people as essentially a benevolent and potentially liberating process is rooted in the tradition of social engineering that continues to dominate intellectual life in Britain. From this perspective, the role of public authority and of the therapeutic professional is an empowering one. Without a hint of irony, Rose observed that "empowerment has mutated from a term utilized by clients and advocates in the challenging of professional power to become part of the obligations of the responsible professional."[90]

The reorientation of the Welfare State towards attending to the therapeutic needs of the public is endorsed by some critics of traditional redistributionist social policy. They claim that in the past, the traditional policy was far too focused on material goods. The argument for a more emotional system of welfare is generally pursued on the ground that a "holistic" approach is needed, one that meets the "emotional as well as physical needs of human beings."[91] This

approach has received an intellectual boost from the claim that social inequalities are experienced through "psychosocial mechanism"
linking structure to individual health. It is claimed that socio-economic factors now primarily affect health through indirect psychosocial rather than direct material routes. From this standpoint, the
call for an egalitarian society is justified on the grounds that it contributes to the best mental and physical health. "Emotions, health
and distributive justice are therefore intimately related in the developed Western world," argues one advocate of this approach.[92]

The representation of therapeutic culture as essentially
unproblematic and potentially even empowering is underwritten by
a political culture that characteristically has a relatively weak sense
of individual rights. A feeble definition of individual rights is the flip
side of the statist intellectual outlook. The kind of libertarian analysis associated with someone like Thomas Szasz is treated as irrelevant by an outlook that treats the idea of individual rights with
suspicion. Rose confirms this standpoint when he notes that British
mental health reformers were deeply hostile to the libertarian/civil
liberty opposition to therapeutic culture. Why? Because, a critique
based on individual rights can make no contribution to improving
the state management of mental health services.[93]

In recent decades, the gradual erosion of the Welfare State has led
to a loss of confidence in the public realm. This process has led to a
growing emphasis on the private self and intimate relationships.
However, this loss of confidence in the public sphere and the turn to
the private self has not led to a rise in the status of the private sphere.
The private sphere is frequently represented as the site of family
violence and abuse and as a terrain that breeds dysfunctional selves.[94]
This mood of mistrust towards the private sphere has provided public authorities with an opportunity to demonstrate their relevance to
the problems faced by the private self. According to one account
"the private self meets public counseling and therapy as sources of
increased health and social improvement and even a recent explicitly political project of 'emotional literacy'."[95] It appears that the
expansion of therapeutic intervention may provide the Welfare State
with a new role and vocation. The cultural problematization of the
private sphere represents an open invitation for professional authority to assume an expanding role for the management of intimate
relationships. The statist legacy of British intellectual life and the
feeble tradition of individual rights along with contemporary culture's

problematization of the private sphere suggest that this trend will meet with little opposition.

Paradoxically, the trend towards the expansion of an orientation towards the self coincides with the decline of the private sphere. This development has encouraged public and professional authority to assume an enormously important role in setting the agenda for the private sphere. The social dynamic behind this trend is invariably misunderstood by much of contemporary social theory, which posits the view that the private sphere is ascendant. Some argue that the assumption of therapeutic powers by public authority is a response to the rise of the private sphere. According to Joe Bailey, "we may now be witnessing not only the rise of the private but its possible dominance and its increasing determination of public discourses of understanding and action; that is, the discourses of intimacy, the self and the unconscious invite a public agenda."[96] In fact, our analysis suggests the very reverse of this trend. The relative ease with which public authority has assumed an interventionist role towards the management of the self indicates that the private sphere is confronted with formidable pressures. The focus of public policy on the private indicates that authority for the management of personal relations is gradually migrating from the domain of the private to that of the state.

Characteristically, therapeutic authority provides a medium through which the public and the private intersect. Berger has argued that "institutionalized psychologism straddles the dividing line between the public and private spheres, thus occupying an unusually strategic position in our society."[97] Today, the line that divides the public from the private has become increasingly porous as public therapeutic authority arrogates for itself new responsibilities for the regulation and management of the self. The rise of therapeutic culture is inexorably linked to the reorganization of the relationship between the public and private. Moreover by gaining a privileged role for the regulation of personal relationship, therapeutic authority can claim constant access to the private sphere. As Gergen has noted, this intervention reduces the ability of people to sort out their affairs; "the tissues of organic dependency are injured or atrophy."[98]

The Diminished Self

In many accounts the growth of therapeutic culture is associated with the process of individuation, which is reflected in a rise towards individualism and a shift of focus towards a preoccupation with the self. As a description of a broad pattern, this interpretation serves to underline an important cultural trend, which is the privatization of identity. However, terms such as individualism and the self are much too general to illuminate the question of just what kind of an individual and just what kind of a self is under discussion. Ideas about the constitution of the self are informed by social judgements and values that are both historically and culturally specific.

It can be argued that the concept of individualism is inappropriate for making sense of the present day cultural demand for individual solutions. Contemporary culture's commitment to recognize and esteem the individual contains a profoundly anti-individualistic dynamic. Recognition, as cultural-political and state sanctioned right is consistent with the bureaucratic imperative of treating the individual according to an impersonal general formula. Despite its individualistic orientation, therapeutic intervention, such as counseling, often leads to the pursuit of the standardization of people rather than encourage a self determined individuality. Universal recognition overlooks individual differences and needs and fails to distinguish between achievement and failure and wisdom and ignorance. A real recognition of the individual requires that choices are made between knowledge and opinion and contributions that are worth esteeming as those that are not. Both the granting and the demand for universal esteem, serve to transform recognition to an empty ritual. Even Fukuyama, who believes that the struggle for recognition is the driving force of history, is forced to recognize the contradiction inherent in the demand for universal recognition. "The problem with the present-day self-esteem movement is that its members, living as the do in a democratic and egalitarian society, are seldom willing to make choices concerning what should be esteemed."[99]

The very demand for the right to be esteemed posits a uniquely feeble version of the self. According to contemporary culture, the self not only needs affirmation, it needs continuous affirmation. Moreover, the failure to affirm is increasingly interpreted as a slight or an injury to the self. "Nonrecognition or misrecognition can inflict harm, can be a form of oppressions, imprisoning someone in a false, distorted, and reduced mode of being," warns the philosopher Charles Taylor.[100] In cultural terms, recognition means accepting people's account of their subjective states as valid. Recognition thus has primarily a therapeutic function. The belief that the defining feature of the self is its vulnerability informs Anglo-American culture's ethnopsychology. In this context, the provision of automatic recognition implies recognizing the condition and experience of vulnerability. As Kenneth Gergen has noted, therapeutic culture offers "invitations to infirmity."[101] For the individual, the disclosure of vulnerability has the status of a moral statement that invites social and cultural affirmation. That is why it has become common for many people to define themselves through a psychological or medical diagnosis.

Indeed there is considerable pressure on British health professionals to recognize a variety of new diseases. Under pressure from advocacy and parents' support groups, a growing number of British doctors now diagnose and treat hyperactivity in children. Those who promote "awareness" of this illness, claim that "identification of the problem is useful in itself" because "any harm done by labeling" is outweighed by the benefits to self-esteem.[102] Medical labels are eagerly sought by some parents for their children. So hyperactive children are now "considered to have an illness rather than to be disruptive, disobedient, overactive problem children."[103] Parents are actually relieved when they "discover" that their child has got some medical problem and is not responsible for his or her behavior. "I got my best Christmas present a few days before the big day this year," wrote a mother in the *Times*. She was referring to the wonderful news that her son was diagnosed as dyslexic and was therefore clearly not lazy as she previously feared.[104] Until this diagnosis, school reports characterized the child as "easily distracted" and "occasionally disruptive." As a victim of dyslexia the child will no longer be subject to official disapproval. Instead, the child can now expect recognition and moral support.

Henrietta Rose, who has written a book - *A Gift in Disguise* - about her difficult experience of bringing up a son with severe learning disability, is still disappointed that her son Tom was never diagnosed with a named condition. She claims, that as a result she "missed the opportunity to start mourning" the loss of her dreams and expectations.[105] This importance attached to recognition means that often parents look for a named condition, even when their children do not have a serious disability like Tom. A medical label eases the difficulty of dealing with problem behavior. There is evidence in Britain that both teachers and parents collude in the popularization of the learning disabled classification in schools.[106] At a time of existential insecurity, a medical diagnosis at least has the virtue of definition. A disease explains an individual's behavior and it even helps confer a sense of identity. The medicalization of everyday life allows individuals to make sense of their predicament and gain moral sympathy.

Therapeutic culture incites people to regard themselves as objects rather than as subjects of their destiny. The intellectual influence of Foucault over proponents of British therapeutic culture reflects this profession's definition of the subject as the docile object of disciplinary knowledge, where empowerment means little more than knowledge of voluntary resignation to authority.[107] The promoters of emotional politics have implicitly adopted the vocation of reconciling the individual to a regime of low expectations. "One poignant contribution that a psychotherapy viewpoint might make to political life is to help people face up to the inevitability of disappointment," advises one of the leading intellectual voices associated with Antidote.[108] This politics of reconciling the individual to the inevitability of disappointment is underwritten by a culture that encourages its people to lower their expectations and acquire a diminished sense of themselves. Encouraging and reinforcing this perception of the self is the precondition for the continued flourishing of therapeutic culture.

Notes

1.   See John Hewitt, *The Myth of Self-Esteem; Finding Happiness and Solving Problems in America*, (New York: St. Martin's Press, 1998).
2.   D. Summerfield, "The Invention of Post-Traumatic Disorder and the Social Usefulness of a Psychiatric Category." *British Medical Journal* (hereafter *BMJ*), no. 322, January 13, 2001.
3.   *Ibid*.
4.   See *Times*, 5 November 1966.
5.   I. McLean, I. & M. Johnes, M., *Aberfan: Government and Disasters*, (Cardiff: Welsh Academic Press, 2000), pp.104-106.
6.   See *Daily Mail*, 19 March 1999.
7.   See for example "164 Known Dead In Flood Disaster." *Times*, 2 February 1953.
8.   "Flooding and Human Health: The Dangers Posed Are Not Always Obvious." *BMJ*, November 11, 2000, p. 1167.
9.   See "Exams Criticized as 'Child Abuse.'" *Times*; 28 July 1999.
10.   See "Looking Back without Anger." *BBC News Online*; 21 November 1999.
11.   "Stress Lessons for Children at Primary School." *Daily Telegraph;* 28 September 2000.
12.   "Pupils to Get Therapy for Big Leap Forward to Secondary." *Observer*; 5 September 1999.
13.   See Ceridian Performance Partners, *The Price of Success*, London, 1999).
14.   B. J. Burchell, D. Dat, M. Hudson, D. Lapido, R. Mankelow, J. Nolan, H. Reed, *et al* (1999) *Job Insecurity and Work Intensification* (York: Joseph Rowntree Foundation, 1999).

15. See "The Samaritans Press Release," 12 December 2000, "Children Suffer Stress over Their 'Love Lives'." *Guardian*, 28 October 2000; and "British Bosses Top of World Misery League." *Observer*; 23 July 2000.
16. "Children Suffer Stress over Their 'Love Lives,'" *Guardian, op. cit.*
17. See Frank Furedi, *Therapeutic Culture; Cultivating Vulnerability in an Anxious Age* (London: Routledge, 2003).
18. Exact figures are hard to compile. The available evidence suggests that there are around 110,000 individuals working as full time and part-time counselors. There are also a far larger number of individuals working in the public sector—teachers, university lecturers, social workers, probation officers, law enforcement person-nel—who practice their counseling skills as part of their job.
19. Nick Totton, "The Baby and the Bathwater: 'Professionalization' in Psychotherapy and Counseling." *British Journal of Guidance and Counselling*, vol. 27, no. 3, 1999, p.88.
20. "Counseling is Offered for the Death of a Council." *Daily Telegraph*; 25 October 1995.
21. Nikolas Rose, *Governing the Soul, The Shaping of the Private Self*, (London: Routledge, 1990), p. 2.
22. See "A New Growth Industry Emerges to Cushion the Blow as More People Lose Their Jobs." *Guardian*, 19 January 1991.
23. See "Taking the Worry Out of Work." *Daily Telegraph*, 6 April 1999.
24. See "The Sharing and Caring Way to Get to the Top." *Times*, 6 January 2001.
25. See "Solving the Mental Problems Caused by Physical Illness." *Daily Telegraph*, 22 March 1997.
26. See the pioneering analysis of the redefinition of health by Michael Fitzpatrick, *The Tyranny of Health: Doctors and the Regulation of Lifestyle* (London: Routledge, 2000), p. 115.
27. See J. Eatcock, "Counseling in Primary Care: Past, Present and Future." *British Journal of Guidance and Counselling*, vol.28, no. 2., 2000, p.161.
28. "Therapy is New Religion Says Carey." *Daily Telegraph*, 1 August 2000.
29. See *Guardian*, 6 January 1996.
30. Tony Walter, *On Bereavement: The Culture of Grief* (Buckingham: Open Univer-sity Press, 1999), p. 196.
31. *Ibid.*
32. See *Pastoral Care Today, Practice, Problems and Priorities in Churches Today; An Interim Report from a Major Survey Initiated by CWR/Waverley Christian Counselling in Association with the Evangelical Alliance Conducted by the Centre for Ministry Studies, University of Wales, Bangor*. (Farnham, Surrey: CWR, 2000).
33. See *Guardian,* 14 September 1999.
34. See Joseph Rowntree Foundation Press Release: 21 June 1999.
35. Rose, *op cit.*, pp. 1-2.
36. A. Arnason, "Biography, Bereavement Story." *Mortality*, vol. 5, no. 2, 2000, p.194.
37. Tony Blair "Speech at Stockwell Park, School, Lambeth, December 1997."
38. It is worth noting that a government commissioned report acknowledged that there is no agreed definition of the term self esteem nor is there any British research that can be used to justify self esteem raising policies. See C. Dennison and J. Coleman, *Young People and Gender: A Review of Research; A Report Submitted to the Women's Unit, Cabinet Office and the Family Policy Unit, Home Office*, (London: Women's Unit, 2000).
39. See *BBC ONLINE NETWORK*, 9 November 1998.
40. Cited in *Guardian*, 12 March 1999.

41.	Cited in *Guardian*, 23 February 1999.
42.	See Cabinet Office Press Release—20 June 2000, "Pressure to Be Thin Affecting Young Women's Self-Esteem: Body Image Summit." 21 June 2000.
43.	See National Strategy for Neighbourhood Renewal: Policy Action Team 3, *Enterprise and Social Exclusion*, (London: H. M. Treasury, 1999); and Northern Ireland Executive, *Investing for Health* (Belfast, 2000), p. 55.
44.	See The Guardian, 23 September 1998.
45.	See DFEE, *Sex and Relationship Guidance* (2000); and Scottish Executive, *Educating the Whole Child: Personal and Social Development in Primary Schools and the Primary Stages of Special Schools* (2000).
46.	See the discussion in *Antidote*, August 2000.
47.	For a discussion of this project, see *Time Out*, 25 October 2000.
48.	See "The Real Life Class." *Guardian*, 11 April 2000.
49.	"New Deal—So Play Your Hand Right." *Observer*, 13 September 1998.
50.	See *Daily Record*, 7 September 1999.
51.	*Supporting Families: A Consultation Document* (London, 1999), p. 30.
52.	This point is elaborated in Frank Furedi, *Paranoid Parenting* (London: Penguin, 2001), chapter 11.
53.	See "Draft Speech for the Home Secretary—Launch of the Lords and Commons Family and Child Protection Group's Report 'Family Matters'," 23 July 1998.
54.	See Home Office "The Crime And Disorder Act. Guidance Document: Parenting Order," 2 June 2000.
55.	See "Social Exclusion: Keeping the Doors Open." *Guardian*, 21 July 1999.
56.	Home Office, Research Development and Statistics Directorate, *An Evaluation of the Prison Sex Offender Treatment Programme* (London, 1998).
57.	"Straw Plan to Tag More Ex-Inmates." *Guardian*, 27 January 2000.
58.	Although different in form, it is arguable that the therapeutic state in Britain is as developed as in the United States. For a discussion of the therapeutic state in the U.S., see James L. Nolan, Jr., *The Therapeutic State*, (New York: New York University Press, 1998).
59.	See "Prime Ministers Speech to the Global Ethics Foundation," Tubingen University, Germany, 2000. See at http://www.number-10.gov.uk/default.asp?PageId=1881.
60.	Sports Scotland, *Social Inclusion* (2000)
61.	Northern Ireland Executive, *Investing For Health* (Belfast, 2000), p. 55.
62.	John Steadman Rice, *A Disease of One's Own: Psychotherapy, Addiction, and the Emergence of Co-Dependency* (New Brunswick, NJ: Transaction Publishers, 1996), p. 36.
63.	Ibid.
64.	The proceedings of this conference are published through a collection of articles in S. Kraemer and J. Roberts, eds., *The Politics of Attachment; Towards a Secure Society* (London: Free Association Books, 1996).
65.	See J. Park, "The Politics of Emotional Literacy." *Renewal*, vol.17 no.1, 1999, p. 52.
66.	See *The Antidote Manifesto: Developing an Emotionally Literate Society* (London: Antidote, 2001).
67.	Andrew Samuels, *Politics on the Couch: Citizenship and the Internal Life*, (London: Profile Books, 2001), pp. 2, 202, and 203.
68.	See Nick Totton, *Psychotherapy and Politics*; (London: Sage Publications, 2000), pp. 50-51.
69.	See Francis Fukuyama, *The End of History and The Last Man* (New York: The Free Press, 1992), pp. 302-303; Charles Taylor, *Multiculturalsim and "The Politics of Recognition"* (Princeton: Princeton University Press, 1992), pp. 25-27 and Axel

Honneth, *The Struggle for Recognition: The Moral Grammar of Social Conflicts* (Cambridge: Polity Press, 1995), p. 135.

70. The role of therapeutic politics in relation to the attempt to tackle the crisis of political legitimacy is well argued by James Nolan in *The Therapeutic State, op.cit.* For the parallel development of this trend, in Britain, see Furedi, *Therapeutic Culture, op.cit.*

71. See Peter Berger, Brigitte Berger, and Hansfried Kellner, *The Homeless Mind* (Harmondsworth: Pelican, 1973), pp. 81-83.

72. See G. Richards, "'To know our fellow men to do them good': American Psychology's Enduring Moral Project." *History of the Human Sciences*, vol. 8, no. 3, 1995.

73. G. Richards. "Psychology and the Churches in Britain 1919-39: Symptoms of Conversion." *History of the Human Sciences,* vol.13, no. 2, 2000, pp.57 & 72.

74. See Rose, *Governing the Soul, op. cit.* For an exploration of developments in the US, see Ellen Herman, E. (1995) *The Romance of American Psychology: Political Culture in the Age of Experts* (Berkeley: University of California Press, 1995).

75. Peter Berger, "Towards a Sociological Understanding of Psychoanalysis." *Social Research*, vol. 32, no. 1, 1965, p. 27.

76. Barbara Wooton, (1959) *Social Science and Social Pathology*, (London: George Allen & Unwin, 1959), pp.17, 203, 207, and 338.

77. Paul Halmos, *The Faith of the Counsellors* (London: Constable, 1965), p. 17.

78. Ibid.

79. Ibid.

80. Ibid., pp.17, 44 and 47.

81. Ibid. p.29.

82. One text, which attempted to build and develop Halmos' insights, was Maurice North, *The Secular Priests*, (London: George Allen & Unwin, 1972).

83. See for example Andrew Scull (1979) *Museums of Madness; The Social Organization of Insanity in Nineteenth Century England,,* (London: Allen Lane, 1979).

84. See Ernest Gellner, *The Psychoanalytic Movement: The Cunning of Unreason,* (London: Fontana Press, 1985).

85. See for example Nick Totton, "The Baby and the Bathwater," *op. cit.*; Nick Totton, *Psychotherapy and Politics, op. cit.,* and J. Russell, J. (1999) "Counselling and the Social Construction of Self." *British Journal of Guidance & Counselling*, vol. 27, no.3, 1999; and R. House, "Therapy and Counselling: Deconstructing a Professional Ideology." *British Journal of Guidance & Counselling*, vol. 27, no. 3, 1999.

86. See for example S. Wessely, "The Rise of Counselling and the Return of Alienism." *BMG,* no. 313, 1996.

87. Anthony Giddens, *Modernity and Self-Identity: Self and Society in the Late Modern Age* (Cambridge: Polity Press, 1991), p. 186.

88. Rose, *Governing the Soul, op. cit.*, p. 257.

89. Ibid.

90. Rose added that "behavioural techniques are no longer viewed as coercive and heteronomous incursions upon subjectivity of the individual, but are widely deployed by doctors, clinical psychologists and psychiatric nurses as well as social workers and many others, as a means for the re-empowering of the disempowered self." See Nikolas Rose, "Psychiatry as a Political Science: Advanced Liberalism and the Administration of Risk." *History of the Human Sciences*, vol. 9, no. 2, 1996.

91. See P. Hoggett, in G. Lewis, S. Gewirtz, and J. Clarke, eds., *Rethinking Social Policy* (London: Sage, 2000), p. 144.

92. See S. J. Williams, "'Capitalizing' on Emotions? Rethinking the Inequalities in Health Debate." *Sociology*, vol. 32, no. 1, 1998, pp. 132-33.

93. Rose, *Governing the Soul*, op. cit., p. 201.
94. The stigmatization of the private sphere is explored in chapter 3 in Furedi, *Therapeutic Culture*, op. cit.
95. J. Bailey, "Some Meanings of 'the Private' in Sociological Thought." *Sociology*, vol. 34, no. 3, 2000, p. 395.
96. Ibid.
97. Peter Berger "Towards a Sociological Understanding of Psychoanalysis," op. cit, p. 38.
98. K.J. Gergen, "Therapeutic Professions and the Diffusion of Deficit." *Journal of Mind and Behavior*; vol. 11, nos. 3-4., 1990, p. 359.
99. Francis Fukuyama, *The End of History*, op. cit., p. 303.
100. Charles Taylor, *Multiculturalism*, op. cit. p. 25.
101. K.J. Gergen, "Therapeutic Professions and the Diffusion of Deficit," *op. cit., p. 356.*
102. E. Taylor, and R. Hemsley, "Treating Hyperkinetic Disorders in Childhood," *BMJ*, April 6, 1995.
103. Peter Conrad, "The Discovery of Hyperkinesis: Notes on the Medicalization of Deviant Behavior." *Social* Problems, 23, 1975, p. 18.
104. *Times*, 26 December 1997.
105. Cited in *Guardian*; 30 September 1998.
106. Interviews with teachers, January 1998.
107. See Michel Foucault, "Technologies of the Self." In L.H. Martin, H. Gutman, and P.H. Hutton, eds., (1988), *Technologies of the Self; a Seminar with Michel Foucault*, (London: Tavistock Publications, 1988).
108. Andrew Samuels, *Politics on the Couch*, op. cit, p. 3.

3

American Sexual Morality Before and After "That Woman"

Jonathan B. Imber

A clearer picture of American sexual morality emerged, following the fusillade of denunciations of the now infamous 1998 Starr Report as everything from puritanical witch-hunting to "sexual McCarthyism" (with accusations of Gestapo tactics thrown in for good measure). Most of this ranting was a special form of male hysteria, replete with implications about why President Clinton's sexual peccadilloes were potentially Everyman's problem. There was also the snobbish reaction of an old-fashioned French sort, where "love" is said always and everywhere to have its own logic. The regulators were upon us, so we were told, at any moment about to burst into American bedrooms. Of course, no one believed this for a moment.

What implications all of this had for the office of the presidency were transitory, with the election of George W. Bush in 2000. In many respects, politics returned to its regular exercises in hopefulness and futility, removing questions of sexuality from family dinner conversation and leaving them for Tupperware-like sex-toy parties, locker rooms, and earnest debates on college campuses. The speculative excesses at the time, whether in the form of *The Death of Outrage* or *Sexual McCarthyism*, sold precisely because they turned morality into a feeling, which is how we prefer our morality, especially when it is *our* morality. An intellectual morality is an oxymoron, suitable to only the most serenely detached. The joining of sex and politics—what Clinton called the "politics of personal destruction"—cannot be neatly separated because each reflects the more impassioned connections made between personal understanding and personal conduct, except in cases of insanity. I examine here the matter of sexual relations because they remain the one thing that so many politicians and pundits said the entire matter was either *all* about or not about *at all*. In the face of such widespread consensus, either way, one reasonable response, at the very least, is to express skepticism.

Incest with Interns

The immediate reactions to President Clinton's public denial about Monica S. Lewinsky in January of 1998 are worth recalling. Women in his cabinet and administration stood by him in his denial, having no particular reason, it seemed, as women and as members of his team to do otherwise. Hillary Clinton went out furthest on the public limb by decrying a "vast right-wing conspiracy" aimed at destroying her husband's presidency. By the time August arrived, and following the elaborate legal theatrics that forced the president to admit that he had, indeed, had a relationship that was "not appropriate" with Ms. Lewinsky, the silence among vastly articulate and otherwise outspoken women who had voted for him twice was downright eerie. Yet, also in the media and among politicians from both sides of the aisle, an outpouring of condemnation came in the wake of events in which the president was publicly forced to admit that he had quite deliberately lied to the American people. The outrage about the lying itself, for a brief time, overwhelmed the ambivalence about what was lied about. As the shock wore off, the lies themselves (and there were many of them) were addressed and the motivations for telling them examined.

And then, with the subsequent release of the Starr Report in September 1998, the moral grounds shifted again, giving credibility to the arguments that the president was only doing what any other man in similar circumstances would have done. At that point, jokes abounded, and they partook of that allegedly vast sexual fantasy world attributed most of all to male adolescence. In the next avalanche of interpretations the president was labeled adolescent, a developmentally challenged male with nothing much more on his mind (when it comes to sex) that is not (apparently) always on the minds of adolescent boys. Besides the slander against male adolescence and causality itself, fantasy and reality were seamlessly merged in the person of the president, something, it seems fair to argue, is not empirically the case among most adolescent males.

The anthropologist, Rodney Needham, in a memorable collection of essays, *Exemplars*, first published in 1985 (and which I reviewed in *Contemporary Sociology* in 1987) recounts Captain Robert Knox's *An Historical Relation of the Island of Ceylon* (1681), a report of Knox's twenty years of captivity (by his own account), though he was free enough to explore in rich ethnographic detail the manners of the king. Needham notes that "It is striking that the king, for all his absolute power, hardly exploits what could be unlimited sexual privileges." When the king "hears of sexual misdemeanors among his nobles he executes them and severely punishes the women." And, as I wrote in my review in 1987: "Nevertheless, Knox relates that the king had incestuous relations with his daughter and explains that although it is abominable in all others, it is permissible 'if only to beget a right Royal Issue.' A proverb then is reported: 'None can reproach the King nor the Beggar.'" The beggar's irremediable pollution, so vile and detestable, was expressed in its most extreme form by incest between father and daughter and mother and son.

The act of incest was thus given exactly opposite meanings—in the case of the king as an act of purity and in the case of the beggar as an act of pollution. Whether above the law or beneath it, the anthropological lesson instructs that the same act may have diametrically opposed meanings. A king preserves his kingdom by incest, enacting the highest form of responsibility; a beggar is seen as so low that incest is both symbol and act of his lowliness, a merging of fantasy and reality that in the late twentieth-century has been recycled as child pornography (or in accusations of molestation against day care administrators), where the helplessness of children below a certain age is linked to their sexual vulnerability. Privacy, after all, must end somewhere, and where it does, the danger of pollution is always present.

The problem with incest in the twentieth century, in such places as Sweden, for example, is that its condemnation is evermore linked with consent, so that where kings are granted a pass on incest for purity's sake, and beggars are held up as an example of what is beneath contempt, everyone else, in the middle, as it were, is subject to reproach, including execution for sexual high crimes and misdemeanors, *if and only if* consent is not given. In America, the sexual predator is an outcast, the beggar who preys on non-consenting flesh. The defense of the "rights" of sexual predators is for many otherwise card-carrying civil libertarians difficult to stomach. The beggars are still among us—we imagine them as sick, criminal, and detestable in their vile lusts. But so, too, in our midst apparently are men who would be kings, and they seek the American equivalent of a royal pardon for their sexual license: favorable public opinion.

From Ceylon to the Book of *Genesis*, chapter 38, a similar problem is raised about responsibility as it pertains to sexual conduct. Here Onan is instructed by his father, Juda, to "Go to your brother's wife, perform your duty as brother-in-law, and raise up seed for your brother," after his older brother Er is slain by the Lord. As is still well remembered among the biblically educated, Onan let his seed be lost on the ground, and for so doing was also killed by the Lord. David Daube, in his Presidential Address to the Classical Association in 1977, entitled *The Duty of Procreation*, noted that Onan was not killed by Yahweh for the act of masturbation, and it was not until the eighteenth century that "Onanism" became a condemnation of masturbation linked with biblical sources. John T. Noonan, Jr., in his book, *Contraception: A History of Its Treatment by the Catholic Theologians and Canonists*, also agreed that Onan's death was the result of his refusal to carry on the family line through his brother's widow. Once the mists of primordial demands for shaping communal identity had lifted, onanism became one of many accounts of the sins of individuals against themselves and against God.

Perhaps it should be called the American concept of sin, since aggressive and judgmental campaigns about what is right and wrong have long been rooted in this country in concepts of individual rather than corporate responsibility. Only in recent years has corporate guilt been thrust upon, for example, race relations, leading to the extremely unpleasant and genuinely hard feelings about affirmative action and reparations. So with the myth of individual achievement also goes the myth of individual sin, or at least up to a point. Conservatives, in particular, who have promoted the rewards of individual achievement and the condemnation of individual sin, are now hard pressed to explain what the majority of Americans think about sin in particular. Most of what was deemed sinful passed first into criminal law, and it is here that sex had its normative expectations shaped over several hundred years. During the past quarter century, the use of criminal law in most matters that pertain to sex has been abandoned, further than many ever imagined was likely to occur in their lifetimes.

Yet, in another sense, not much has really changed. The clamoring for recognition of same-sex marriage is as much about middle-class entitlements as it is about the conferring of dignity upon or affording respect to homosexual unions. The outcomes of various state referenda suggest that electoral majorities do not confuse the withholding of entitlements for disrespect of persons. This may be ungenerous of Americans, but it hardly qualifies as bigotry. The pressure will remain to treat adult sexual relations in terms of privacy and choice, in other words, not as matters of sinfulness or criminality but exclusively of rights. The American public by and large refuses to condemn homosexuality as sinful, and it certainly has even less interest in defining different kinds of sexual acts as criminal. Occasionally, particularly in the case of homosexuality, there are outbursts of medical conviction that it can be "treated." But this medicalization of sexual "orientation" seems more suited to the talk show debates about the generic (i.e., equally applicable to homosexuals and heterosexuals) diagnosis of "sex addiction."

Clinton's behavior with Monica Lewinsky was run through the gauntlet of every possible interpretation, though few defended it as a matter of legal right, which, if one accepts the full implications of contemporary doctrines of consent, including those promulgated by sexual harassment codes, it is. He was legally entitled to receive sexual stimulation from an intern so long as she consented. This right also trumped any claim about adultery, since marriage vows and various "agreements" within marriage are now entirely a personal matter, or so some would insist. We may celebrate a marriage, toast to its future, but we must not pry and judge and moralize when things go wrong. Much was made of Clinton's adultery, but what was missed was his self-understanding of his purely legal rights. He did point out to Monica Lewinsky that the tag of officership that she wore chained around her neck, which allowed her access to the White House as an intern, might create a problem. It is the kind of problem that a king might recognize as he transformed his own daughter into his highest responsibility to preserve his kingdom. In the fictional kingdom of Washington, the transformation was first and foremost about turning a person into a thing of pleasure, and all the more pleasurable and pure for its furtiveness. His family may have been eventually mortified, but only the long legacy of informal, moral sanction remained a barrier to open and public celebration of his legal right to pursue pure pleasure.

The Consensual Concubine

Consensual concubines are a new version of youth. In this instance, they are the daughters of the baby-boomers who, in being given up sacrificially for sexual use by the baby-boomers themselves, muddy the already murky waters about where the lines get drawn over consensual sex. Perhaps Monica Lewinsky's relationship with the president of the United States should also be called a "multicultural moment," partaking of the traditions of other cultures and other times, where the availability of women to the sovereign was carefully controlled and supervised by one kind of eunuch or another. (Surely, the eunuchs in service to modern power are called, with egalitarian charm, spokespersons.) This would certainly make a novel defense in the future world courts of global governance. And King Solomon had seven hundred wives and three hundred concubines, which diminishes Clinton's actions in ways that his most ardent defenders, stuck on privacy and rights, missed.

The twenty-something concubine in America has nevertheless been culturally prepared for her role in history, in a culture of supine consent, cultivated among California connoisseurs of the endless uses of flesh, where principled objection to sexual opportunism is always countered by public assertion of private rights. Monica Lewinsky is the product of in-vitro Californian socialization, delivered to the president for sexual ministering. In one sense, there was nothing random about it, nothing that could not have been predicted, had only the prognosticators examined the moral implications of our present socialization to adulthood. Like millions of other girls who must today choose between the feminist morality of "you are your own person" and the consensual morality of "you may do with your body as you choose," Monica Lewinsky, to whom the media referred as "Ms. Lewinsky," was held personally responsible for both her adoration and anger.

Some defenders of former President Clinton (mostly men and women over sixty, I would wager) argued that powerful and influential men have robust sexual urges and "needs," offering the kind of sociobiological account of manhood that is simultaneously raised up as science and condemned as patriarchal by those younger and more experienced with being ideologically intimidated in the new ways. And further, attacks against Clinton's personal behavior had to be understood in light of the alleged sexual peccadilloes of former presidents. But the presidency, unlike other offices, is an active N of 1, that is, where other professions may have a certain, and expected, percentage of "deviant" practitioners (say, physicians or lawyers), the presidency represents a one-to-one correspondence between what that person does and how that office at that moment is regarded. Looking at presidents over time and drawing conclusions about any one of them in particular risks judging them out of the context of their times. This is why those over sixty are more inclined to give credence to the "pressures" of the office for men in particular (since all the presidents have been men), while younger interpreters see a classic case of a double standard (without naming it as such) because "boys will be boys" is no longer an all-purpose excuse, except when justifying the medicating of young boys who will not be docile in classrooms.

While some defended Clinton as if he were a king above the law, in pursuit of royal pleasures if not issues, others half whining and half opining, insisted that a college teacher or business executive could not have gotten away with similar pursuits, regardless of consent. And, the military at the time in the wake of Tailhook and other public trials found itself reprimanding subordinates for pointing out the hypocrisy of their commander-in-chief acting above the same laws that they had sworn to uphold with their lives. But all other offices, insofar as individual conduct is subordinated to expectations about the office itself, operate in neither total purity nor total pollution, where those in them are understood to be more and less saintly. Those judged less so, if they slide too far down the scale— for instance at my own institution, if they have sexual relations with a student enrolled in one of their classes—are subject to losing their jobs. But we college teachers are not presidents; we are not kings. We are also, most of us, not beggars.

Fresh as we are from continuing revelations about the genetic make-up of descendants of Thomas Jefferson (along with other claims about George Washington's descendants), the reactions have been entirely predictable about what it means to be in a consenting adult relationship. Some say that Jefferson could not have had consensual sex with a slave because she was defined as property and thus could not in any legally understandable sense give such consent. (More or less the same has been said about Strom Thurmond, whose fathering of a child with a black teenage housekeeper, was only widely publicized after his death.) We will never know *for cer-*

tain what Jefferson may or may not have done. That kind of certainty would nevertheless be mitigated by an understanding of the subjective points of view of both Jefferson and Sally Hemings, could they but give testimony to what each understood about the other.

It is peculiar nonetheless to think how much the present "certainty" about the nature of Jefferson's conduct turns on genetics, given the general revulsion toward genetic determinism that otherwise operates in debates about race. I say this not to provoke denunciations and defenses of the uses or misuses of genetic knowledge. Proof of paternity is an ancient problem, and its implications for American identity and morality in particular are crucial because at the same moment that Jefferson is being trotted out as the embodiment of some past evil, the old racist defenses of so-called racial purity are hardly any longer part of mainstream sensibilities. Jefferson's descendants are living proof that many Americans, both white and black, in such biologically vital respects do not know who they are. And without speculating about what the relationship between Jefferson and Hemings may mean to us or may have meant to them, it no longer appears to matter decisively to those who feel kinship with a legacy that is about neither racial purity nor pollution. In literal and moral respects, we are witness to a mixed legacy of pain and hopelessness, dignity and endurance, emblematic both of our human condition (neither above the law nor beneath it) and of the trials and tribulations that will always be part of that condition. It is also a legacy that opens upon further forms of vindication.

The intern is not a slave, but in a society that sometimes praises metaphor more than reason, we express less doubt about imposing our point of view on the absolutely unknowable past than on a present into which we may still inquire and about which we may know more. In that present, the operative term is "consent," as in "age of consent" and "informed consent." We attribute a great deal to the fiction that consent carries with it the agency of personal autonomy, and this is why at the end of the twentieth century the only remaining barriers against the most minimal standards of autonomy applicable to and exploitable by everyone, rest upon delicate assumptions and careful conclusions we make about whether some people (e.g., young children, the unconscious injured, et al.) can truly offer consent about what they may want to do or have done to them. An immense industry promotes surrogate voices for everyone in our culture of consent. At the same time, concepts such as "agency" trickle down from elite academic glacial peaks into the public discourse, substituting the idea of "a business of one entrusted to another" for the elementary fiction that trust is first about trusting yourself. This new "agency" has given subjectivity a bad name because it conflates the inevitable need to trust others with some sort of blaming of the victim who does not recognize and assert his or her "agency."

Monica Lewinsky was a special agent of sorts in the corridors of power. She provided sexual stimulation of several kinds, which was reciprocated by the former president in the very act of his paying attention, in a manner of speaking, to her in particular. She was not certain that he knew her name after their first sexual encounter. As late as the presidency of James Abram Garfield, a man could walk directly up to the front door of the White House to seek the president's attention. Garfield was fatally shot by someone who felt that he had not been given sufficient attention to his concerns for employment. There is no evidence that his assassin, Charles Julius Guiteau, had in any way earned such attention, but this is what power always provokes, the sense that one has something to gain by being associated with it, whether or not that sense is reasonable. The presidential "gaze," to give it a postmodern update, is something special in and of itself. It is the attention of power exercised at the will of one person who is at any given moment in a special position to use that power to get what he wants, when he wants it, and for whomever he wants it. Since the exercise of such power is not unique to the office of the president (only dramatically amplified by that office), such reciprocity is ubiquitous in a society where doors are rarely opened anonymously.

For her part, Monica Lewinsky was vilified, although the sheer asymmetry between his power and her powerlessness puts a lie to the claim that she could understand in any reasonable sense what she was doing. But that was not the point, because Clinton presumably did know what he was doing and to her. To argue, as some have, that he did not know what he was doing, that is, to "medicalize" his deviance, is to advance the argument that as neither a sinner nor a criminal, he was, at least in this regard, a mentally sick man, not with the kind of mental sickness that cost Thomas Eagleton his spot on a presidential ticket, but rather sick in our new ways—either addicted or, as he obviously preferred, sick in his soul. Addiction is the preferred choice of weakness of secular selves in our clinical times, while spiritual sickness opens upon a much broader landscape of possible excuses and forgiveness. To announce himself as a sinner was the only rational choice that Clinton could make. If he defended his actions as a matter of legal right, those Americans still in the ambivalent throes of moral judgment, would have been appalled, and even those operating only on the pretense of moral judgment would have had to fake a certain air of indignation that still separates the president of the United States from the publisher of *Hustler Magazine*. It may be that some, particularly sociologists, still believe that legal right does not resolve entirely the problem of moral choice, but they must consider, especially with the example of Clinton's behavior, whether a broader convergence has already occurred, and from now on, what is legal is also approved and celebrated. So, too, what is made illegal also becomes immoral, as the campaign against cigarette smoking confirms. If you smoke, you can be a bad role model, but if you have sexual relations with a clearly defined subordinate, the talk of role models is subversive conservatism at work.

President William Jefferson Clinton could not be delivered to psychiatrists, though legions of TV evangelical clinical psychologists enthusiastically volunteered to "treat" him. For his sexual ministering, he still required those real ministers, all men of the cloth, for whom the healing of the sin sick soul is something of a rare occurrence among the powerful, something publicly requested as often as an exorcism. It is one thing to be seen walking down the stairs of a church, as many Presidents regularly have been, it is quite another to announce that you have handed yourself over to its healing ministrations. The public is always more comfortable inferring an association between being seen at church and the purpose of going to church—the ante is raised considerably when some proof of process, of outcome, of personal and spiritual transformation is at stake.

What could the spiritual counselors offer? Could they really exorcise from a President the dictates (read, "demons") of his libido? Their authority was entirely therapeutic-lite. They signed on to that part of the racket that requires the all-too-careful separation of character and conduct. The religious authority figures brought in for soul site-visits at the White House were the spiritual equivalents of the absurd techno-censors known as "v-chips." They were put there to ease the older forms of conscience of a nation that endorses controls easily gotten around at the push of a button or by the jaded sneer of sophistication. Where once condemning the sin and not the sinner had hell as its backdrop, we have the mere illusion of personal defeat against the therapeutic guarantee of endless second chances. Clinton's impeachment was a fateful reminder that the land of opportunity in which second chances rule is also a nation of laws, however disregarded. As Congressman Robert Livingston fell upon his own sword after revelations about his "personal" life, raising morality above law, Clinton chose at the same moment to raise his own sword, carefully crafting his response to the law, while asking the nation for yet another chance.

Sex without Guilt

Frigidity, the accusation of sexless womanhood has long since been superseded by impotence, the proof of failure of male will, suggesting something about the cultural triumph of feminism that has gone virtually unremarked, especially in recent years. Viagra is more than wish-fulfillment, its immense popularity confirms that male libido has a chemical clause in its contract with desire. Clinton confided that his relationship with Monica Lewinsky made him feel young again. In this respect, she served better living through an old-fashioned chemistry that probably cannot be matched for its authenticity. It is this authenticity that attracts those who would be powerful, the rest may have to settle for Viagra, a middle-class love-potion if ever one were invented. Just as the pill was invented for younger, fertile women, so Viagra has been invented for older, impotent men. These drugs have deeply altered consciousness about sex, and in so doing, have broken up an older consensus about the pursuit of happiness whereby sex was not a pursuit in itself, but rather a part of something greater than itself. With the alleged end of a double standard about who can have sex without consequences, the most profound effects of this broken consensus are suffered in silence, in the breaking of vows, in the despoiling of trust, and in the poverty of consent.

The vanguard movements for sexual liberation of the masses have succeeded in creating the likes of Monica Lewinsky, neither pitied nor respected. Her modeling for *Vanity Fair*, the *New York Times'* columnist, Maureen Dowd, remarked, belied a babyish quality about her (e.g., in her hands and fingers) that was the physiognomic sign that gave her carnal innocence away. She was out of her league *all the way*. Clinton did recognize when he was not in intimate contact but rather *in loco parentis*, that he felt sorry for her. He did want to help her, about that there can be no real doubt. He really did "like" her in his own way. When he was forced to stand before the nation and thus referred to her as "that woman," he called forth a hoary prejudice that proper men and women express when they have been betrayed. He meant for the nation to know that he knew her, but that she had betrayed him in some way. In this way he told everyone that he had been hurt, too, which he determined to call the politics of personal destruction, his own first and foremost. The asymmetry of who was destined to be hurt most, was concealed by his implication that her motives were not pure. She became a suspect as a result of the urgency that power gives to privilege and paranoia. It took the Office of Independent Council to extract, however inadvertently and after a time, an apology to her.

"That woman" does not immediately convey an evaluation of a woman's mental condition. It is simply a way of putting a person outside the pale of acceptable company. She went from a person of pleasure to a person of pain, and in the months following the January denial, the public appetite for truth was fed on still further denials of such pleasures on one side, and an insistence that an immense conspiracy was afoot, on the other. Once the truth was out, the country divided among those who said they had known the truth all along, those who had wanted to believe that it was not true, and those who did not care either way. Wanting to believe is properly called assent. It should not be confused with consent. You cannot give yourself permission to believe, except to make-believe, anymore than you can forgive yourself. Permission is always and everywhere about conduct, not about belief. In the wake of a crushing blow to the nation's ability to assent came a spectacular display of disappointment but also an equally powerful desire not to think about it, to put all the implications in the same place that Clinton had originally put "that woman."

The proper world wished from the start to forget Monica Lewinsky. She wore the blue-stained dress of the consensual concubine. Forced to confess at the risk of punishment, she was still barely pitied, because such pity (where was the clergy on her behalf?) would bring her back into the consciousness of those who elected to banish the immediacy of his and her sexual behavior and honor instead the abstractness of his political causes. She became the contemporary harlot and tart who "seduced" and "stalked" the president of the United States, making him innocent and her guilty. Subsequent brief appearances in the media by Lewinksy, capitalizing on her fame, sealed her fate. But her innocence was first and foremost her age. It turns out that when the young commit real violence, we cannot bear to treat them as adults. But when they are used for sexual purposes by the most powerful people on earth, they are fully consenting, autonomous creatures of ribald pleasure, though, they become sinister in their disappointments or gauche in their post-presidential pursuits for public attention.

The absence of the now ritual denunciations by the legions of feminists who used the phrase "You just don't get it" to establish their political mark on the 1990s, was a calculated gamble to sacrifice one of their really "abused" own for the sake of their abstract cause about "real" abuse. In reality, if you do get it, then it means that sexual banter, sex in the workplace, and certainly sex with subordinates, are the biggest no-no's to have been dictated by the nonpartisan spirit of assent that rolled across the country when Clarence Thomas endured his quite public trials and tribulations. Regardless of the facts of that case, it was argued, "You just don't get it." Closing ranks now in favor of Clinton's political "agenda" and against those who were accused of using his private behavior to upset that agenda, the inversion of our inherited sensibilities about sexual morality was almost complete.

When Anita Hill came seemingly reluctantly forward to accuse Clarence Thomas of saying "inappropriate" words to her, constituting in her mind "sexual harassment," she had waited enough years to raise credible suspicions that her earlier silence had mostly to do with her opportunism. Thomas's star may have been rising, but not so fast that anyone would reasonably expect, no doubt including Anita Hill, that he would someday become a justice of the Supreme Court of the United States. Hill was depicted as having suffered from a kind of syndrome in which men get to say certain kinds of things even as women ask for their recommendations and remain silent.

In coming to Clinton's defense, Anita Hill dismissed any comparisons between her suffering and Monica Lewinsky's. On September 28, 1998, she concluded in the New York Times: "According to their testimony, Mr. Clinton and Ms. Lewinsky viewed their relationship as consensual. While their immoral and undignified behavior no doubt had a negative effect on others in the office and in the Clinton household, it was not coerced, unwanted or illegal."

But it was the president who conjured up the name of Clarence Thomas when defending himself against what appeared, at first, to be a growing tide of accusations against him and his behavior. Perhaps Anita Hill missed this bit of the testimony. Unable finally to prevent the confirmation of Clarence Thomas, she referred, with studied indifference, to "a negative effect" as incidental, rather than central to, the very problem for which she claimed to be a martyr. The weakness of her own sexual harassment charges had required an extraordinarily special context in order for them to become explosive. The "negative effect" that she has determined to overlook required special douses of denial, including, "Clearly the President and Ms. Lewinsky used sex for their own purposes ..." This conferring upon Ms. Lewinsky of her own agency is one of the earmarks of libertine earnestness and political expediency.

But what will be said if Monica Lewinsky, someday in the future, awakens to the fact that she had been drugged by the aphrodisiac of power? Anita Hill had her chance to change her mind, failing in the particular case, but succeeding so profoundly in general that she became a legend in her own time. Her failure *against* Justice Thomas is part of her success, for it seems more than likely that had Clarence Thomas not been confirmed, the name of Anita Hill would have been disappeared along with the man she was sent to bring down. He had to win confirmation in order for her losing against him to be a winning thing. The lives of secular saints (those losers against such secular evils as "glass-ceiling" patriarchy) will undoubtedly be written, replete with accounts of celebrity martyrs.

Should Monica Lewinsky someday revolt against her submissiveness to America's most visible symbol of patriarchy (the office of presidency), it would become the basis for another lawsuit in the longest continuing grievance in human history. That blue dress contains more than a former President's DNA; it represents positive proof of power expressed in its most literal sense, not as violence, but as decreation. Centuries of patriarchal deliberations on "onanism" have now been abandoned in favor of the "healthfulness" of a fully expressive sexual life. The blue dress is Onan's redemption, and he has nothing more to answer for to those expansive middle classes and their many admonitory guides who across vast space and time insisted that the pursuit of sexual pleasure always had consequences for more than oneself.

Of course, there is supposed to be in our present insights about "healthy sexuality" nothing wrong with masturbation, but Clinton did not, after all, appear too close by when Joycelyn Elders was forced to resign for too openly defending it as good fun and healthy sport. He owes more of an apology to her than to Lani Guinier. Sex is never too far out in the open. It is mostly two-dimensional when it is. The Internet is only the latest escalation of masturbatory fantasies, allegedly for the improved health of the indulging populations who consume it, with the proviso that those who consume it in certain forms (e.g., child pornography) are still beggars. Finally, it is no longer even a matter of public health. It is a right, the final entitlement, superseding sin, crime, and health. The inversion of our inherited sexual morality is complete.

Doubts were raised about the future effectiveness of one kind of feminist intimidation, which so relentlessly impugned a person when his politics were incorrect but spared him rather shamelessly when his politics were correct. The era of an exclusively feminist intimidation appeared at an end, and was renamed neo-Puritanism, though it is difficult to explain how Larry Flynt was a neo-Puritan. The weakening of political influence that came along with accusations about personal behavior came full circle. It may be that nothing could stop this juggernaut of relentless scrutiny of personal conduct, since it invites voyeurism on a national scale. In the end, democratic leadership in particular requires trust, a kind of covenant in which any detail at any moment may be relevant to the authority that one individual has over another.

The case of Congressman Livingston's resignation illustrates the difference between an honorable politics and the so-called politics of personal destruction. Throughout the Clinton years a variety of existential politics ensued, first in the calls to pursue the "politics of meaning," and, after impeachment, in the calls to stop the politics of personal destruction. The witch-hunts against conservative jurists, for example, were down and dirty politics, pursued by individuals without the slightest qualms about their moral responsibilities. Congressman Livingston made clear by his resignation that leadership cannot afford to be compromised by an uncertainty about personal character. We are told that we must believe that "good" men will not run for office, for fear of what are now called, generically, "sexual" outings.

Disclosures about Henry Hyde may have been calculated to harm him, yet he was obviously not deterred in his role as chairman of the House Judiciary Committee. In using himself as an example to Clinton, Robert Livingston contradicted the thoroughly false and misleading idea about a politics of personal destruction. Politics is only about winning and losing, and in a democracy, at the time elections are held. If, somehow, there were a national blackout on polling, politicians would appear to have only the law and themselves to fall back upon to guide their actions. To invoke "conscience" or "duty" seems alien and suspect to those who play to win. There was never any politics of personal destruction at work in efforts to oppose conservatives, it was politics operating with every weapon short of *physical* destruction. If the calls for civility lately are about calling a moratorium on the use of certain kinds of weapons, it seems unlikely to result in anything more than producing outcomes in which some men will resign rather than endure their shame publicly any longer while other men will insist on holding on to their power until the last hour of the last day of their elected office.

As to shame, sex, and politics, the chilliest and warmest indications were contained in a perfectly straightforward feminist criticism of the president as a sexist by Martha Ackermann, a professor of women's studies at Mt. Holyoke College, followed a week later by a letter in response to her analysis by John P. Siegel of San Jose, California. (Both appeared in the *Wall Street Journal* in mid-September 1998.) Professor Ackermann chastised her fellow feminists for accepting the president's behavior in order to support the larger causes he claimed to represent. Feminists were settling for too little, but their ambivalence was "rooted more in fear of what could be next than in support for what is." This is ambivalence about the wrong thing. What could after all be next? The return of Anthony Comstock? The outlawing of all abortions? The return of unsanctioned male sexual bravado at the water-cooler? The removal of women from all the professions? The Christianizing of the nation? Where is this specter that is supposedly haunting women's achievements in America? When the lives of women around the rest of the world are in truly precarious states, this holy paranoia about American society among its highly educated elites, is precious to a fault. At the same time, the election and re-election of George W. Bush may be enough for some to hold to this apocalyptic faith, despite all evidence to the contrary.

At the very end of *The Protestant Ethic and the Spirit of Capital-ism*, the still reliable Max Weber observed: "In the field of its highest development, in the United States, the pursuit of wealth, stripped of its religious and ethical meaning, tends to become associated with purely mundane passions, which often actually give it the character of sport." Substitute "sexual pleasure" for "wealth," and something can be made of John P. Siegel's oddly hopeful account of Clinton's behavior: "The Clintons, perhaps because of their experience dur-ing the 1960s' so-called 'sexual revolution,' have learned guilt-free separation of sex and intimacy. A sexual act is not about domination or submission, nor is it about making love or an expression of inti-macy, nor even a fleeting moment of passion or overwhelming ani-mal attraction. It is simply fun, another individual-performance sport in which one casually engages one's friends and acquaintances, like golf, tennis, jogging or shooting baskets." The denials at the White House were no doubt issued swiftly and widely, but Citizen Siegel had a point that should not be lost on those still struggling to under-stand why ambivalence about sexual morality is different than the abandonment of moralizing about sex altogether.

4

The Dubious Triumph of the Therapeutic: The Denial of Character

Alan Woolfolk

> *"And, after boasting this way of my tolerance, I come to the admission that it has a limit. Conduct may be founded on the hard rock or the wet marshes, but after a certain point I don't care what it's founded on. When I came back from the East last autumn I felt that I wanted the world to be in uniform and at a sort of moral attention forever; I wanted no more riotous excursions with privileged glimpses into the human heart."*
> —*F. Scott Fitzgerald*, The Great Gatsby *(1925)*

> *"In a society with so many inducements to self-interest, "self-realization" seems a noble and healthy end. The least valuable competitive position is to be self-defeating. The therapeutic cannot conceive of an action that is not self-serving, however it may be disguised or transformed. This is a culture in which each views the other, in the fullness of his self-knowledge, as 'trash.' Freud used the word to summarize his general opinion of people. But, the question remains: How to discipline the 'trash'? To be liberated from renunciatory character ideals by the analytic attitude might give the 'trash' (Freud's term) too much liberty to do its worst, whereas in the older system the 'trash' would not do its best. One may think, therefore, an ethic of perfection to be more prudent, even on Freud's own assumption about the human animal, than an ethic of tolerance. Yet, probably the ethic of tolerance is the one more appropriate and safe for use in the age of psychological man. It is the ethic of a wayfarer rather than that of a missionary; it is the ethic of a pilgrim, who, out of his experience, became a tourist.*
> —*Philip Rieff*, The Triumph of the Therapeutic *(1966)*

> *"The world is not hospitable to pilgrims any more...The hub of postmodern life strategy is not identity building, but the avoidance of being fixed."*
> —*Zygmunt Bauman*, Life in Fragments *(1995)*

The moral revolution that defined the twentieth century may be drawing to at least a temporary close insofar as the worldview now commonly characterized as "therapeutic" has triumphed. In American, European, and other post-industrial societies, this triumph has meant the defeat of moralities of self-denial based upon the assumption that the path to individual salvation is through submission to doctrines of communal purpose and adherence to narratives of spiritual ascent. Likewise, it has meant the victory of moralities of self-affirmation authorizing experimentation with an endless variety of what are now called "lifestyles."[1] Our most recent *kulturkampf* has been more transitory and less consequential than it first appeared.[2] Under the symbolic-moral regime of modernity, the therapeutic worldview made significant gains in industrial societies, but these gains were often checked by a bourgeois ethos that bore an ambivalent relationship to the modernist intellectual and artistic adversaries who were the primary predecessors of a full-blown therapeutic culture. Today, what remains of this bourgeois ethos has come unraveled.

The modernists of Lionel Trilling's "adversary culture"[3] have won a posthumous victory that most of them would not have wanted as the earlier tensions between modernity and modernism, bourgeois and bohemian, have been resolved in favor of releases from cultural controls, which made earlier spiritual rebellions possible. Rimbaud's attack upon the "specious good" (or, as Philip Rieff has explained, Oscar Wilde's attack upon the "philistines"[4]) has been so massively reproduced and cheapened as to subvert the integrity of such rebellions. Under the symbolic-moral regime of postmodernity, the therapeutic has penetrated even more deeply into our hearts and minds than when Rieff first announced with exquisite irony the ascent of psychological man amidst the turmoil of 1960s.[5] The pockets of moral resistance—cultural, social, personal—are in rapid decline, most notably among educated elites. Indeed, it is the demise of what used to be called *character* that may be the most significant. As David Brooks has observed, members of the contemporary educated class have "cultivated an ethos that celebrates, actually demands, endless innovation, self-expression, and personal growth."[6] More precisely, in the name of individual health and psychological well-being those towards the upper end of the class scale (and those who aspire to join them) have been re-educated to accept what they previously rejected. They have learned to renounce inherited renunciations that once functioned, however intermittently, to link the individual's well-being to the health of the community. To put the matter differently, if *The Great Gatsby* had been written during the early twenty-first century rather than the 1920s, Nick Carraway would have learned to get over his "provincial squeamishness"[7] about the conduct of the Buchanans (or perhaps not experienced it in the first place) and never returned to his Midwestern home.

Therapeutic Hegemony: A Synopsis

As the reigning symbolic-moral regime of postmodernity, the therapeutic worldview has become hegemonic by penetrating the structure of impulse and inhibition in the personality as well as the established institutional order of power and privilege. The rise of therapeutic professions in recent decades is by now well documented. But the influence of therapeutic psychology extends far beyond the burgeoning numbers of doctorates in psychology, clinical psychologists, psychiatrists, social workers, family counselors, assorted therapeutic paraprofessionals, and a vast self-help and co-dependency industry. As James Nolan has recently argued, the therapeutic ethos has made dramatic inroads into the state itself in civil case law, the criminal justice system, welfare policy, public education, and the very rhetoric of national political life among *both* cultural progressives and cultural conservatives.[8] The therapeutic has triumphed by penetrating the hearts and minds of the very individuals whom one might expect to be most opposed to any such victory. Increasingly, we all live inside a symbolic world, or rather it lives inside of us, that rejects definitive moral judgments in favor of "emotivist" values that proclaim the sovereignty of the self and the supremacy of psychology. "Where once the self was to be surrendered, denied, sacrificed, and died to, now the self is to be esteemed, actualized, affirmed, and unfettered."[9] Where once religion, morality, and custom accounted for human conduct in terms of good and bad, right and wrong, today psychology guides us towards criteria of well-being and sickness, functional and dysfunctional, even in matters of religion.

At an earlier stage in the development of therapeutic culture before its triumphs were less obvious and less complete, Ralph Turner stipulated the changing relationship between self and society in terms of a shift away from an institutional focus and toward that of impulse as the locus of one's identity. "Self-as-impulse," Turner argued, "tends to transform the institutional order into a set of norms, all cramping the expression of the true self. Self-as-institution subordinates the normative sense to a set of values, such as integrity, piety, patriotism, considerateness, and many others."[10] The therapeutic division of the self from institutional role, value from norm, builds upon the theoretical pitting of human nature against the social order that runs from Rousseau through modernist philosophy and literature to a variety of psychologizers, who have favored individualist conceptions of the self that classical sociology argued against. The moral revolution that erupted in the mid-twentieth century, which was prepared for and informed by psychologizers (ranging in intellectual depth from Nietzsche and Freud to the likes of Carl Rogers and Abraham Maslow), transformed this problematic conception of the self into the reality of a therapeutic personality type. As John Steadman Rice has cogently argued, the "liberation psychotherapy" of the time articulated a "revolutionary discourse" based upon "the seemingly innocuous conviction that the individual's subjection to communal purpose is the cause of psychological sickness." Out of this discourse arose an ethic of self-actualization or -affirmation based upon dubious anti-cultural and anti-institutional premises that specified therapeutic criteria of health and sickness as the new standards by which to measure spiritual growth. "For self-actualized individuals, then, any action governed by social convention rather than individual preference—staying in an intimate relationship or abiding by the demands of educational institutions or an inherited religious faith—is tantamount to self-violation. To be well, to be ethical, requires leaving a marriage, finding a new faith, and so on....To conform to social expectation is to be, in varying degrees, psychologically sick."[11] Well-being, or more accurately, a sense of well-being, replaced an inhibitive sense of guilt as the sixth sense necessary for negotiating the endless choices that define the experience of living. To play a role without thought of change became an indication of arrested individuality and dishonesty towards the self.

This impulsive-expressive configuration of the self revenged itself in the form of obvious symptoms when it broke to the surface of public and private life on a broad scale with the post-war "baby-boom" generation. Rates of suicide, homicide and other serious crimes, drug and alcohol abuse, illegitimacy and abortion, divorce, and a host of other social pathologies dramatically increased in the 1960s and continued to do so on the whole until the 1990s, when they seemed to be abating. Intellectuals fighting a rear-guard action in defense of the collapsed bourgeois ethos, such as Gertrude Himmelfarb, have argued that a religious and moral revival favoring cultural conservatives against cultural progressives accounts for the improvements in "moral statistics." However, Himmelfarb seriously underestimates the extent of the very therapeutic revolution that she opposes, not to mention the ambivalent structure of the exhausted bourgeois ethos that she defends; for a therapeutic ethos has been able to penetrate and co-opt the bourgeoisie precisely because of the antitraditional character of the most ambitious and successful segments of that class.[12]

As Joseph Schumpeter, and before him Karl Marx and Max Weber, understood, the dynamic of capitalism is driven by an evolutionary doctrine of progress—a process of "creative destruction" that does not favor cultural conservatism. Furthermore, Schumpeter (once again, drawing on themes in Marx and Weber) contended that the habits of rational analysis cultivated under capitalism eventually turn on the capitalist ethos and institutions themselves because these habits develop into a critical frame of mind that respects no moral authority whatsoever. "Capitalist rationality does not do away with sub- or super-rational impulses," Schumpeter argued. "It merely makes them get out of hand by removing the restraint of sacred or semi-sacred tradition." Lack of "*emotional* attachment to the social order," in particular, leaves capitalist society defenseless before "the hostile impulse" that is a part of the experience of daily trials in any society. "If there is no emotional attachment," Schumpeter concludes, "then that impulse has its way and grows into a permanent constituent of our psychic setup."[13] Contrary to what "neoconservative" intellectuals argue, then, the ethos of the bourgeoisie *in toto* does not support cultural conservatism. That case can only be made if one is able, as in the case of Christopher Lasch, to defend those virtues of the bourgeois ethos that have been historically as much associated with socioeconomic failure as success—namely the ethos of the *petty* bourgeoisie.

Therapeutic culture attempts to control and exploit hostile impulses toward the social order, as well as other anti-institutional and anti-cultural impulses, not through repressive controls but by means of tolerant remissions on the assumption that many impulses are less harmful than they first appear, while others may be made safe through controlled, cathartic releases. However, the case for such mild forms of control is questionable at best. Safe expressions of previously forbidden impulses may have entertainment value, but they also function to prevent direct challenges to a social order that is uncertain about what it stands for. Vulgarity in public life gives the illusion of freedom; exclusive devotion to private well-being, as Tocqueville understood, forestalls revolutionary efforts. Furthermore, cathartic releases of impulses may only enhance the risk of dangerous and destructive forms of behavior and arrest the development of the self. Indeed, a permissive morality would appear to be conducive to a mild but spiritually debilitating social order of the sort that Tocqueville foresaw and Huxley parodied.

Under what Alasdair MacIntyre has called the doctrine of emotivism, therapeutic culture has attempted to heal the tearing apart of self and institution that the impulsive-expressive definition of the self has set in motion. According to this doctrine, all moral judgments or evaluations are subjective preferences—they are understood as "*nothing but* expressions of preference, expressions of attitude or feeling"[14]—with the consequence that the self can be reconciled to institutional roles insofar as the normative controls are experienced as voluntary and therapeutic. The emotivist reduction of moral judgements to subjective preferences encourages in theory an ethic of tolerance under which there are no authoritative points of moral reference beyond the self. Successfully implemented, such an ethic would make Turner's self-as-impulse indistinguishable from the self-as-institution. But it would also contradict the established function of culture "to bind and loose" individuals in communal purposes, primarily through *institutionalized* disciplines of interdiction limiting the self.

Mitigating Practices

In recent years, a growing body of scholarly work has attempted to make the case for the maturation of forms of control in therapeutic culture. In *One Nation, After All,* for example, Alan Wolfe has discovered an anti-political "morality writ small" among contemporary Americans that has as its primary commandment "Thou shalt not judge." In Wolfe's reading, Americans are united precisely because they are "accommodating, pluralistic, tolerant, and expansive." Americans are "reluctant to pass judgment, they are tolerant to a fault.... Above all moderate in their outlook on the world, they believe in the importance of leading a virtuous life but are reluctant to impose values they understand as virtuous for themselves on others; strong believers in morality, they do not want to be considered moralists."[15] Likewise, Brooks describes members of the educated class as recoiling "from those who try to 'impose' their views or their lifestyles on others. They prefer tolerance and civility instead."[16]

Furthermore, as analysts of contemporary culture have discovered an ethic of tolerance succeeding what Rieff called an ethic of perfection, they have frequently (as in the cases of Wolfe and Brooks) offered an implicit defense of that very tolerance. One especially effective approach employed in such efforts has been to appropriate MacIntyre's concept of practices in order to mitigate in varying degrees the acceptance of the very emotivism that he rejected.

In *Habits of the Heart*, Robert Bellah contends in apparent opposition to the therapeutic culture of emotivism that Americans continue to engage in practices that belie their "inarticulate" language of individualism. With the concept of practices, Bellah follows MacIntyre in referring to cooperative activities in which the participants strive to conform to established standards of excellence that are essential to the cultivation and sustenance of virtues. "The tensions of our lives would be even greater," reads one passage, "if we did not, in fact, engage in practices that constantly limit the effects of an isolating individualism, even though we cannot articulate those practices nearly as well as we can the quest for autonomy."[17] Likewise, in a follow-up essay entitled "The Idea of Practices in *Habits*: A Response," Bellah writes that "practices necessarily persist in our lives even when we find it difficult to articulate them." He continues: "we locate these persistent practices in those spheres of our lives where biblical religion and civic republicanism still survive."[18] Although Bellah argues that many Americans have retreated into "lifestyle enclaves" in pursuit of an expressive individualism, he maintains that "concrete commitments" have persisted in "communities of memory," especially in the lower and upper reaches of the class structure. What he calls "practices of commitment" still embody the conventional moral languages of American culture in contemporary society, even if those languages are poorly spoken.[19]

Bellah places such a heavy emphasis on MacIntyre's concept of practice because social practices constitute, as Lasch has pointed out, "the discipline of character formation"[20] that is necessary for the narrowing of possibilities and the establishment of a firm sense of identity in the personality. However, in order to instill character practices cannot be separated from the symbolic-moral system that informs them. Moreover, it is the personal capacity to reject or resist, rather than to accept, possibilities that is the litmus test of character formation. By that test, the practices which Bellah defends fail because they have, at best, become detached from the moral traditions

(Biblical and Republican) that MacIntyre contends are necessary for sustaining them and, at worst, succumbed to the regnant therapeutic regime. Nothing in Bellah's analysis explains how the "practices of commitment" embedded in "communities of memory" can instill the personal capacity to resist a postmodern, therapeutic culture when those practices and communities have become infected with therapeutic assumptions. Indeed, when Bellah approvingly states in *Habits of the Heart* that for ecologist Marra James the "'whole world' is a community of memory and hope and entails "practices of commitment," or that labor activist Cecelia Dougherty "describes her solidarity with working people and 'the have nots' as an expression of concern for human dignity,"[21] one must question how much Bellah's own theory has absorbed self-deceptive therapeutic assumptions. What Bellah elides, according to Charles Taylor, is "the search for moral sources *outside* the subject through languages which resonate *within* him or her, the grasping of an order which is inseparably indexed to a personal vision."[22] Without such personal knowledge, Bellah misses the decline of militant character ideals that defines what is most significant about American culture at the turn of the century.[23]

Following Bellah, Robert Wuthnow has also employed MacIntyre's concept of practices but towards the end of defending a "practice-oriented spirituality" as an alternative to a traditional "spirituality of dwelling" and a postmodern "spirituality of seeking." Wuthnow finds neither *habituation* to a specific moral tradition (*apropos* of a spirituality of dwelling) nor the *negotiation* of identity (*apropos* of a spirituality of seeking) to be adequate for our unsettled times. "Habituation spirituality encourages dependence on communities that are inherently undependable and fosters an idolization of particular places to the point that energies gravitate too much to those places rather than being deployed to the full round of human needs in a complex world," Wuthnow contends. "A spirituality of seeking, in contrast, is invariably too fluid to provide individuals with the social support they need or to encourage the stability and dedication required to grow spiritually and to mature in character." Thus, Wuthnow emphasizes, not surprisingly, that "the increasingly complex social and cultural environment in which Americans live" is the single most important factor affecting our spiritual lives.[24]

With a clearer eye for the requisites of character formation than Bellah, Wuthnow contends that the spiritual excesses and superfici-

ality that resulted from the 1960s are in the process of being overcome with the recent growth of spiritual practices that are "morally
binding." Practice-oriented spirituality "requires devoting a significant amount of time and effort to praying, meditating, examining
deep desires, and focusing attention in a worshipful manner on one's
relationship to God."[25] It accents "the value of rooting...spiritual
practice in a specific *tradition*."[26] Yet, Wuthnow underestimates the
difficulties of character formation in a therapeutic culture. A practice-oriented spirituality may well concede too much to the fluidity
of postmodern life. While recognizing that habituation to a specific
moral community has become dysfunctional for the individual,
Wuthnow fails to consider the pervasiveness of deracination in a
culture "with nothing at stake beyond a manipulatable sense of well-
being."[27] All roots grow increasingly shallow in a therapeutic soil.
None may sink deeply enough into the individual to prevent an endless shuttling among lifestyle options. What Charles Horton Cooley
called a "credible creed"[28] may be more necessary than Wuthnow
imagines to the development of the individual and the stability of
society.

To be more precise: Wuthnow's focus on the complexity of the
contemporary social and cultural environment emphasizes "the social factor" at the expense of an analysis of the cultural system and
its implications for the formation of identity. On the basis of
Wuthnow's own limited description, that system can be described as
anticredal because little or no consensus of belief exists. In such a
culture, according to Wuthnow, the development of the inner life
depends upon the spiritual search of the individual being subject to
the discipline of practices. Yet, even here, the individual self-consciously searches out and submits to any one of an endless variety
of traditional spiritual practices with the consequence that intentional
conduct takes precedence over habitual conduct. But just such a
self-conscious search is, in the words of Cooley, "a task to which
few are equal." Most will "undergo distraction, or cease to think
about such matters," if they can, because for Cooley the formation
of character is largely a matter of habit and affection.[29] Wuthnow, in
contrast, operates from a theory of culture that is unduly shaped by
the prevailing anticredalism of our own culture. He emphasizes the
cognitive dimension of conduct and, as a consequence, grossly over-
estimates the capacity of most individuals to form self-consciously
their own worldviews and character for the better.

Therapeutic Culture: Intimations and Formulations

Of the classical sociologists, Max Weber is the most important theorist for helping us to understand the traditional role of religion and culture in character formation and the failure of that function in the twentieth century. As is well known, Weber understood the history of religion and culture as the history of the rationalization and disenchantment of the world. But what is frequently obscured is that Weber conceived of this process as developing in two movements: disenchantment began with the ascendance of religious prophecy over magic that led to the evolution of rational, ethical religion. And it continued with the disenchantment of high culture, especially ethical religion, by the modern intellect.

The first movement is significant because it marked the rationalization or systematization of conduct through physical and psychic regimens that functioned therapeutically to provide some assurance of salvation and continuity of religious mood. Such regimens, whether ascetic or mystical, were anti-instinctual and aimed at the control of everyday life in the service of religious ends. Among the various religious paths to salvation, Weber maintained that inner-worldly asceticism created the greatest degree of rationalization of conduct in worldly activities. But neither monastic, world-rejecting asceticism nor mystical contemplation affirmed the world as such. All forms of asceticism and mysticism created tensions within one's inner life and with the world. When these systematic "techniques for attaining sanctification stressed *ethical* conduct based on religious sentiment," according to Weber, "one practical result was the transcendence of particular desires and emotions of raw human nature which had not hitherto been controlled by religion." Depending upon the religion, "cowardice, brutality, selfishness, sensuality, or some other natural drive" was "the one most prone to divert the individual from his charismatic character."[30] In its most advanced stages, rational ethical religion resulted in what Weber called a *Gesinnungsethik*, literally a disposition ethic, that established an integrated, ethical personality.

Thus, for Weber, character-forming regimens against "raw human nature" that stressed ethical conduct were directly linked to fundamental dispositional changes in the personality that established a spiritual *habitus*. Commitment to ethical values or ends contained repressive implications for the individual that created tensions in one's inner life as well as with the external world. Rationalization was inseparable from resistance to what Weber called the "polytheism of experience."

Under modernity, rationalization had precisely the opposite effect because it advanced in a symbolic-moral world lacking a unifying vision. With the differentiation of modern societies into separate spheres of activity, Weber argued that rationalization had resulted in the emergence of conflicting value spheres. Rationalization "pressed towards making conscious the *internal and lawful autonomy* of the individual spheres"—economic, political, aesthetic, erotic, and intellectual—with each value sphere containing its own immanent interests and inherent logic.[31] Writing in the early twentieth century, Weber assumed that neither an ethic of conscience nor a *traditional* ethic of responsibility was credible because the fragmentation of modern culture had destroyed the illusion that we live in an ethical world. Traditional Protestant asceticism had failed, and the German character ideals that succeeded it in the nineteenth century were no longer viable. Neither the Kantian idea of the moral personality nor the discipline of personal cultivation, *Bildung*, could any longer maintain the integrity of the self. Consequently, Weber advanced his own famous and problematic ethic of responsibility for a world he imagined to be without limits.

Late Weberian theory suggests that the rationalization and fragmentation of modern culture has been closely linked with the atrophy of what Rieff calls interdictory controls, with the consequence that characterological resistances to the immediacy of experience have been weakened. Indeed, Rieff has built upon Weber's theory, arguing that religion may be understood as performing two distinct functions that, when successful, tend to spread out into the larger culture—either a therapeutic control of life or a therapeutic remission from that control. Insofar as faith controls everyday life, it is "doctrinal, and that doctrine is internalized thus becoming functionally anti-instinctual." As in Weberian theory, such faith "tends to be methodical and systematic." It limits experience and inhibits expression. Defined as remission of control, faith is, Rieff argues, once again following Weber, "ecstatic, or erotic...and the religious mood covertly provides an opportunity for the instincts to express themselves more directly—for example, in orgiastic behavior, or in mystical states of mind which release the subject from traditional authority." Such faith "tends to be anti-methodical and unsystematic."[32]

According to Rieff, not only has the controlling, interdictory function of religion failed, but the remissive function of faith has become increasingly self-conscious and dominant in modernity, as the larger culture itself has grown increasingly remissive. The consequence of this growing remissiveness has been the emergence of a new personality type that was beyond Weber's historical grasp—the therapeutic.[33]

For Rieff, the remissive function of faith can never become primary for long because the individual's sense of well-being has always depended upon mandatory commitment to a communal purpose that limited the freedom of the self. As in Weberian theory, the sense of reassurance and ego security have been a direct result of submission to regimens that rationalized and systematized conduct, establishing characterological dispositions in the personality. "In the culture preceding our own," Rieff states, in one formulation, "the order of therapy was embedded in a consensus of 'shalt nots.'"[34] Under a remissive regime, the link between commitment and therapy, character and cultus, is broken. That is, character can no longer be securely formed in the traditional sense because therapeutic enhancements of the sense of well-being can be obtained more directly, without the self-denying provisos of earlier ascetic and mystical religious-cultural modes. In what Rieff calls a therapeutic culture, affirmation of life as such triumphs.

"It is out of a highly differentiated society, spheres of action separate, none subject to the same interdicts, and all to fewer," Rieff argues, "that the therapeutic has been born." The therapeutic personality type is "free, in the first place, because he can live his life among authorities so long divided that none can assert themselves strongly even in their own sphere—quite the contrary of Durkheim's quasi-syndicalist hope."[35] In particular, the therapeutic has broken free of the inhibiting, guilt culture of the past that relied upon the authority of example to instill both ethics of conscience and ethics of responsibility. "Freedom" has been translated into a freedom from militant ideal images of the self and mandatory cultural forms, as the inner life has been increasingly defined by its lack of character-defining resistances to the immediacy of experience. As the enchantments of Weber's pre-ethical universe have returned, each sphere of activity becomes what Weber called "autonomous"—business is business, politics is politics, erotics is erotics, just as artistic and intellectual life achieve their respective freedoms.[36]

Recently, sociologists of culture have suggested that the differentiation of modern life has been reversed with the rise of postmodernity, as seen especially in the melding or even collapse of the aesthetic into economic, social, and political domains. But in Rieff's vision the aesthetization of life is one of the definitive hallmarks of therapeutic culture. Postmodernity marks no definitive break with modernity but rather is an extension of it as older religious, moral, and legal criteria are increasingly subverted by the language of psychology and the aesthetic refinements of lifestyle priorities. Art and life merge, as life is increasingly conceived as a work of art, executed with greater or lesser degrees of talent and skill.

Postmodern Reforms

For Weber, the tension between habituation and intentionality, credal and anti-credal motifs, was played out in the form of a great and delicate balancing act between, on the one hand, the concept of *habitus* or disposition in the studies of religion and traditional cultures and, on the other hand, the concept of value-rational action in modernity. Indeed, Weber helped to drive a wedge between *morality as character* and *morality as values* that has only grown wider since his day. In the work of Rieff and MacIntyre, we see the implications of the wholesale acceptance of morality as values in the twentieth century traced out under the respective rubrics of "therapeutic culture" and "emotivism."

For Rieff, the narrative of modernity is the story of the rise of an anti-credal, analytic attitude that has led to the detachment of the individual from communal purposes (and what we today call "grand narratives"). "The social type most obviously so detached is the intellectual," Rieff argues. "By our time, the detachment of the late nineteenth-century intellectual from a predominately middle-class culture has been rendered general."[37] Rieff picks up Weber's theme of the rationalization and intellectualization of the world and drives it to its logical conclusion with the ideal of psychological man who discovers no normative order or objective goals inherent in the universe and, therefore, strives above all not to be deceived into further unconditional commitments. With the example of Freud informing him, Rieff describes the precarious ideal that arose out of modern democratic culture:[38]

> To reserve the capacity for neutrality between choices, even while making them, as required by this new science of moral management, produces a strain no less great than

choosing itself. The analytic capacity demands a rare skill: to entertain multiple perspectives upon oneself, and even upon beloved others. A high level of control is necessary in order to shift from one perspective to another, so to soften the demands upon oneself in all the major situations of life—love, parenthood friendship, work, and citizenship. Such conscious fluidity of commitment is not easily acquired. In fact, that attainment of psychological manhood is more difficult than any of the older versions of maturity; that manhood is no longer protected by a fantasy of having arrived at some resting place where security, reassurance, and trust reside, like gods in their heavens. The best one can say for oneself in life is that one has not been taken in, even by that "normal psychosis," love.

The ideal of psychological manhood is, as a point of recent sociological and psychiatric experience, untenable, except for perhaps a few exceptional individuals. Indeed, an exploration of the tensions that arise between the ideal of an honest, undeceived life and the temptation of therapeutic consolations is a motif that runs throughout Rieff's work. That is, the narrative of modernity is *also* the story of the strains created by detachments from communal purposes that have resulted in efforts to establish post-communal therapeutic faiths (as illustrated by the examples of C.G. Jung, Wilhelm Reich, and D.H. Lawrence in *The Triumph of the Therapeutic*). The narrative of postmodernity, insofar as it has one, may increasingly center on the question of whether therapeutic culture can moderate its excesses without resorting to a revitalization of interdictory controls that would be tantamount to its defeat.

Rice has taken up precisely this question in his recent study of the co-dependency movement, arguing that co-dependency represents a "discourse of reform" within the larger "discourse of revolution" that defines the triumph of the therapeutic. Aptly summarizing the fundamental assumption of this cultural revolution, Rice states that "liberation psychotherapy ultimately has but one explanatory mechanism for any and all psychological problems: societal and cultural repression of the self."[39] Consequently, according to this revolutionary discourse, a release from inhibiting cultural controls and institutional forms is the secret to achieving personal well-being and curing our social pathologies. But if total liberation is not possible, then the anti-cultural and anti-institutional impulses of therapeutic culture need to be either mitigated or repressed. As a discourse of reform addressing the excesses of the therapeutic revolution, Rice contends that the co-dependency movement operates as what Clifford Geertz calls "a set of control mechanisms," which function to re-establish limits upon the self and to commit the individual to new forms of communal purpose and "mediating institutions," such as "families of affiliation." Yet, as Rice implies, these controls may not be controls at all; in the end, they subserve the liberationist assumptions of the prevailing therapeutic discourse *and* offer a way to stabilize social relationships and personal identity, providing one does not interrogate them too closely. Consequently, they cannot be construed as equivalent to the interdictory controls that Rieff deems necessary to all culture and inner development of character. Nor do they appear to be consistent with Geertz's focus on a definition of man stressing "the mechanisms by whose agency the breadth and indeterminateness of his inherent capacities are reduced to the narrowness and specificity of his actual accomplishments."[40] Indeed, both Rieff and Geertz point toward the necessity of the very repressive function of culture that liberationist psychology identifies as the only source of our social and psychological problems.

Co-dependency epitomizes, then, the complete democratization of the modernist intellectual-artistic attack upon the repressive function of culture *per se* carried out under the shibboleth of *épater la bourgeoisie*. With the triumph of the therapeutic, that attack has been rendered superfluous as earlier character ideals have failed and an ambivalent bourgeois ethos has given way to a radical aestheticization of reality under the rubric of *lifestyles*.

The Intellect of the Guilty Conscience

By the early twentieth century, the Kantian ideal of the ethical personality, the virtuous dispositions of the Victorian age, the German character ideal of *Bildung*, and the nineteenth-century American ideal of "the balanced character"[41] were among the character ideals discredited among the culturally sophisticated through the idealization of an intellectual-aesthetic approach to life *and* by the widespread public acceptance of a variety of habits formerly considered unacceptable among the general populace of the United States and Europe.[42] With respect to the former, Weber's use of the term value (*der Wert*) was not simply inherited from both Nietzsche and the Southwestern School but was itself indicative of the advance of the "intellectualist civilization" which he otherwise diagnosed and opposed. In criticism of this civilization, Weber wrote that "the rejection of responsibility for ethical judgment and the fear of appearing bound by tradition, which come to the fore during intellectualist periods, shift judgments whose intention was originally ethical into an aesthetic key. Typical is the shift from the judgment 'reprehen-

sible' to the judgment 'in poor taste.'"[43] Nonetheless, by employing
the concept of value to describe the various priorities of highly differentiated spheres of life in an increasingly fragmented culture,
Weber helped to ratify the recession of morality as character that
stands at the center of the intellectualization and disenchantment of
the world. That intellectualization has overseen the emotivist reduction of moral judgments to mere personal preferences in the twentieth century and ushered in the therapeutic commandment "Thou shalt
not judge," which has marked the apparent defeat of the most visible
class symbol of traditional moral judgments—the bourgeoisie.

This defeat is not as significant as it appears. As explained earlier,
the bourgeoisie were never the traditionalists they appeared to be,
especially the *haute bourgeoisie* among whom aesthetic concerns
have triumphed in recent years. E. Digby Baltzell's aristocrats within
the old Protestant Establishment, who preceded Brooks's contemporary bourgeois bohemians, were hardly the moral elite Baltzell
imagined them to be.[44] Rather, it has been more a case of intermit-
tent adherence to ideals of self-denial and public service among the
American upper class, with the most public and visible members of
that class (e.g., the Roosevelts, the Kennedys) adhering to criteria
that were far more aesthetic than moral in content.[45] Today, even
that aristocratic aplomb and courage are gone with the rise of an
educated elite that Lasch has characterized as "the cosmopolitanism
of the favored few...uninformed by the practice of citizenship."[46]
That leaves the *petite bourgeoisie*. For Lasch, it is the lower middle
and working classes that have "a more highly developed sense of
limits than their betters."[47] Against the liberal and republican interpretations of American history, Lasch defends "the moral conservatism of the petty bourgeoisie, its egalitarianism, its respect for work-
manship, its understanding of the value of loyalty, and its struggle
against the moral temptation of resentment."[48] Lasch's defense of
petty-bourgeois virtues is itself significant because of his intellectual acceptance of limits, even upon the intellect itself.

Lasch, then, joins MacIntyre, Rieff, and a few other contemporary intellectuals (e.g., Roger Shattuck) who have raised a question
that modern and postmodern intellectuals understandably have found
distasteful—the question of forbidden knowledge. At the heart of
Rieff's work in particular is a profound tension between the intellect
of psychological man, which would remain undeceived and
unreconciled to any limits, and the intellect of the guilty conscience,

rescued from the withering criticisms of Nietzsche and Freud. In the most revealing passage of *The Triumph of the Therapeutic*, Rieff candidly states "I, too, aspire to see clearly, like a rifleman, with one eye shut; I, too, aspire to think without assent. This is the ultimate violence to which the modern intellectual is committed. Since things have become what they are, I, too, share the modern desire not to be deceived."[49] Rieff has rejected the transgressions of the undeceived intellect but only after undergoing his own descents along what he calls the vertical of authority; indeed, his *oeuvre* reads like a series of reaction-formations that map the temptations of the therapeutic. These maps may well serve to cultivate a sense of limits in our own intellects so that we may better chart a theoretical course out of the therapeutic thought-world.

Notes

1. "If the *modern* problem of identity was how to construct an identity and keep it solid and stable, the *postmodern* problem of identity is primarily how to avoid fixation and keep the options open" (Zygmunt Bauman, *Life in Fragments: Essays in Postmodernity* [Cambridge, UK: Blackwell, 1995], p. 81).
2. The definitive work on the American culture war remains James Davison Hunter's *Culture Wars: The Struggle to Define America* (New York: Basic Books, 1991). See Alan Woolfolk, "A House Divided? Diagnosing the American *Kulturkampf*," in *Qualitative Sociology* (Volume 18, Number 4, 1995), pp. 487-493, for a discussion and critique of Hunter's thesis. In *The Death of Character: Moral Education in an Age Without Good or Evil* (New York: Basic Books, 2000), Hunter trumps his own argument concerning the depth of our culture war, tracing out implications implicit in earlier works that suggested the triumph of the therapeutic among cultural conservatives and cultural progressives alike.
3. Lionel Trilling, *Beyond Culture* (New York: Harcourt Brace Jovanovich, 1965), preface, n.p.
4. Philip Rieff, *The Feeling Intellect: Selected Writings of Philip Rieff*, edited by Jonathan B. Imber (Chicago: University of Chicago Press, 1990), p. 283.
5. See Philip Rieff, *The Triumph of the Therapeutic: Uses of Faith after Freud* (Chicago: University of Chicago Press [1966] 1987). Psychological man was first announced in *Freud: The Mind of the Moralist* (Chicago: University of Chicago Press [1959] 1979), pp. 329-357.
6. David Brooks, *Bobos in Paradise: The New Upper Class and How They Got There* (New York: Simon & Schuster, 2000), p. 226.
7. F. Scott Fitzgerald, *The Great Gatsby* (New York: Charles Scribner's Sons, 1925), p. 181.
8. James L. Nolan, Jr., *The Therapeutic State: Justifying Government at Century's End* (New York: New York University Press, 1998). For the author's review, see *Society*, Volume 37, Number 5 (July/August 2000), pp. 79-80.
9. Ibid., p. 3.
10. Ralph H. Turner, "The Real Self: From Institution to Impulse," *American Journal of Sociology* (Volume 81, Number 5, 1976), p. 1009.

11.   John Steadman Rice, *A Disease of One's Own: Psychotherapy, Addiction, and the Emergence of Co-Dependency* (New Brunswick, NJ: Transaction Publishers, 1998), p.29.
12.   See Gertrude Himmelfarb, *One Nation, Two Cultures* (New York: Alfred A. Knopf, 1999). For a critique of Himmelfarb's argument, see Alan Woolfolk, "Two Cultures After All?" (*Society* January/February 2002), Volume 39, Number 2, pp. 83-88.
13.   Joseph Schumpeter, *Capitalism, Socialism, and Democracy* (New York: Harper & Row Publishers, Harper Torchbook, third edition, 1962), p. 144.
14.   Alasdair MacIntyre, *After Virtue: A Study in Moral Theory* (Notre Dame, IN: University of Notre Dame Press, second edition, 1984), pp. 11-12.
15.   Alan Wolfe, *One Nation, After All* (New York: Penguin Books, 1998), pp. 54, 278.
16.   Brooks, *Bobos in Paradise*, p. 247.
17.   Robert Bellah, et. al., *Habits of the Heart: Individualism and Commitment in American Life*, updated edition (Berkeley: University of California Press [1985] 1996), p. 151.
18.   Robert Bellah, "The Idea of Practices in *Habits*," in Charles Reynolds and Ralph Norman, editors, *Community in America* (Berkeley: University of California Press, 1988), p. 271.
19.   Bellah, *Habits of the Heart*, p. 154.
20.   Christopher Lasch, "The Communitarian Critique of Liberalism," in Reynolds and Norman, editors, *Community in America*, p. 179.
21.   Bellah, *Habits of the Heart*, pp. 159, 162.
22.   Charles Taylor, *Sources of the Self: The Making of Modern Identity* (Cambridge, MA: Harvard University Press, 1989), p. 510.
23.   For a discussion and critique of Robert Bellah's work and its relation to the concept of the therapeutic, see Alan Woolfolk, "Readings of Therapeutic Culture: From Philip Rieff to Robert Bellah," in *Community and Political Thought Today*, edited by Peter Augustine Lawler and Dale McConkey (Westport, CT: Praeger, 1998), pp. 109-119.
24.   Robert Wuthnow, *After Heaven: Spirituality in America Since the 1950s* (Berkeley: University of California Press, 1998), pp. 15-16, 11.
25.   Ibid., p. 178.
26.   Ibid., p. 188.
27.   Rieff, *Triumph of the Therapeutic*, p. 13.
28.   Charles Horton Cooley, *Human Nature and the Social Order*, introduction by Philip Rieff (New York: Schocken Books, 1902, 1964), p. 400.
29.   Ibid.
30.   Max Weber, *The Sociology of Religion*, translated by Ephraim Fischoff, introduction by Talcott Parsons (Boston: Beacon Press, 1964), p. 163.
31.   Max Weber, "Religious Rejections of the World and their Directions," *From Max Weber: Essays in Sociology*, translated, edited, and with an introduction by H.H. Gerth and C. Wright Mills (New York: Oxford University Press, 1946), p. 328.
32.   Rieff, *Triumph of the Therapeutic*, pp. 34-35.
33.   Philip Rieff, *Fellow Teachers: Of Culture and Its Second Death* (Chicago: The University of Chicago Press, 1973, 1985), p. 23.
34.   Rieff, *Triumph of the Therapeutic*, p. 15.
35.   Rieff, *Fellow Teachers*, p. 45.
36.   Among the founders of modern sociology, several theorists, in addition to Weber, had intimations of an emergent therapeutic culture in advanced, specialized societies. In the late nineteenth century, for example, Emile Durkheim argued that the common conscience became more general and abstract as the division of labor advanced. There was an "uninterrupted decline of formalism." Tradition became

"more supple," as it transmitted "more and more indeterminate predispositions, general ways of feeling and thinking which can be specialized in a thousand different ways." Common heritage was "no longer, as it was formerly, a set of complete mechanisms exactly set up for special ends, but of very vague tendencies which do not definitely prejudge the future" [Emile Durkheim, *The Division of Labor in Society*, translated by G. Simpson (New York: Free Press, 1964), p. 327]. Durkheim, as suggested above, was overly sanguine about the prospects for highly differentiated societies developing new modes of symbolic control and moral discipline that were less unitary and interdictory. One consequence of the increasing generality and suppleness of cultural forms is that such forms, paradoxically, have taken on pejorative connotations of rigidity and repressiveness even as those forms have grown more remissive and fewer in number.

Georg Simmel, to take another example from the classical sociologists of the early twentieth century, was more perceptive and apprehensive than Durkheim about the ineluctable remissive dynamic of modern culture. In the well known essay "The Conflict in Modern Culture," written during the First World War, Simmel argued that cultural forms *per se* had come under attack more directly and openly than in the past. According to Simmel, all spiritual life had always expressed and realized itself in cultural forms with which life, in turn, inevitably found itself in a "latent opposition." This tension had expressed itself in different spheres, but eventually it resulted in "the old struggle" entering "a new phase," in which life perceived "the form as such" as having been "forced upon it." Thus, Simmel wrote in a passage that evokes the unrestrained vitality that was breaking to the surface of modern consciousness—life "would like to puncture not only this or that form, but form *as such*, and to absorb the form in its immediacy, to let its own power and fullness stream forth just as if it emanated from life's own source, until all cognition, values, and forms are reduced to direct manifestations of life." No longer was it "a struggle of a contemporary form, filled with life, against an old, lifeless one, but a struggle of life against the form *as such*, against the *principle* of form." In erotic life, marriage and prostitution alike appeared as "oppressive forms which thwart immediate and genuine life." In religion, likewise, there was "a tendency for forms of religious *belief* to dissolve into modes of religious *life*, into religiosity as a purely *functional* justification of religion" [Georg Simmel, *The Conflict in Modern Culture and Other Essays*, translated, with an introduction, by K. Peter Etzkorn (New York: Teachers College Press, Columbia University, 1968), pp. 12, 22-23]. In short, Simmel discerned an animus toward forms as one of the distinguishing marks of this new phase of cultural development. But he also perceived that the emergent culture was inclined toward functional views of religion that were in effect anti-credal. Both traits are symptomatic of the anti-interdictory cultural revolution that has defined the twentieth century and undermined the dispositional supports of character.

37. Rieff, *Triumph of the Therapeutic*, p. 74. Thomas Mann once remarked that all of his writing could be understood as an effort to free himself from the middle class [cited by Lionel Trilling, "On the Teaching of Modern Literature," in *Beyond Culture: Essays on Literature and Learning* (New York: Harcourt Brace Jovanovich, A Harvest Book, 1965), p. 26]. Likewise, Flaubert saw hatred of the middle class as "the beginning of all virtue" [quoted in César Graña, *Fact and Symbol* (New York: Oxford University Press, 1971), p. 31].
38. Rieff, *Triumph of the Therapeutic*, p. 51.
39. Rice, *A Disease of One's Own*, p.37.
40. Geertz, *The Interpretation of Cultures* (New York: Basic Books, 1973), p. 45.

41. See Daniel Walker Howe, *Making the American Self: Jonathan Edwards to Abraham Lincoln* (Cambridge, MA: Harvard University Press, 1997).

42. See John Burnham, *Bad Habits* (New York: New York University Press, 1993).

43. Max Weber, *Economy and Society*, Volume 1, ed. G. Roth and C. Wittich (Berkeley: University of California Press, 1978), p. 608.

44. See E. Digby Baltzell, *The Protestant Establishment: Aristocracy and Caste in America* (New York: Vintage Books, 1966).

45. See Nelson Aldrich, *Old Money: The Mythology of America's Upper Class* (New York: Alfred A. Knopf, 1988), especially pp. 70-105.

46. Christopher Lasch, *The Revolt of the Elites and the Betrayal of Democracy* (New York: W.W. Norton & Company, 1995), p. 47.

47. Ibid., p. 27-28.

48. Christopher Lasch, *The True and Only Heaven: Progress and Its Critics* (New York: W.W. Norton, 1991), p. 17.

49. Rieff, *Triumph of the Therapeutic*, p. 13.

Part 2

The Therapeutic March through Institutions

5

Therapeutic Adjudication: The Un-Common Law Judge of America's Drug Court

James L. Nolan, Jr.

> *"One dramatic departure from the traditional model*
> *is the role of the drug court judge. These judges are not*
> *neutral fact finders . . . . This novel judicial role confers great*
> *institutional power . . . . it departs considerably from the*
> *traditional American conception of the judicial role."*
> —*Harvard Law Review (May 1998)*

The first U.S. drug court was started in 1989 in Florida's populous Dade County. Miami is well known as a heavily trafficked drug area. With jails, prisons, and court dockets overcrowded with new and repeat drug offenders, officials became convinced something new had to be tried in criminal justice efforts to handle drug crimes. Under the leadership of Janet Reno, Florida's state attorney at the time, Dade County launched America's first drug court. Judge Stanley Goldstein, a former police officer and prosecutor, would preside over what would become a model for over 1,000 similar drug courts established throughout the United States since.

With the promise that successful completion will result in the dismissal of a charge or the expungement of an arrest, offenders are offered court-monitored therapy as an alternative to the normal adjudication process. Defendants participate in various treatment modalities including acupuncture, individual and group counseling sessions, and Alcoholics Anonymous (AA) and Narcotics Anonymous (NA) twelve-step groups. Offenders also submit to periodic urinalysis testing and regularly (every one to four weeks) report back to the judge, who oversees their overall treatment program. The program is usually expected to last one year, but often lasts much longer. Most drug courts offer defendants, as an incentive for participation, the dismissal of their criminal charge or the expungement of their drug arrest upon successful completion of the program.

For successes in the program—such as graduating to a higher level (courts may have as many as three or four stages of treatment)— judges offer participants praise, applause, and prizes. Among small incentives handed out for good performance are tee shirts, key chains, donuts, pens, mugs, colored star stickers, and candy. Graduation ceremonies are celebrated with cake, speeches, graduation certificates, individual testimonies by graduates, and visits from politicians and other local luminaries. Failure to comply with treatment, on the other hand, can result in the imposition of sanctions. These may come in the form of increased participation in twelve-step groups, community service, one or two days sitting in the jury box during drug court sessions, or short stints (usually several days to two weeks) in the county jail.

Responses to the drug court by the media and across the political spectrum have been largely celebratory. Conservatives support it because of its tough intrusive nature and liberals because of its ostensibly more humane and compassionate approach toward offenders. In many important ways the style and scope of the drug court transcend conventional political categories. Irrespective of the drug court movement's widespread popularity, the change represented in this new judicial model is anything but modest. As Judge Jeff Rosnik of the Miami drug court put it, in drug court, "the players' roles are altered, modified, inextricably changed . . . . Legal justice becomes therapeutic jurisprudence. And crime and punishment becomes holistic justice." Drug court, according to Judge Rosnik represents a fundamental "change in our judicial system. What was so sacrosanct has changed so drastically." As Rosnik's statement makes clear, among the important changes central to the drug court model is a radical transformation of the conventional roles of courtroom actors.

Lawyers, for example, who traditionally relate to one another in an adversarial manner act cooperatively in the drug court, working together to see their clients progress toward recovery. Not only is the relationship between public defender and prosecutor no longer adversarial, but lawyers generally play a less prominent role. In many drug courts lawyers do not even attend the regular drug court sessions; and when they do, it is often difficult to determine just who they are in the courtroom drama. Drug courts also depart from normal criminal courts, in that treatment providers play a more prominent role. Among other duties, counselors administer urinalysis tests, run individual and group therapy sessions, provide acupuncture treatment, and help clients with GED testing and job placement. When defendants regularly return to court (as often as once a week) treatment providers update the judge on the defendant's performance, and provide information on urinalysis test results, attendance records, job status, receptivity to different treatment modalities, and participant attitudes. Inside and outside the courtroom, treatment providers advise the judge on how and when to reward or sanction various participants, advice that is rarely ignored.

Defendants or "clients" as they are referred to in the drug courts, also have a dramatically altered role in this novel judicial setting. Instead of remaining silent while defense attorneys speak on their behalf, drug court clients talk openly with the judge about their drug use and other personal (and sometimes criminal) activities. Indeed, the main action in the drug court drama is between client and judge. At graduation ceremonies clients often give public testimony about their "recovery" to an applauding audience, an audience which includes not only their families and friends, but the judge, attorneys, treatment counselors, and court clerks.

While the roles of all actors in the courtroom drama are altered in drug court, the redefined role of the drug court judge is the most pronounced. Even those with only limited exposure to the United States criminal justice system would find the actions of the drug court judge clearly out of the ordinary. The profundity of the change, however, is even more significant than it at first appears. This chapter focuses on the redefined role of the drug court judge. In highlighting the therapeutically oriented actions, words, and judicial disposition of drug court judges, I will argue that this legal innovation represents an important departure from America's common law tradition, a change that is, as we will see, commensurate with broader changes taking place in the American judiciary.

The Common Law Judge

But first, what is the common law from which the drug court has allegedly disengaged? The common law refers to several different things. For one, it is to be distinguished from the Roman based civil law tradition of continental Europe, what Max Weber described as the prototypical embodiment of formal legal rationalism. The common law, contrastingly, is judge-made or case law, and has its origins in the English system dating back to the medieval period. In the common law tradition judicial decisions are not made through reference to an aggregate and comprehensive legal code—as is the case in the civil law tradition—but to judicial precedent and in accordance with a particular method of decision making. In other words, the common law refers both to an evolving body of law that is developed on a case by case basis, and to the particular process of reasoning that goes into deciding these cases. As Roscoe Pound, then dean of Harvard Law School, put it over half a century ago, the common law is both a "body of authoritative materials" and a "judicial process"—a process which itself is defined by a particular cognitive disposition or "frame of mind." The judicial "frame of mind" endemic to the common law tradition requires a high level of restraint, discipline, craftsmanship, and careful reasoning. It is a legal orientation that has "always," as Pound explains, "imposed upon itself limitations."

Writing in the early 1960s, Karl Llewellyn offered a similar understanding of the common law. For Llewellyn, like Pound, the common law refers to a distinctive "way of thought and work," a particular "manner of doing the job," a kind of "craftsmanship in office." The common law judge, according to Llewellyn, strives toward impartiality, avoids cases in which he may be personally interested, and endeavors to discern the "true essence" of a conflict from "accidents of person, personality, and the like." The impartial, common law judge, moreover, works within a tradition that is deeply connected to the past yet allows for the "ongoing renovation of doctrine." This renovation, however, occurs only gradually. In Llewellyn's words, it does not have the "smell of revolution or...of campaigning reform." Adjudicating within the common law tradition, then, is not for the maverick or the revolutionary. Rather, as classically conceived, the role of the common law judge requires a great deal of restraint.

Mary Ann Glendon characterizes the nature of this restraint as threefold: "structural restraint" or those limits placed on the judge by the other branches of government, by the federalist system, and by the court's place in the hierarchy of the judiciary; "interpretive restraint" or those limits required by judicial deference to Constitutional precepts, statutory law, and legal precedent; and "personal restraint" or the limits the judge places on himself in his efforts to be fair, impartial, objective, and dispassionate. The common law, as such, requires a certain kind of judge, trained in a particular tradition, who operates within the confines of important structurally and personally imposed limitations. It is a passive rather than an active posture which, again, distinguishes it from the civil law tradition.

The common law judge, as Lawrence Friedman explains, "sits on the bench as an august, reverend umpire," whereas the civil law judge is one who will actively "investigate" and "develop evidence" for a particular case. The common law judge literally and figuratively stays behind her bench, while the civil law judge, often behaving more like an American lawyer, does not. According to comparative law scholars these contrasting judicial roles represent a major point of difference between the two legal systems. The more passive role of the common law judge was, in fact, a defining feature of the American judiciary that so impressed Tocqueville in his famous early nineteenth century investigation into American culture and society. American "judicial power is, by its nature," Tocqueville observed, "devoid of action; it must be put in motion in order to produce a result . . . . It does not pursue criminals, hunt out wrongs, or examine evidence of its own accord." To do so would "do violence to the passive nature of his authority." As traditionally understood, then, the common law judge is a judge who operates within a particular system, is committed to carrying on a certain tradition, while employing a unique frame of mind. He or she approaches the adjudicative process with disinterest, impartiality, passivity, and restraint.

Abraham Lincoln once worried that a thirst for distinction might remain a defining feature of American leadership, and that in an established democracy like the United States a passion for distinction would prove "highly dangerous." In its place Lincoln argued for "the sober judgment of Courts," for "unimpassioned reason . . . general intelligence, sound morality, and, in particular, a reverence for the constitution and laws." Could passionate leaders desirous of distinction, Lincoln asked, be content to support and maintain a system handed to them by others? "Think you these places would satisfy an Alexander, a Caesar, or a Napoleon? Never! Towering genius disdains a beaten path." The common law, and the kind of deference to tradition and precedent that defines it, is precisely this, a beaten path, deviations from which are forged only very slowly, cautiously, and with considerable judicial restraint. But are American judges still willing to exercise the restraint necessary to carry on a tradition, a system, a temperament, a manner of reasoning, a form of adjudication, "an edifice," as Lincoln put it, "that has been erected by others?"

Observers of the Supreme Court in the second half of the twentieth century argue that they decidedly are not. Nathan Glazer first observed in 1975 that the American courts have "changed their role in American life." They are "now more powerful than ever before" and "reach into the lives of the people . . . deeper than they ever have in American history." The kind of judicial activism which defined the Warren court between 1954 and 1968 did not retreat with the confirmation of four Nixon appointed justices in the years following. Instead, what Glazer calls the "imperial judiciary" sailed at full tilt through the Burger court years, with justices laying down decisions "even more far-reaching" than in the Warren court years. Glazer predicted then that the assertion of judicial authority realized in the twenty years between 1955 and 1975 was not a passing fad, that it had become the expected posture of the court, transcending the varying philosophical tendencies of the different justices.

Glendon, writing nearly two decades after Glazer, argues that the trend has indeed continued. In fact, Glendon holds that the "'conservative,' 'moderate' justices on today's Supreme Court are often more assertive and arrogant in their exercise of judicial power than the members of the 'liberal,' 'activist' Warren Court." The classical judge characterized by "impartiality, prudence, practical reason, mastery of craft . . . and above all, self restraint" has given way to the romantic judge who is disposed instead to be "bold, creative, compassionate, result-oriented, and liberated from legal technicalities." The romantic judge is less bound by tradition, by precedent, and by a cautious and careful approach to judicial decision making. The traditional ideals of disinterest, humility, and restraint have given way to the new ideals of "judicial boldness, energy, and compassion." Consider one rather telling anecdote. On June 29, 1992, the day of the *Casey* decision, Justice Anthony Kennedy invited a reporter to follow him around for the day. While a crowd gathered outside of the Supreme Court building, in view from Kennedy's office window, he said to the reporter, "Sometimes you don't know if you're Caesar about to cross the Rubicon or Captain Queeg cutting your own tow line."

More significant than Kennedy's unusual invitation of a reporter to shadow him on the day of a widely observed ruling or the disturbing hubris of his self-comparison to Caesar is the degree to which the attitude reflected in this statement characterizes the disposition of the Supreme Court in the last several decades, and the extent to which this new orientation represents a notable departure from the common law tradition. No longer, it seems, is the judiciary primarily a custodial vocation for those willing to quietly carry on and carefully advance an inherited tradition. Rather, in direct contrast to Lincoln's musings, the imperial leanings of a Caesar may well find (or at least seek) satisfaction in the role of a judge.

Glendon and Glazer concentrated their observations on developments at the Supreme Court level. Here I will show that the same type of transformation is mirrored in the judicial activity of the local drug courts. Here too judges are casting off the shackles of common law constraints in their efforts to make a mark, exercise compassion, and bring about real change. Like the romantic Supreme Court judges, the drug court judges have jettisoned traditional adjudicative restraints, finding them "too confining, boring, unrewarding, [and] insufficiently responsive to social problems." Instead, they have championed a reinvention of the adjudicative process, one which allows them to be more proactive, personally interested, and responsive to the needs of the clients who come before them.

Judicial Activism

To begin with, the drug court judge deliberately departs from the kind of passive role Tocqueville saw as a defining quality of the American judiciary. Instead, the drug court judge is, on a number of fronts, an activist judge. The drug court judge is the main actor in the courtroom drama. But the judicial robe of passivity is to be shed off the bench as well. That is, judges actually involve themselves in the lives of clients outside the courtroom. Consider an example from the Boston drug court program. Cathy Delaney, the director of treatment at Boston's drug court, tells the story of Judge Ziemian visiting a client who for months had been unable to secure employment. Judge Ziemian finally "got tough" on this client telling him, "You are going to get a job or you are going to do community service, whichever you want. You can work for free or you can work for money. Take your pick." Brad, after weeks of no success, finally got a job. Judge Ziemian was so pleased with the news that he personally visited Brad at his new place of employment. And according to Cathy Delaney, "Brad has never forgotten it, ever."

In another case a drug court judge's activism led to the establishment of contact with a client's employer. A participant in Judge
McKinney's Syracuse, New York drug court lost his job. McKinney
called the employer and learned that the client was regarded as a
"damn good employee" and that the boss would "hire him back in a
heartbeat" if the judge could guarantee that he was drug free and
that he wouldn't miss any work. So the judge made a deal with the
employer. He said to him: "Okay, I'll make a deal with you, you
take him back and I'll add another weapon to your arsenal. If he
doesn't come to work when he is supposed to, doesn't come to work
on time, if he comes to work under the influence of any kind of
drugs, I'll put him in jail, on your say so."

McKinney filled the client in on the new arrangement, telling him:
"I'll get your job back for you, but you've got to promise you'll be
at work when you are supposed to and not take any drugs. Your
employer is now on the team of people who are reporting to me.
When he calls up and tells me that you are late, or that you're not
there, I'm going to send the cops out to arrest you." The client agreed
to this arrangement which, according to McKinney, "worked for
awhile." McKinney acknowledged that these actions probably violated "the canon of judicial ethics" and that he "would never have
done it before as a judge." He justified the actions, however, on the
grounds that in the drug court such prohibitions have to be "soft-
ened a little bit" because of the "overall purpose and methodology"
of the program.

The drug court judge's involvement in the community, however,
is not just in relating individually to drug court clients or their em-
ployers. The drug court judge also plays a significant leadership
role in bringing the whole program together. As described in a State
Justice Institute (SJI) document on drug courts, "the judiciary as a
whole and the drug court judge in particular must take the lead in
promoting the drug court concept in both the justice system and
larger community; in developing awareness of the goals it seeks to
achieve; and in marshaling the support required to sustain a viable
program that meets community needs."

Judges are aware that this extra-adjudicative activism represents
a departure from traditional understandings of the judge's role. Jeffrey Tauber, for example, acknowledges that "traditionally, judges
have played the passive role of objective, impartial referee, only
reluctantly stepping beyond the boundaries of their own courtroom."

In the drug court, contrastingly, the judge "should be a strong leader with enthusiasm for the court's mission." It's a judicial orientation that "requires a willingness to work outside the confines of the traditional judicial role," which involves, among other things, exerting leadership "in the promotion of coordinated drug control and treatment efforts, both within the criminal justice system and [in] local communities."

Among other tasks, drug court judges often lead efforts in procuring funds from nontraditional sources. Judge Jack Lehman of the Las Vegas drug court, for example, started a 501c3 to support his court. Judge John Schwartz, the first judge of the Rochester, New York drug court, likewise led efforts to round up support for his emerging drug court. Judge Schwartz tells of having been inspired to start a Rochester drug court following a visit to Miami. Though state and local government officials thought his drug court idea a good one, because of budgetary constraints they were not at the time in a position to financially support it. Undeterred, Schwartz turned to "non-traditional sources."

> I went to the local United Way and asked them if they would be the fiduciary for all funds I received for drug courts. They agreed. Therefore all the money I raised from city government, county government, charitable foundations, private foundations, is donated to the United Way Service Corporation and that money is dispensed as our drug court team directs it shall be. Whether you like it or not you as a judge are considered a leader of your drug court team. Your team looks to you for inspiration and guidance. So as the leader of that team you must take a very active part in the raising of funds. For the Rochester drug court, I went out and raised all the money from local foundations.

Other drug courts (approximately one in five), following the example of Judge Schwartz and Judge Lehman, have obtained some form of private funding. The 1997 Justice Department survey of drug courts found that nine drug courts had solicited a total of nearly half a million dollars in support from private foundations. Judge Steven Marcus, of the Los Angeles drug court, worries some about these practices. He thinks drug court judges should "be especially careful about fundraising." "Most judges in most jurisdictions," Marcus notes, "have some strict prohibitions about being directly involved in fundraising. It's an easy ticket to have yourself investigated." To those who may question the ethics of judicial fundraising from non-legislative sources, Judge Schwartz answers that prohibitions against such activities are but a "myth," that "the judicial cannons of ethics do not prevent a judge from raising money." Ethical or not, it is an uncommon practice, and one in which American judges historically have not engaged.

Beyond fundraising, judges also seek the support of other community resources, including groups and agencies that provide health care, education, and job training. Judge Weitzman, for example, sees the judge as uniquely positioned to solicit support from "job training and placement, life skills training, and medical, health services." Syracuse, New York's Judge McKinney tells of how he introduced GED training into his drug court program. He arranged with a particular GED training program to bypass certain eligibility requirements in order to facilitate and expedite the enrollment of drug court clients. Reflecting on this arrangement McKinney noted the novelty of his role outside the courtroom. "This is something as a judge I would never have done before, because . . . my role was just whatever happened right here in the courtroom. If it didn't happen here, it didn't happen at all." With the drug court, such restrictions are less binding.

Whether recruiting external resources, lobbying, campaigning, coordinating, fundraising, or talking to the media, the drug court judge is an activist judge. It is a role that represents a clear and intentional departure from the more passive orientation of the classical judge of the common law tradition. As Judge Tauber explains, "It is a system and it is a philosophy that says it is not enough to be a good referee. It is not enough to be up on the law and to know the law." Rather, the drug court judge exercises active "leadership . . . outside of the courtroom." There is nothing to be ashamed of, drug court judges argue, regarding this new role. As Judge Schwartz asserts, "I think the judiciary is an independent branch of the government. We should be leaders. And we shouldn't be afraid to speak up as leaders." That this is a significant departure from previous practices is made clear by Judge Peggy Hora of Hayward, California. "The drug court judge is no longer either the neutral umpire calling the balls and strikes, or the case manager. Instead the drug court judge has taken on a totally different role; a role that judges have never had before in the world, in the history of jurisprudence."

Judicial Compassion

If the classical trait of judicial passivity is absent in the drug court, even less evident are the common law notions of disinterest and impartiality. Drug court judges are actually instructed to be interested and invested in the clients who come before them. As Judge Tauber instructs: "Be less the dignified, detached judicial officer. Show your concern, as well as your toughness. Treat the offender as a person and an individual . . . . Don't lecture the offender, but engage him or her in conversation . . . . Make a connection." In the drug court, then, the "assertive and compassionate" judge is preferred over the "restrained and impartial." As previously noted this empathetic connection between the judge and the client is a central focus of the courtroom drama. As opposed to disinterest, the judge is actually encouraged to cultivate interest in and concern for the defendant. When a dozen drug court judges were asked to list the "six most important characteristics of an effective drug court judge," the most often reported response was "the ability to be empathetic or to show genuine concern." Other responses included "acceptance of an unconventional role," having a "sense of humor," and "having experienced personal crises."

According to Judge Jamey Weitzman of the Baltimore drug court, making this kind of personal connection is crucial for motivating clients. In the context of drug court, says Weitzman, an "incredible relationship" develops between judge and client.

> During periodic progress conferences, as the judge comes to know better the defendants' background, problems, what makes them tick, an incredible rapport develops almost spontaneously between the judge and the defendant. They start doing things because of you. I remember one defendant who said, "Judge, I'm now doing well because I know you were so disappointed in me."

Weitzman does many creative things to encourage her defendants. "We smile and laugh at them. We have them turn around in the courtroom and give speeches. I read the poems they write for me. I play the songs that they record for me. I show pictures." Weitzman may well be understating things when she concludes that this kind of courtroom activity gives "a whole new meaning to the term, 'judicial action.'"

Judge Weber of the Louisville, Kentucky drug court demonstrates his compassion and understanding during drug court sessions by literally shedding his judicial robe and the traditional notions of authority that it symbolizes. He intentionally does not wear the judge's customary black robe in order to communicate a message to his clients. "It's a conscious statement that I'm not the regular kind of judge that you would expect in a criminal court," Weber explains, "This is different. My being there without a robe makes it different."

The precise message that he wants to get across through this difference: "I'm a real person. I listen to them. I care about them."

Judge Fogan of the Fort Lauderdale, Florida drug court, while he
still wears the traditional judicial robe, wants the same message of
friendliness to be conveyed to defendants. For example, he regularly asks clients if he can call them by their first name, "as a sign of
friendship." He also on occasion hugs clients during graduation ceremonies. As demonstrated in a promotional video of the Fort Lauderdale drug court: "At graduation participants receive a certificate
of achievement, a t-shirt, and a hug from the judge." In her study of
fifteen drug courts, Sally Satel likewise found that "judges sometimes hug participants after graduation," and that in the vast majority of the courts (fourteen of fifteen) there was some form of physical contact between judge and client. Some judges, though certainly
not all, forcefully defend this practice. When Judge Ellen DeShazer
of the Compton, California drug court, for example, was asked by
another judge whether judges should hug clients, she replied with an
unequivocal, "Absolutely." She then told the story of one drug court
client who "just wanted a hug," and had come to her judicial cham-
bers (a practice she permits of her drug court clients) to receive one.

> I let them come into my chambers. When they say, 'can I speak to the judge?' I never
> say, 'no, you cannot.' All she wanted was a hug. And I had to set aside the criminal
> history information that I had on this person, and say, 'this young lady just wants me to
> give her a hug. And can I do that?' I mean, you are thinking just instantly. You don't
> have time to think about it later on. So, I just gave her a hug. I mean, what would you do
> if your child came up to you, and said, 'may I have a hug?' You wouldn't say, 'well let
> me think about this now. You have been bad fifteen times.' You would just do it. So, that
> is what I did. And yes you should [give hugs]. You get a whole lot back. You really do.

One wonders, given this more intimate relationship between the
judge and defendant, whether a level of judicial impartiality can be
sustained, or even if impartiality and consistency in sentencing are
still valued judicial standards. An interesting interchange between a
group of judges at a Washington, D.C. drug court conference would
suggest that, at the very least, this is no longer a value that can be
taken for granted. At this particular session, a discussion ensued about
the different ways judges impose sanctions on drug court clients
who have somehow not complied with the treatment program. The
drug court judges who were present offered various strategies.
Emerging out of the discussion was the common theme that sanctions should vary according to the individual and according to the

particularities of the case. As one drug court judge put it, "justice" in the drug court "is taking an individual, it is looking at that individual case, and it is fashioning a disposition in that particular case that is going to benefit not only society, but that particular individual." Such flexibility is important because as Los Angeles drug court judge, Steven Marcus opined, "so many people in front of you have individual situations." Subsequently, though the Los Angeles drug court "started out with set [sanction] goals, it has become more individualized as we have gone along."

Following this interchange, Judge Patrick Michot from Lafayette, Louisiana hesitantly took the floor. He was at the time in the very early stages of starting a drug court in his jurisdiction and was visibly perplexed by what he was hearing. "I'd like to ask a question" he posed, "is it okay then to be inconsistent in your sentencing? Is that basically okay?" Almost before he could finish his question several more seasoned drug court judges sought to enlighten him. The first was Judge Weber from the Louisville, Kentucky drug court, who was also moderating the discussion. "Can I ask you a question right back? In your regular court setting are you always consistent?" Somewhat taken aback Michot responded, "I try to be consistent. What I am hearing here, though, suggests that maybe I ought to rethink that."

Another judge rose to try to bring clarity to the situation. He explained that because the drug court employs a "reinforcement model" the relationship between judge and client is more like "parenting." Therefore, like a parent "you just cannot have absolute rules." Instead "you have got to be responding." This judge, in fact, based upon input from a therapist, preferred the use of the word "response" over "sanction." Next, Judge Stanley Goldstein, the country's first drug court judge, stood up to offer his input on the issue.

> I just want to make one comment. Just don't lose sight of what you are doing. We are there to get these people off of drugs, to retrain them, rehabilitate them, put them back on the street, let them become tax paying citizens. We are not there to fast track them into jail. We are not there to trick them. We are not there to play any games. We are there for specific purposes. As long as whatever you do is designed to get them off drugs and put them back out on the street in a position where they can fight using drugs, whatever you do to accomplish that is fine.

A little later Judge Roosevelt Robinson, Portland Oregon's drug court judge, with a tone of indignation, argued strongly against the notion of uniformed sentencing. "If you want machines that can

determine" a sentence then "you can put a computer up there . . . .
The drug court program is a situation where we get an opportunity
to deal with human beings, with human problems . . . . and when we
are through with them, they are better persons, and we have a better
society. I would rather be a jurist doing that, than a computer just
giving people time."

With his original question apparently answered, Judge Michot
never spoke again. Flexibility and individually tailored sanctions,
indeed, "whatever" you need to do to accomplish the goals of the
drug court are fair game. Recall that each of these judges once vowed
that they would "administer justice without respect to persons," that
they would "do equal right to the poor and to the rich" and would
"impartially discharge and perform" their duties in accordance with
the "Constitution and the laws of this country." Even in the "grand-
est common law" tradition, no one expected or asked more of a
judge than that he or she aspire with Judge Michot to "try to be
consistent" realizing that the human factor will never make the dis-
pensing of justice as consistent as a "computer." A wholesale disregard for this standard, however, is a new notion altogether. Classical
judges, as Glendon observes, realized the elusiveness of "total objectivity." Yet, borrowing Clifford Geertz's imagery, "they also knew
that a doctor who cannot have a completely sterile operating field
does not need to perform surgery in a sewer."

The higher goal of getting the drug court client well, however,
now supersedes in importance the goal of consistency and impartiality. A common frustration expressed by drug court judges is the
unwelcome constraints they experience from legislatively imposed
mandatory minimum sentences. Drug courts are liberating in that
they allow more flexibility in the way a judge can respond to a client. Drug court judges have a myriad of sanctions available to them.
They can put clients in jail for two weeks, mandate increased attendance of AA and NA meetings, require community service, and so
on. These sanctions are typically imposed individually and creatively.
Often there are no hard and fast rules.

The enhanced discretion that the drug court allows is one of the
attractive features of the program to Judge Barbara Beck from Santa
Barbara, California's drug court.

> You know, the legislature in the state of California has just about taken away all the
> discretion we have as judges. They now tell us exactly what sentence to impose, and

how to do it, and when to do it, and where to do it. This is one of the few areas that we have where we still have some discretion. And that is really what I became a judge for. I wanted to help people. I wanted to make a difference in people's lives. And the drug court is one of the areas that we are still allowed to do that.

In other words, it is the court's adoption of the treatment perspective that makes the expansion of judicial authority possible. As Judge Swett of Charlottesville's emerging drug court sees it, "under the traditional courts there are very few effective options available to a judge." With the drug court, however, "because of the emphasis on treatment, it enlarges the number of options that a judge has available." One of the main reasons judges appreciate the drug court and the kind of judicial discretion it allows is the belief that this new form of adjudication actually works, that is, that the drug court is effective. It has a utilitarian value.

Judicial Expediency

A utilitarian orientation has been an important justificatory principle legitimating the expansion of the drug court movement. In as much as this "frame of mind" is employed by judges and directs their adjudicative practices, it ultimately represents another way in which the drug court departs from the common law tradition. Glendon identifies expedience as one of the defining features of the late twentieth century Supreme Court. In keeping with the same romantic disposition, the drug court also aims at "problem resolution." As Judge Weber puts it, the drug court "actually let's us go to the heart of the matter and solve the problem." The classical arrangement did not. As a result, drug offenders were repeatedly recycled through the criminal justice system, a system, as the judges see it, which did nothing to rehabilitate offenders from their root problem, i.e., drug addiction. Therefore, something new had to be tried. "What we did before simply was not working," is the common refrain.

Thus, judges justify a departure from the common law tradition on the grounds that previous methods were ineffective. These methods failed to rehabilitate offenders. Because of this, many judges have no scruples about trying something new even if it fundamentally departs from an age-old system. This is clearly the case with Judge Schwartz of Rochester, New York. He acknowledged that departing from the common law may be hard for some judges. But, as he puts it, "It was never a concern of mine. As a common law judge presiding over trials, I knew we weren't making an inch of headway in the drug problem." Schwartz is, in fact, very proud of the innovative effort represented in the un-common law format of the drug court. "Oh it's much different. I'm proud that it is different. It means that we're willing to advance with the times. I truly believe in separation of powers and the independence of the judiciary, but that doesn't mean that the judiciary has to do the same thing for over 300 years." Again, the willingness to be different is justified on the grounds of efficacy. Consider Schwartz's further explanation.

> We weren't making any headway and we are not stupid. So why don't we try different approaches. Our job is to make sure justice is done. Our job is also to punish, but what's the point of punishing if it doesn't work. I mean, 70% of our clientele in the criminal justice system had drug problems. It's about time we learned how to deal with them. When they developed the common law, they didn't have the problem. They didn't have this problem 20 years ago when I started, 25 years ago, 30 years ago, actually, when I started practicing law. But we do now, so let's deal with it. Take the business world, they come along with new ideas all the time. Government unfortunately doesn't, and the court system is even slower than government. We have to deal with the problem. It is our problem.

Explanations such as these are repeatedly offered by judges. The utilitarian argument is presented with the perception (an apparently justifiable one) that it has an ultimate trump value. If it works, then how could anyone conceivably question it? As Judge Stanley Goldstein argues, "You see the thing here that is different than anything else that has ever been done before is that it works. It really works! People come in who are hooked on drugs, look so bad that they can't stay off it for ten minutes. And a year later they are out working. What the hell is wrong with that?"

So concerned are judges with the inefficiency of traditional methods that without some radical changes, it is feared the judiciary will become irrelevant. "If you don't make some changes" Judge Hodos argues, "you're going to become irrelevant. I think we really need to change the way we are doing things. We need to listen to the community because they are losing faith in what is happening in the justice system." Judge Weber agrees. As he puts it, "the system has to change." Why? Because "anybody who works in the criminal justice system realizes how little effect we're having on things . . . . There is a recognition that the traditional way of doing things may not be the best." Like Schwartz, Weber is glad that through developments like the drug court movement, "the legal system is slowly evolving into something else." The only thing slowing it down are "those folks that have an investment in the status quo . . . who don't want to change." A break with the common law tradition, then, is only seen as something that the change-resistant need to get over. Any misgivings about such a break with the past are overshadowed by greater concerns with establishing a system that effectively deals with the enormous problem of drug dependency and associated criminal activity.

With the expansion of judicial authority and the perceived efficacy of the drug court program judges are more excited than ever about their new judicial role. They have finally been given the tools and the philosophy that allows them to help clients in ways they were previously unable. Like activist Supreme Court justices, the drug court judges have "decided that the other two branches won't act." Therefore they have determined "to act on their own, and increasingly are intrigued by the opportunity to go to the root of the problem." For the drug court judge, going to the root of the problem is a more gratifying model of adjudication.

Judicial Enthusiasm

That the drug court is a more satisfying role is repeated over and over by drug court judges. Judge Tauber sums it up best. "Drug Court represents one of the most challenging and exciting innovations in the Criminal Justice System in a long time." Moreover, he asserts, "I have never talked to anyone who has done drug court for any length of time who hasn't said that this is the most satisfying thing they have done in their career." Almost without exception this is the sentiment expressed by drug court judges.

With the zeal of a missionary Louisville's Judge Weber, for example, says, "Drug court is something I want to do and it's something that I strongly believe in. When I'm in my regular court it's more like work. It's my assignment. Drug court, I don't have to do it. I'm there because I want to do it." Weber reports that people who have observed him in both situations say "I look like a different person when I'm doing drug court." Like Judge Weber, Judge Diane Strickland, of the nascent Roanoke, Virginia drug court works both in drug court and with a regular court docket. The contrast for her is striking. "I get more personal satisfaction out of what I'm doing with the drug court population than with anything I do for the remainder of the week, because I do feel that there is a contact with the offenders that allows me to get at a more personal level and to see true success stories."

Rochester's Judge Schwartz is equally gratified by the drug court experience. "In the other role all we saw was failure," Schwartz explained. In drug court "we see success and it's very heart warming," it's "my most rewarding judicial experience." Judge Carl Goldstein of Wilmington, Delaware likewise finds the drug court experience an emotionally satisfying one. "There are very few emotional rewards in this job. They come along occasionally but very seldom and I think in this case I think that's what you're dealing with. You're dealing with being able to see in a very direct way, at a very personal level, people benefiting from what you have provided them." In the same way, Judge Schma finds the experience "very rewarding, very satisfying, terribly commonsensical and useful." Judges even go so far as to argue that the drug court has positive therapeutic outcomes for the judge. As two judges write, "judging in this non-traditional form becomes an invigorating, self-actualizing and rewarding exercise."

Following a meeting with a group of judges, I was joined at lunch by a British criminologist who had been sent by his government to study and report back on the American drug court movement. One thing this British academic could not understand was why judges would choose to participate in a program like the drug court. I related my discovery that the judges almost uniformly report their involvement in the drug court to be a very exciting personal/vocational endeavor, indeed the highlight of their careers. He noted that he too had picked up on this sentiment. After a pause he then stated, "I find the notion that judges need excitement to be a very frightening one." After a moment of further silence, he then added, "If the need for excitement is what drives changes such as these, what will they do next?"

Conclusion

In sum, then, drug court judges find this therapeutic form of adjudication personally fulfilling, liberating in comparison to their traditional role, and invigorating in its allowance of extra-adjudicative activism. To top it off, they believe the drug court works and that they are making a difference in the lives of individual clients. These perceived positive outcomes overshadow any concerns about departing from the common law tradition. Commensurate with developments in other arenas of the American judiciary, drug court judges assume an activist, "problem solving" orientation. In their efforts to help clients overcome drug addiction, they engage in unconventional judicial activities and even acknowledge compromising standards of judicial ethics. Any scruples with these means, however, are justified by the more important end of helping the clients on their road to recovery. In short, as Judge Peggy Hora puts it, "It works. It makes sense. It's cost effective. And it makes you feel good."

Bibliography

"Alternatives to Incarceration for Drug-Abusing Offenders." Developments in the Law. *Harvard Law Review* 111 (May 1998): 1898-1921.

Glazer, Nathan. "Towards and Imperial Judiciary?" 41 *Public Interest*, 1975, pp. 104-123.

Glendon, Mary Ann. 1994. *A Nation Under Lawyers: How the Crisis in the Legal Profession is Transforming American Society.* New York: Farrar, Straus and Giroux.

Hora, Peggy Fulton, William G. Schma, and John T.A. Rosenthal. "Therapeutic Jurisprudence and the Drug Treatemnet Court Movement: Revolutionizing the Criminal Justice System's Response to Drug Abuse and Crime in America." *Notre Dame Law Review* 74, 2 (January 1999): 439-538.

Nolan, James L., Jr. 2001. *Reinventing Justice: The American Drug Court Movement.* Princeton, NJ: Princeton University Press.

Satel, Sally. "Observational Study of Courtroom Dynamics in Selected Drug Courts." *National Drug Court Institute Review* 1,1 (Summer 1998): 43-72.

6

The Therapeutic School: Its Origins, Nature, and Consequences

John Steadman Rice

In 1983, the federal government released a report on the status of education in the United States; somewhat ominously entitled *A Nation at Risk*, the report spoke in terms of "a rising tide of mediocrity" (National Commission on Excellence in Education, 1983, p. 16), marked by precipitous declines in academic standards and embodied in what the report's authors saw as the poor quality of teacher preparation and, by extension, the progressively worsening performance of American school children on both national and international tests. These disturbing indicators, moreover, came about in conjunction with continually increasing per-student expenditures. This combination of escalating costs and flagging performance initiated what has now been nearly two decades of educational reform, as most recently manifested in the "No Child Left Behind" legislation sponsored by the Bush administration.

This chapter shows that both this "crisis in education" and the education establishment's responses to ensuing reform efforts should be understood in relation to fundamental cultural changes that have transpired in the last thirty years in the United States and other Western, industrial societies. I will argue that the rise of what I call the therapeutic school (about which, more follows) has played a significant role in the perceived crisis in contemporary education. In addition, therapeutic ideology, by dint of its circular logic, has precluded the possibility of substantive reform, a point I will substantiate by briefly examining the emergence of so-called "whole language" as one of the mainstream educational establishment's responses to the growing demand for reform in the methods of teaching reading. In what follows, then, I will discuss the rise of the therapeutic culture, the subsequent construction of the therapeutic school, and, finally, will examine whole language's emergence in response to mounting public criticism of education.

Therapeutic Discourse and the Therapeutic Culture

It is all but axiomatic, now, to state that, over the course of the past generation, American culture has undergone profound trans-formations. For some, these changes comprise a bona fide revolu-tion (Rieff [1966] 1987), albeit perhaps more "expressive" (Martin 1981) than instrumental, more "silent" (Inglehart 1977) than deaf-ening. For others, the changes are somewhat less epochal, but none-theless of great significance, representing a "master trend" (Russell 1992), or a "culture shift" (Inglehart 1991). As many observers have noted, one thread that runs brightly throughout the overall tapestry of cultural change is the growing and powerful impact of psycho-logical thought upon how we Americans think about ourselves and our social world. This impact is reflected in studies documenting the rise of "psychological man" [sic] (Boyers 1975), the "triumph of the therapeutic" (Rieff [1966] 1987), and the birth of the "psychologi-cal society" (Gross 1976). Over the course of the past generation, researchers repeatedly documented and discussed the rise of a "thera-peutic attitude" (Bellah et al., 1985) marked by an excessively so-lipsistic world view, and the creation of an intrinsically "subjective self" (Gehlen 1980) given to retreat from and indifference toward public life (Sennett 1976); a generation of "free agents" (Russell 1992) holding no loyalties beyond the self.

This chapter aims to contribute to the recent research that has focused on the pivotal issue of institutionalization, examining spe-cific institutional carriers of the therapeutic culture, such as the state (Nolan 1999), the corporation (Tucker 2000), and the self-help move-ment (Rice 1996). As Max Weber (1958, 1968) has demonstrated, culture is the source of specific "action orientations" of which orga-nizations and institutions are the "carriers." (See also, Geertz 1973; Douglas 1966, 1970.) To speak meaningfully of cultural change, then, requires careful attention to the systematic embodiment of given beliefs, attitudes, values, and the like, in organizational and institu-tional form.

To fully appreciate the nature of cultural change in the United States requires a consideration of the claims put forth in psychotherapeutic discourse. Not only is this discourse the principal source of the changes; it is also clear that not *all* therapeutic ideas and ideals have been involved. Rather, the cultural changes to which a wide variety of research has pointed issue from and are grounded in a set of ideas and ideals associated with what has been called "human potential psychotherapy"—what I have elsewhere called "liberation psychotherapy" (Rice 1996)—as embodied especially in the thought of such writers as Abraham Maslow and Carl Rogers.[1]

Liberation psychotherapy refers to any and all therapeutic styles and modalities—gestalt, transactional analysis, reality therapy, client-centered therapy—which, despite superficial differences, nonetheless share a core set of assumptions about the self and the social world. The next section of this chapter discusses those assumptions in some detail. However, it should be emphasized, here, that what is at issue in the prominent cultural role of therapeutic discourse is not simply an increase in the public's consumption of clinical therapy. Although that consumption has increased, what is of far greater importance is the widespread dissemination of liberation psychotherapy and its acceptance by a large portion of the general public. For millions of Americans, the therapeutic worldview has become an *ethic* (Weber 1958; 1968), a set of interconnected tenets that provide guidelines for moral conduct. These guidelines define organizational and institutional purpose and structure people's behavior—both as individuals and in the aggregate—into distinctive patterns. It is crucial, then, to understand the nature and core premises of the therapeutic ethic.

The Therapeutic Ethic Articulated

Before turning to therapeutic discourse in education, per se, it is important to briefly examine liberation therapy's four core assumptions, as they are articulated in its advocates' discourse. The first core assumption of liberation psychotherapy is an adamant rejection of the premise that humans are by nature self-seeking, aggressive, and potentially destructive creatures; instead the therapeutic ethic is structured around the conviction that *human nature is intrinsically benevolent, positive, and constructive*. This assumption is a recurrent theme in the discourse. Thus, Carl Rogers observes that, "I have little sympathy with the rather prevalent concept that man is basically irrational, and that his impulses, if not controlled, will lead to destruction of others and self." Indeed, contrary to this view of human nature, Rogers asserts that "the basic nature of the human being, when functioning freely, is constructive and trustworthy" (1961, p. 194). Echoing precisely the same themes, Abraham Maslow maintains that

> [t]hroughout history, human nature has been sold short primarily because of the lack of knowledge of the higher possibilities of man, of how far he can develop when permitted to . . . . [M]y studies of 'self-actualizing people,' i.e., fully evolved and developed people, make it clear that human beings at their best are far more admirable (godlike, heroic, great, divine, awe-inspiring, lovable, etc.) than ever before conceived, in their *own* proper nature. (1964, p. 37; original emphasis)

Assumptions about human nature serve as the foundation from which derives all of the other presuppositions in any social theory. Of particular importance, here, is how conceptions of human nature shape conceptions of the relationship between the self and the social world.[2] Consistent with psychoanalytic theory, liberation therapy's second core assumption is that *cultural and societal repression of the self is the cause of virtually all forms of psychological sickness.* However, unlike psychoanalytic theory, liberation therapy—because of its core assumption about the essential goodness of human nature—does not see such repression as an inescapable by-product of or the foundation for the existence of civilized society. Indeed, for the liberation psychotherapist, such repression is doubly tragic, insofar as it not only distorts the self, but that it does so unnecessarily.

These premises also define and suffuse the entirety of the liberation therapy corpus, reflected, for example, in Rogers's position that societal repression creates what he calls the "defensively-organized personality"—his term for psychological maladjustment. Given the presumptively benevolent nature of our species, Rogers asks that we consider the development of a sort of "everyman" figure. If left to his own innate devices and propensities,

> We do not need to ask who will socialize [this everyman], for one of his own deepest needs is for affiliation and communication with others. As he becomes more fully himself, he will become more realistically socialized. We need not ask who will control his aggressive impulses; for as he becomes more open to all of his impulses, his need to be liked by others and his tendency to give affection will be as strong as his impulses to strike out or to seize for himself . . . . His total behavior . . . will be . . . behavior which is appropriate. (1961, p. 194)

Because of the assumption of innate human benevolence, adherents of liberation psychotherapy contend that cultural control of the self is unnecessary. Indeed, as Rogers puts it, the "real person"—

"discover[s] to an ever-increasing degree that if they are open to their experience, doing what 'feels right' proves to be a competent and trustworthy guide to behavior" (1961, p. 189).

These first two core assumptions of liberation therapy—human nature's benevolence and cultural distortion of our true nature—suffuse the entirety of Abraham Maslow's corpus, as well. For example, Maslow asserts that by nature, and *under good conditions*, people will make good choices. By "'good conditions,'" moreover, he means situations in which

> There is no external constraint to choose one action or thing rather than another. The organism has not already had a choice build [sic] in from past habituation, familiarization, negative or positive conditionings or reinforcements, or extrinsic and (biologically) arbitrary cultural evaluations . . . . In other words, 'good conditions' means mostly (entirely?) [sic] good conditions permitting truly free choice by the organism. This means that good conditions *permit the intrinsic, instinctoid nature of the organism to show itself by its preferences. It* tells us what it prefers, and we now assume these preferences to express its needs, i.e., all that which is necessary for the organism to be itself, and to prevent it from becoming less than itself. . . . [T]his free-choice 'wisdom' is easily destroyed in the human being by previous habituation, cultural conditioning, neurosis, physical illnesses, etc. etc. (1964, pp. 101-102; [emphasis supplied])

Maslow's reference to the "instinctoid nature of the organism" obliquely highlights the centrality of the assumption of innate human benevolence to the entire liberation psychotherapy enterprise. The term "instinctoid" is Maslow's neologism, intended to connote the premise that humans are instinctively endowed with morality: we are, again, born moral. This assumption, in turn, explains why Maslow speaks, in the same passage, of "cultural evaluations" of conduct as "(biologically) arbitrary": *because* we are by nature moral creatures—i.e., biologically "hard-wired," as it were, to *be* moral—cultural attempts to impose moral strictures on the self are "arbitrary."

The third core assumption of liberation psychotherapy holds that *the psychological sickness born of repressions is, in the aggregate, the cause of a wide variety of public problems.* This, of course, is the standard psychologistic conceit that the entity we call society is really no more than the sum total of individual action and interaction—a collection of individuals whose ties to one another begin and end with the enlightened pursuit of self-interest. Hence, social problems are merely a collection of individual problems—drug and alcohol abuse, teen pregnancy, crime and delinquency, poor school performance, and so forth, are thereby all understood as deriving from the shared root of repression.

In Maslow's work, this assumption is expressed in terms of the "total collapse of all values outside the individual" (1968, p. 155)—a collapse that is understood as a predictable product of the attempt to impose collective standards upon the self, rather than allowing the natural fruition of each individual's innate benevolence. Thus thwarted, individuals become psychologically unwell and, again, in the aggregate, society itself is also sick. In the wake of this collapse of values, Maslow avers, we find ourselves in a position in which

> We can no longer rely on tradition, on consensus, on cultural habit, on unanimity of belief to give us our values. These agreed-upon traditions are all gone. Of course, we never *should* have rested on tradition—as its failures must have proven to everyone by now—it never was a firm foundation. It was destroyed too easily by truth [and] by honesty . . . ." (1964, p. 9; original emphasis)

For his part, Rogers also concludes that psychological sickness is a widespread phenomenon: "In our daily lives," he maintains,

> there are a thousand and one reasons for not letting ourselves experience our attitudes fully, reasons from our past and from the present, reasons that reside within the social situation. It seems too dangerous, too potentially damaging, to experience them freely and fully. (1961, p. 111)

For Rogers, "the real self is something which is comfortably discovered in one's experiences, not something imposed upon it" (1961, p. 114). Again, given the universality of the socialization process, and the nature *of* that process—which is ineluctably a matter of the imposing of collective meanings and morality upon the self—there can be little doubt but that psychological sickness is rampant.

Given the combination of these first three assumptions, it is inevitable that devotees of this set of therapeutic ideas should arrive at the concluding assumption *that people must be set free from cultural and societal repression*—hence, the appellation, *liberation* psychotherapy. The reasoning, here, is that by negating the repressive, standardizing demands imposed upon them by conventional culture and society, individuals can gradually cultivate innate potentials heretofore lost in the process of socialization. Moreover, these innate capacities are understood as the elements comprising a *true self*, that person we were meant to be but that the socialization process has prevented us from becoming. The presumption is that to the extent that a sufficiently large number of people are thus emancipated from the externally imposed demands of conventional society and culture, both those individuals, and, by extension, society itself, will be "cured."

As the next section demonstrates, the four core assumptions of the therapeutic ethic have been wholeheartedly embraced and adopted by educationists. Over the past thirty-plus years, advocates of liberation psychotherapy have been constructing and maintaining the therapeutic school.

Constructing the Therapeutic School

The generalized cultural impact of liberation psychotherapy began in the 1960's. Its influence on people's conceptions of organizational and institutional performance, and the schools in particular, has played itself out since that time. The means of transmission of the therapeutic ethic into education was educational discourse regarding the purposes of public education, particularly as that discourse informs the professional socialization of new teachers.

Given the assumptions of the therapeutic ethic, as adumbrated above, for schools to be the carriers of that ethic requires, first of all, a redefinition of education, teaching, and the teacher's role. Since the devotees of liberation therapy see the imposition of external standards upon the individual as repressive, and the cause of psychological sickness, education must be understood as a means to ensuring each student's positive self-image. Teachers and schools, then, must adapt themselves to, and accommodate, the students' individual needs, tapping into and helping them to cultivate their own natural interests and abilities. The infusion of the therapeutic ethic in education also requires that teachers not be authority figures. They should not impart a body of facts, information, and skills against which students' performance is to be rated. To the degree that they are required, by law or administrative policy, to cover certain substantive areas corresponding to specific grade and age levels, they must relax the standards students are expected to meet, to minimize the possibility of low ratings and/or negative evaluations which might have a deleterious effect on students' self-images.

The work of adapting schools to the requirements of the therapeutic ethic can be traced in any number of educational treatises published in the last three to four decades. Consider, for example, the premises articulated in an edited volume, on the purposes of schooling, published in 1977 by the Association for Supervision and Curriculum Development (which is an influential voice in American education). The general theme throughout this volume is the value of so-called "Affective Education"—a theme that owes its provenance to the core principles of the therapeutic ethic.

In keeping with the notion that the school should adapt to each individual's unique personal interests and abilities, one contributor maintains that the education process has much to learn from how children play naturally: "the child at play is a constant reminder that, no matter how convincing the argument might appear for the moment, an interpretation of education in manufacturing terms misses something of import, something of human significance. A child is not raw material to be treated in the school factory to meet someone else's specifications" (Yamamoto 1977, p. 27).

Invoking the same premises, the co-authors of another piece in the volume point out that "this [therapeutic] view of humankind requires the educative process to free people to be themselves. It values autonomy and independence as well as concern for others and interdependence. It decries stereotypes which societies can press upon their people, and the imposition of constraints and conventions through roles which can retard the individual's growth." (Hedges and Martinello 1977, p. 231) Rather than "the imposition of constraints and conventions," these authors

> believe that for maximum learning and for maximum richness of living, each person must be valued for himself with his uniqueness recognized and not only respected, but revered: *I am a self and you are a self and I don't want to be made to feel guilty if I am not like you nor should you be made to feel guilty if you are unlike me.* (Hedges and Martinello 1977, p. 241; original emphasis)

Consistent with the therapeutic ethic, the premise informing these observations is that the schools' practices thwart uniqueness by holding all students to a standardized set of expectations. Because not all students can meet these expectations, it is likely that some students' self-images will take a beating. A better approach, they contend, would involve increasing the odds for success: "[A]ll learners search eagerly for evidence of their self-worth. Schools, as presently designed, deny evidence of adequacy to many through denying opportunities for successful learning experiences" (Hedges and Martinello 1977, p. 244).

Although they do not specifically refer to the works of Rogers or Maslow, the ideas each of these authors espouse plainly reveal those influences, calling for the organization of school activities that will accord with the core therapeutic premises. These influences are *explicitly* acknowledged in another contribution to the volume. Outlining the "psychological foundations of humanistic and affective education," Patterson explains that

> [T]he goals which those interested in humanistic education are proposing for the schools . . . are aspects of what [Carl] Rogers calls the fully functioning person, a person who is open to and aware of his feelings, who is able to relate to others, and who is developing and utilizing his potentials. Other terms referring to the same concept are self-realization, self-enhancement, and self-actualization. The last, *self-actualization, is becoming generally accepted . . . [a]s the primary goal of humanistic education.* (Patterson 1977, p. 164; emphasis supplied)

As the highlighted passage in the foregoing quote reveals, the construction of the therapeutic school requires a fundamental transformation in how one understands the purposes of education. Again, "the primary goal of humanistic education . . . [is] self-actualization." Moreover, it is not only the school that should embody, carry, and pass on the therapeutic ethic. Indeed, for Patterson, "The production of self-actualizing persons is—or should be—the goal of all our social institutions: the family, the church, the economic system, and the social and political systems" (1977, p. 165).

Certainly, Patterson concedes, schools must still engage in conventional conceptions of education—after all, "The self-actualizing person must be able to read and write, and must be well informed if he is to utilize his potentials"—but, he avers, it is important to recognize that "cognitive development is only one aspect of the total development of the individual." (1977, p. 165) The problem with traditional education, Patterson contends, is that there is an "overemphasis upon techniques and structured, teacher-controlled procedures, complete with predetermined specific objectives" (1977, p. 171). This emphasis, and the practices it begets, does not facilitate learning. Indeed, "The school environment, rather than facilitating learning, often retards or destroys it . . . . Education must become involved in the child's personal development—his [sic] feelings, emotions, values, and interpersonal relationships. This aspect of education is becoming known as affective education, or psychological education" (1977, p. 168, 169).

Under the aegis of affective education, the classroom, Patterson asserts, can and should take on the aspects of Rogers's "encounter groups":

> Affective education should include group experiences of a natural, spontaneous nature, such as the basic encounter groups of Carl Rogers . . . . While the facilitation of encounter groups requires some training of a psychological nature, such training need

not be extensive. The conduct of encounter groups consists of providing the same conditions as those [necessary] for humanistic teaching— empathic understanding, respect and genuineness or honesty. Teacher education students should, and could easily, be provided the necessary preparation in teacher education programs. (1977, p. 173; see also Patterson 1973)

Uniquely underscoring the degree to which the therapeutic school's purposes are fundamentally different from those associated with conventional understandings of education, Patterson describes the educational tasks to be undertaken in the therapeutic classroom:

In the small [encounter] group of six to ten students, without assigned subject matter or an agenda other than to talk about themselves or whatever is of concern to them, students can learn through experience:

> To listen to others
> To accept and respect others
> To identify and become aware of one's feelings
> To express one's feelings
> To become aware of the feelings of others
> To experience being accepted and understood by others
> To develop greater awareness of oneself
> To be oneself
> To change oneself in the direction of being more the self one wants to be.[3]

The foregoing conceptions of organizational purpose plainly hearken back to the core principles of liberation psychotherapy. The school's reason for existence is to facilitate the development of the self-actualizing individual. Organizational purposes are defined in terms of accommodating each individual's unique qualities and interests, rather than evaluating student performance in accordance with centralized, standardized, criteria. These conceptions of organizational purpose rest upon the notion that repression damages the innately benevolent, constructive self, and that this damage translates into a variety of costs not only to self but to society as a whole. Rather than imposing criteria against which some proportion of students are certain to fare poorly, then, schools should provide—as Hedges and Martinello put it earlier—more "opportunities for successful learning experiences" (1977, p. 244).

This emphasis on making success more widely available also reveals the powerful influence of William Glasser, whose ideas have long held much currency in American education. Glasser's *Schools Without Failure* (1969) helped to define the therapeutic school. And his more recent work, on what he calls *The Quality School* (1992), is a fixture on most principals' and superintendents' bookshelves.[4]

Glasser's earlier work is of particular importance for the purposes of understanding the construction of the therapeutic school. At every stage in his argument, Glasser's constructs embody the central principles of the therapeutic ethic: the schools' shortcomings are a function of their failure to accommodate individuals' psychological needs (1969, pp. 13, 25, 27). The imposition of external standards—such as the memorization of facts—guarantees failure, and this failure, in turn, produces a negative self-image (the failure identity); by extension, this negative self-image is transmuted into social problems (students "strike out in delinquent acts")(1969, pp. 29-30).

Glasser goes on to discuss several of what he sees as the most problematic elements of the conventional conception of educational purpose. First among these problem areas is grading. Here, we have reached the core of what Glasser means by "schools without failure." In accordance with the therapeutic ethic, when Glasser speaks of "schools without failure," he does not mean that students successfully master a body of standardized knowledge and information. Rather, what he means is a school that simply does not fail students—i.e., does not give failing grades. "[B]ecause most grades are primarily measures of the student's ability to remember designated facts rather than to think, grades are often unable to indicate those who can do the most in the world. . . . [T]he grading system sets the stage for failure, frustration, and lack of motivation. These results can only be changed by means of a different system that eliminates grades" (1969, p. 61).

In addition to grading, Glasser objects to and calls for the elimination of memorization of facts, closed-book examinations, homework, and ability grouping—all of which represent the imposition of external expectations upon the self. At bottom, the goal of education is to make students "feel good."

> Thinking and involvement with teachers in a cooperative educational effort lead a student to feel good. This kind of education is psychologically rewarding because it allies with school the good feelings associated with problem solving. These good feelings lead to continued use of the problem-solving process. Students who feel good, who solve problems, who are involved with teachers in cooperative efforts, do not create disturbances in school (1969, p. 81).

There is no question as to the charitable, humanitarian, impulses underlying Glasser's ideas, and they inform the work of those he has plainly influenced. There is ample evidence that the ideas of

Rogers, Maslow, Glasser, and a panoply of lesser-known educational theorists came to be widely-embraced and endorsed among American educators. Moreover, and much more importantly, there is a direct connection between the dissemination of the therapeutic ethic and the nearly two decades of educational reform referred to at the start of this chapter. These linkages are explored in more detail in the next section.

Incommensurability, Circularity, and Educational Reform

The rise of the therapeutic school has yielded multiple results, of which two are especially pertinent for understanding the nearly generation-long efforts at educational reform in the United States: the problems of *incommensurability* and *circularity*. In the first instance, as noted earlier, the academic performance of American children took a downward direction as educational philosophies and practices came to embody the core assumptions of liberation psychotherapy. Hence, for example, the aforementioned findings and concerns regarding the "rising tide of mediocrity" expressed in *A Nation at Risk* (National Commission on Excellence in Education1983, p. 16). Data on a variety of indicators revealed American school children's progressively worsening results—both longitudinally and cross-culturally—on a variety of measures (see also Sykes 1995). These data, although undeniably calling for attention, must also be understood in more complex ways than they are usually portrayed. Some have pointed out, for example, that the downward trajectory on such measures as the Scholastic Aptitude Test is to no small extent a byproduct of much larger numbers of children being tested now than in the past (see, for example, Berliner and Biddle 1997).

A more subtle point that is reflected in the data on flagging student achievement is that the rise of the therapeutic school created the problem of *incommensurability*. Traditional barometers of academic ability do not measure the "curriculum" of the therapeutic school. As we have seen, the therapeutic school is the institutional carrier of cultural premises that are at best loosely connected with traditional conceptions of the purposes of education. Thus, Glasser's "school without failure" will no longer require the memorization of facts or closed book examinations, nor will they assign grades for student performance. So, too, the "affective education" classroom will be modeled after Carl Rogers's "encounter groups." It is less than surprising, then, that educational beliefs and practices that preclude the imposition of external demands and expectations—emotional, behavioral, academic, cultural—should reveal sharp downward turns in traditional academic abilities. The tests were measuring different capacities than what the schools were teaching.[5]

Be that as it may, the data trends accompanying the rise of the therapeutic school fueled the efforts of the past two decades to introduce and institutionalize sweeping educational reforms. As early as 1981, the therapeutic school had been identified, albeit not by that name, as a source of some concern. Until *A Nation at Risk* was published in 1983, however, that concern was limited to a small number of voices. Perhaps chief among these minority voices was Richard Mitchell, the founder and editor of, and principal contributor to, *The Underground Grammarian,* a trenchant chthonian broadsheet devoted to the critique of mainstream educational practices.

Mitchell's editorials and articles were collected and published, in 1981, under the title, *The Graves of Academe.* The central argument in this book is that schools of education, educational research, and educational theory, as a whole, are dominated by an anti-intellectual point of view—one in which the therapeutic ethic's influences are plainly evident. Mitchell unpacks the logical paradox of such anti-intellectualism in a field ostensibly devoted to intellectual development. His ire is directed at university-based teacher preparation programs:

> If intellectualism is undesirable, its opposite must be desirable; but the opposite of intellectualism, by whatever name, is hard to champion in a supposedly academic context. It would take a bold professor indeed to come out in favor of ignorance and stupidity and offer in their favor arguments based on knowledge and reason . . . . It requires only a presumptuous professor to plump for ignorance and stupidity on other grounds . . . . For the institution of teacher-training as a whole, however, something more publicly defensible is needed, and, since the defense can afford neither kookiness nor the appeal to knowledge and reason, *it must rest upon what is likely to prove emotionally acceptable to the largest possible audience.* . . . And there is such a defense. Over and against the overweening demands of scholarly intellectualism, the teacher-trainers have set the presumably unquestionable virtues of what they call 'humanism.'" (1981, pp. 38-39; emphasis supplied)

But Humanism, Mitchell continues, is not quite the right term. The way therapeutic professors of education use the term,

> the meaning is something closer to "humaneness," as that word is used by what used to be called the "Humane Society," an organization that publicly deplored the cruel treatment of horses. *One of the aims of "humanistic" education is to deplore the cruel treatment of children subjected to the overbearing demands of knowledge, scholarship, and logic by the traditional powers of authoritarian intellectualism.* (1981, p. 39; emphasis supplied)

It is clear that what Mitchell objects to is a conception of education grounded in the therapeutic ethic's hostility toward any and all external control of the individual. As if speaking directly to Glasser and other advocates of the therapeutic school, Mitchell observes that "the educationists . . . justify and formalize their hostility to the intellect, with which they never *did* feel comfortable, by inventing the 'affective domain' of feelings and attitudes and appreciations and setting its gracious virtues over against the tedious and unimaginative 'rote' learning of the merely 'cognitive domain'" (1981, p. 83).

At bottom, what Mitchell is describing is the rise of the therapeutic school. In the years prior to Mitchell's critique, Rogers, Glasser, and other mainstream educationists had called for a redefinition of the purposes of schooling such that, as we have seen, classrooms were to become Rogerian encounter groups. Understood in this way, teacher preparation programs had to be aligned with these new purposes. Thus, Mitchell concludes that "The training of teachers is [now] . . . a miniature lampoon of the training of the psychoanalyst, who must first be analyzed so that he may do unto others as has been done unto him. *The incipient teachers are, in fact, therapists, keen to discover, if unable to treat, vast arrays of 'learning disabilities' and 'problem youngsters'"* (1981, p 67; emphasis supplied).

Mitchell, as noted, was an early voice of concern regarding the rise of the therapeutic school; indeed, the research reported in *A Nation at Risk* (1983) was still being conducted when *The Graves of Academe* (1981) was published. With the publication of the federal government's report on education, however, many educationists clearly realized that reforms were inevitable and that their field would be asked to respond to the mounting public criticism. The form those responses have taken provides important insight into the second key by-product of adherence to the dictates of liberation psychotherapy. This by-product is the problem of *circularity*, which manifests itself in mainstream education's either unwillingness or inability to undertake meaningful reform. The problem of circularity stems from the fact that the therapeutic ethic has one, and only one, means of accounting for "deviance," of whatever form: that is, ignorance, criminality, alcoholism, drug addiction, depression, and so on, are *all* understood to stem from the same source: namely, the repression of the "true self." When presented with evidence indicating that schools and teachers steeped in the liberation therapy ethic are failing to produce success, as success has conventionally been understood, therapeutically-inclined professors not only *do* not, but *can* not, arrive at any other conclusion than that the negative results are, as *all* negative results are according to the therapeutic ethic, the product of yet another instance of collective control over, and denial of, the true self. As such, when called upon to solve the problem of declining academic performance, education's responses were to further loosen the grip of external control over students. The next section briefly illustrates this problem of circularity as it applied to teaching of reading.

The Problem of Circularity, Recycling, and "Whole Language"

The problem of circularity by necessity translates into the recycling of old ideas under new names. Called upon, in the mid-to-late 1980s, to reform the therapeutic version of education (which, in the argot of the field, was known as "Open Education" [Grossen 1998]) theorists and practitioners in the field of reading seized upon so-called "whole language" as the preferred reform in that sub-field. As the brief discussion below reveals, the widespread adoption of whole language uniquely illustrates the twin phenomena of circularity and recycling: whole language is simply therapeutic education, recycled and given a new name.

Whole language is "primarily a system of beliefs and intentions" (Moats 2000, p. 5; see also Smith 1978; Goodman 1967), rather than a method of reading instruction, per se. The product of Kenneth Goodman's (1967, 1986) and, later, Frank Smith's (1977, 1978) "introspection into their own mental processes" (Moats 2000, p. 5), the central premise underlying whole language is that learning to read is as natural to humans as is learning to speak. The scientific research on the processes by which we learn to read, however, has incontrovertibly demonstrated that learning to read is immensely more complicated than learning to speak.

Although it may seem a matter of common sense to say that reading requires fundamentally different skills than does learning to speak, it may be helpful to briefly adumbrate some of the skills research has shown to be required to become an effective reader. Becoming a reader requires, first of all, developing skill at hearing and manipulating the basic sounds (phonemes) in words: the "b" in "ball," for example, is one phoneme. Second, becoming an effective reader requires mastery of the *alphabetic principle*, which is the principle of letter (or symbol)-to-sound correspondence. "Spoken language may be hard-wired in the human brain, but written language is an acquired skill that requires special, unnatural insights about the sounds in words" (Moats 2000. p. 6). Beginning readers, then, must be aware of the fact that each word comprises a combination of phonemes—an awareness that demands, first of all, that they can *decode* the word (know the sound corresponding to each letter), and, second, that they be able to *blend* the sounds together into the single word. These abilities, in good readers, over time and with much practice, lead to *fluency*, the ability to decode and blend with ever-greater speed and accuracy. Progressively, as fluency improves, children build *vocabulary*, such that they can both correctly identify words more and easily and quickly, and know the meanings of a growing number of words. Finally, all of these skills are the requisites for *comprehension*. To the extent that children become fluent at decoding, reading becomes less a halting labor than a smooth process of interaction with text (for example, National Institute of Child Health and Human Development 2000; Adams et al. 1998; American Federation of Teachers 1999; Simmons and Kame'euni 1997; Carnine, Silbert, and Kame'enui 1997; Ehri 1991; Foorman et al. 1997; Hasbrouck 1998; Juel 1988; Liberman and Liberman 1990; Moats 1999; Texas Center for Reading and Language Arts 1998; Yopp 1992; Moats 2000; Fletcher and Lyon 1998).

Contrary to the scientific research on learning to read, in the 1960s and 1970s, as noted above, Smith and Goodman asserted that meaning should be the primary goal of reading instruction. The memorization and repetition of essential basic skills that have been at the heart of initial reading instruction throughout much of the history of literate cultures are, they pronounced, unnecessary. Indeed,

> Smith asserted that the decomposition of words into sounds was pointless; that attention to letters was unnecessary and meaningless; that letter-sound correspondences were "jabberwocky" to be avoided; and that skill development was largely boring, repetitive, nonsensical, and unrelated to developing *real readers*. (Moats 2000, p. 6, original emphasis; citing Smith 1978)

As we have seen, during the same period of time that Smith and Goodman were developing whole language, the field of education was embracing the core premises of liberation psychotherapy. It is not altogether surprising to hear these themes repeated, then, in Smith's insistence that it is unnecessary and boring to subject new readers to a sequential and often painstaking process of cumulatively developing the skills needed to become fluent, accomplished readers[6] Each of these contentions reflects the therapeutic premise that we must reject institutional infringements upon children's innately constructive and positive natures. Such infringements are yet one more example of, as Patterson described it earlier in this chapter, conventional education's "overemphasis upon techniques and structured, teacher-controlled procedures, complete with predetermined specific objectives" (1977, p. 171). In the same vein, whole language advocates' references to becoming "real readers" hearkens back to, for example, Carl Rogers's "real person," or Maslow's "self-actualizing individual."

Plainly, then, whole language contained the requisite features to be widely accepted by mainstream, therapeutic educationists searching for responses to the growing public concern about education in the 1980's. Whole language shares liberation psychotherapy's assumptions regarding the appropriate relationship between the self and social institutions and, as such, is grounded in the therapeutic school's conceptions of educational purposes. Reflecting the circularity built into the logic of liberation psychotherapy, then, whole language represented a recycled version of beliefs and practices that were already in place in the schools. As such, the whole language advocates' ideas

> were eagerly and readily embraced by progressive educators turned off by drab basal reader [and] mechanistic drills . . . . Teachers were persuaded that the cause of most reading failure was insufficient emphasis on reading real books for real purposes. By the mid-1980's, schools were ready to throw out basal readers, phonics workbooks, spelling programs, and other "canned" material so that teachers could create individualized reading instruction with "authentic children's literature. (Moats 2000, p. 6)

The whole language approach was enthusiastically endorsed by reading experts in education and rapidly caught on nationwide. As Moats explains,

> The International Reading Association and the National Council for Teachers of English vigorously promoted the philosophy and practices of whole language. Publishing houses, university reading departments state education agencies, and professional development providers jumped on the bandwagon. The ideas were disseminated through internet connections, teacher journals that do not require articles to meet standards of scientific accuracy, courses and textbooks used in schools of education, and instructional manuals for teachers. (2000, p. 6)

A Brief Illustration: Whole Language in California

The circularity of liberation psychotherapy precludes the development and implementation of meaningful reform. Indeed, whole language's ascendancy as the preferred reading reform in education merely exacerbated the problems that had arisen in the context of therapeutic education. Perhaps nowhere was this reality more apparent than in California, which, in the late 1980's, made the decision to adopt whole language reading instruction statewide. As Stewart explains:

> In 1987, whole language theory began its sweep across California in the form of a nationally acclaimed reading "framework" adopted by the state Board of Public Instruction that downplays the teaching of traditional reading skills. "The core idea of whole language," says one of its most vocal proponents, Mel Grubb of the California Literature Project, "is that children no longer are forced to learn skills that are disembodied from the experience of reading a story. The enjoyment and wonder of the story are absorbed, just as the skills are absorbed." (Stewart, 2001, p. 2)

Whole language's adoption in California is a lengthy and tangled tale, fraught with the political infighting that has consistently characterized the so-called "reading wars" in education. Those "wars," waged between the fervent advocates of whole language and those arguing for reading instruction grounded in the research based on how children learn to read, have been ongoing over the past fifteen to twenty years. That there is such a "war," and that it has been so long-lived, is grounded in the circularity of the therapeutic ethic, and the assumption—underlying that circularity—that all problems can and must be explained as the product of societal and cultural control over the individual. This repudiation of external authority is reflected in whole language's rejection of teaching the basic skills needed to learn to read; so too, it is reflected in the advocates' rejection of data that refute their assertions: science, too, represents authority external to the individual.

> Unfortunately, whole language theorists were promoting . . . [their] beliefs without the benefit of controlled studies or methodologically accepted research. According to articles published in 1995 by the respected American Federation of Teachers, to date no meaningful research has ever verified [whole language's] claims. "The movement's anti-science attitude forces research findings into the backroom," the Federation's articles noted. Ominously, the Federation noted, the primary tenet of whole language philosophy, that learning to read is akin to learning to speak, "is accepted by no responsible linguist, psychologist, or cognitive scientist in the research community." (Stewart 2001, p. 7)

Insofar as the adoption of whole language, by dint of its status as a recycled version of therapeutic education, is ill equipped to solve educational problems stemming *from* therapeutic education, the results of California's decision to adopt whole language are less than surprising. In less than a decade, the state went from being one of the best performing public school systems in the nation to being one of the worst performing. Indeed,

> [W]hole language, which sounds so promising when described by its proponents, has proved to be a near-disaster when applied to—and by—real people. In the [short time] ... since whole language first appeared in the state's grade schools, California's fourth grade reading scores have plummeted to near the bottom nationally, according to the National Assessment of Educational Progress. Indeed, California's fourth graders are now such poor readers that only the children in Louisiana and Guam—both hampered by pitifully backward education systems—get worse scores. (Stewart 2001, p. 3)

In the past few years, California has taken steps to redress these problems, encountering staunch opposition from devotees of the whole language philosophy. Moreover, the "reading wars" continue unabated nationwide.

So, too, have efforts at educational reform writ large continued since the mid-1980's. The field of education over the past nearly two decades has adopted strategies designed to strengthen the professionalism of teachers and educational administrators. Such measures have included the creation of National Board Certification for teachers; the introduction of new or sharply revised proficiency standards for educators; tougher admissions standards for aspiring teachers; de-centralization of decision-making (called "site based management," which putatively empowers educators to shape school policy at the individual school level); and, the creation of so-called "professional development schools," which serve as, in effect, the "teaching hospitals" of the teaching profession (Holmes Group 1986; see also Carnegie Forum Task Force on Teaching as a Profession 1986).

By most accounts, progress has been made on each of these fronts. How much progress, and whether it is real or imagined, are questions that remain to be answered. Solid empirical data on the reforms just outlined are not available, and are often either not gathered or are poorly conceptualized; in some cases, reported findings have been based upon highly problematic research methodologies (Ballou and Podgursky 1998a; 1998b; 1999; 2001).[7]

What seemed apparent to many lawmakers in the early 1990's, however, was that measurable academic progress was very slow in coming. To no small extent, this slow progress reflected the reality that there had been virtually no change in the pedagogical instruction students in schools of education received during this time. Research indicated that reforms aimed at kindergarten through twelfth grade public schools had little impact upon university-based teacher preparation programs. Though expressed in different terminology— e.g., self-esteem, rather than self-actualization; child-centered classrooms, rather than encounter groups—researchers found that the therapeutic ethic remained (and remains) the dominant voice in schools of education, shaping both the curriculum for, and the socialization of new teachers. (See, for example, Sykes 1995; Kramer 1991; Lerner 1996; Baumeister 1996a, 1996b.)

In light of these circumstances, many policy makers concluded that it would be necessary to put more pressure on mainstream education. Reflecting this impetus, in the years immediately following the first President Bush's National Education Summit — held in Charlottesville, Virginia in 1990 — virtually every state in the Union passed some form of accountability legislation, attempting to produce tangible improvements in American education. The preferred approach for accountability uniting most of these reforms is state-mandated standardized testing, combined with some (variable) combination of incentives—both positive and negative—aimed at raising the academic achievement of all students; closing the "achievement gap" between and among racial, ethnic, and socio-economic groups; and ensuring that teachers, principals, and superintendents are held accountable for their own performance and for the well-being of the constituents of schools and districts. Moreover, the federal government has recently acted to take accountability to the national level, with the "No Child Left Behind" legislation, which is structured in much the same way as the putatively more stringent state laws.[8]

In short, then, although the past twenty years have seen quite extensive and comprehensive legislative and policy initiatives aimed at redressing the consequences of the rise of the therapeutic school, results thus far are, at best, mixed.[9] Public education, faced with state mandates, has increasingly been forced to attend to the achievement of all students, and preliminary results, in some states at least (Texas and North Carolina are often singled out for the comprehensiveness of their accountability laws, and the results they appear to be producing), suggest that the therapeutic ethic has been placed on the proverbial back burner. University-based schools of education, to date, have not faced the same tangible incentives as have their K-12 colleagues. This, however, is a state of affairs that is likely to change: in some states, the level of analysis of testing data is presently shifting to focus on individual teachers and, by extension, the schools in which those teachers learned their profession.

The Therapeutic Roots of Disappointment and Recalcitrance

As noted earlier, both the disappointing and/or unfortunate results of therapeutic schooling, and the (thus far) lack of response to reform legislation on the part of university-based schools of education stem from the same source: to wit, the assumptions upon which liberation psychotherapy discourse is structured. In the first instance, declining student achievement on objective measures of competency, as well as a general reduction of academic and intellectual rigor, are undeniably lamentable developments; but they are also utterly predictable, as well. Education, after all, is, or at least has historically been, at bottom about students' ability to learn and internalize an inherited system of symbolic forms (language, grammar, mathematics, science), about which, as everyone more or less agreed, their teachers knew more; thus, the teachers had to teach. The body of knowledge was understood to be external to the individual, and was also seen as comprising information about, and in relation to, which it was entirely possible to rank students in terms of their grasp of and ability to use that knowledge effectively. Because the therapeutic ethic defines precisely that form of social interaction as "repressive," and as a violation of the true self, what is surprising is not so much that, as discussed in regard to the problem of incommensurability (above), measures of academic achievement, thus understood, should show signs of trouble, but that anyone would be surprised by the story those measures tell. Under the influence of Rogers, Maslow, Glasser, and their adherents, education has ceased to be about instruction, or the passing on of an accumulated body of knowledge; in essence, it has become group therapy. It is not the case, then, that students do not receive an education; rather, they receive an education, but in the vocabulary of emotion and in the practice of self-absorption. Tests designed to tap into *those* competencies would likely tell a different story than data from, say, the Scholastic Aptitude Test—which continues to measure academic, rather than therapeutic, ability.

The unresponsiveness of therapeutic schools of education is but a facet of the same gem, as it were. Although turn of the century American institutions are the least controlling, the least repressive, social institutions in the history of our species, it is increasingly common to read, from the pens of contemporary educational theorists, that the source of the problems in education now, is the prepossessing desire of institutions to control the individual. It is too late, at this juncture, to delve into this emergent and burgeoning literature. For present purposes, suffice it to say that the rise of the therapeutic culture represents a binding commitment, on the part of its adherent, to a single explanation—cultural control of the individual—for every social problem that might arise. Unflagging allegiance to the tenets of liberation psychotherapy, when applied to public education, yields not only a fundamentally transformed conception of educational purpose, it also, precisely *because* of the problem of circularity, forestalls the construction of meaningful reform from within the field of education.

To be sure, there is no small amount of irony involved in this state of affairs: therapeutic educators' aversion to external control, manifested in the therapeutic school, has yielded data showing a sharp decline in American school children's traditional academic skills and abilities. Those data, in turn, initiated the ongoing effort to reform public education. Those efforts, as we have seen, engendered the imposition of far greater external control over the field, in the form of the state and national accountability legislation passed in the last decade.

Notes

An earlier version of this chapter appeared in *Society* 39 (2), January/February 2002: 19-28. I would also like to acknowledge my colleague, Dr. Martin Kozloff for sharing his encyclopedic knowledge of the scientific research on developing children's reading skills. Dr. Kozloff's exhaustive web site can be accessed at http://people.uncw.edu/kozloffm/ .Anyone interested in resources related to effective public education will find a visit to his site worthwhile.

1.   Human potential psychotherapy came to be the preferred term among the advocates of therapeutic ideology. I opt for "liberation" to underscore the much more fundamental point in the discourse: it is unmistakable that adherents of this ideology believe that reaching one's potential as a human being is contingent upon being liberated from the constraints of conventional society. (For fuller exposition, see Rice 1996.)

2.   For example, as is well known, Freud believed that humans were instinctively aggressive creatures; as such, he concluded that for civilization to be possible those instincts must be controlled, or, in the parlance, "repressed." In thus controlling

human instinct, by way of the childhood socialization process, society inevitably engendered individual psychological "discontents" (Freud 1961). For Freud, then, these discontents were an inescapable by-product of civilization itself. (See also Frank, 1966.)

3. I have abbreviated Patterson's list; the essential themes remain unchanged, however.
4. I taught in a school of education for nearly six years, and, as result, had numerous occasions to visit both principals and superintendents with whom I worked in a number of capacities. Invariably, they owned a copy of at least one of Glasser's books.
5. I use the past tense in this case because during the 1990s nearly all states adopted some form of educational accountability measures; moreover, the No Child Left Behind Legislation mandates such measures nationwide. Although the forms of accountability still vary widely from state to state the measures effectively force schools to teach a traditional curriculum.
6. Smith's views largely reiterate ideas first articulated in Goodman's initial article (1967) laying the foundations of the whole language philosophy.
7. For example, Ballou and Podgursky (1998a, 1998b; 2001), in regard to studies on the merits of National Board Certification, note that "Although the board [National Board for Professional Teaching Standards] has spent considerable time and money developing standards for accomplished teaching, many of these standards are vague platitudes. . . . Give the vagueness of the standards, and the subjective element that enters any performance assessment, one would expect that the board would have done extensive research to show a correlation between its assessments and more objective measures of teacher performance (for example, student test scores). In fact, the board has never provided any evidence of this kind to validate its certification procedures" (1998a, p. 1).
8. Indeed, the federal legislation closely resembles the laws passed in Texas when Mr. Bush was governor of the state.
9. Longitudinal data on the effects of the accountability legislation (laws which are very unpopular with most teachers and professors of education) that will allow for meaningful comparisons and ensuing evaluation and refinement of policies are coming in only now.

References

Adams, M. J., Foorman, B. R., Lundberg, I., and Beeler, T. 1998. "The elusive phoneme: Why phonemic awareness is so important and how to help children develop it." *American Educator*, 22 (1-2), 18-29.

American Federation of Teachers. 1999. *Building on the Best, Learning from What Works: Seven Promising Reading and English Language Arts Programs*. Washington DC. In http://www.aft.org/edissues/whatworks/index.htm

Baker, Simmons, and E. J. Kame'enui. 1997. Vocabulary acquisition: Research bases. In Simmons, D. C. & Kame'enui, E. J. (eds.), *What Reading Research Tells Us About Children with Diverse Learning Needs: Bases and Basics*. Mahwah, NJ: Erlbaum.

Ballou, Dale, and Michael Podgursky. 1998a. "The Case Against Teacher Certification." *Public Interest* (Vol. 132, Summer): 17-29.

_____. 1998b. "Some Unanswered Questions Concerning National Board Certification of Teachers." *Education Week on the Web* (http://web.missouri.edu/-econwww/nbart1.html: 1-3).

_____. 1999. "Gaining Control of Professional Licensing and Advancement." Pp. 69-109 in *Conflicting Missions? Teachers Unions and Educational Reform*, edited by Tom Loveless. Washington, DC: Brookings Institution Press.

_____. 2001. "Reforming Teacher Training and Recruitment." *Government Union Review* 17 (4): 1-26. (http://www.psrf.org/doc/v174_art.html).

Baumeister, Roy. 1996a. "Relation of Threatened Egotism to Violence and Aggression: The Dark Side of Self-Esteem." *Psychological Review*, vol. 103 (1).

_____. 1996b. "Should Schools try to Boost Self-Esteem? Beware the Dark Side." *American Educator*, Summer: 14-19, 43.

Bellah, Robert N., Richard Madsen, William M. Sullivan, Ann Swidler, and Steven M. Tipton. 1985. *Habits of the Heart: Individualism and Commitment in American Life.* New York: Harper and Row.

Berliner, David. C., and Bruce J. Biddle.1997. *The Manufactured Crisis: Myths, Fraud, and the Attack on America's Public Schools.* White Plains, NY: Longman.

Berman, Louise A., and Jessie A. Roderick. 1977. *Feeling, Valuing, and the Art of Growing: Insights into the Affective.* Washington, DC: Association for Supervision and Curriculum Development.

Boyers, Robert (ed.). 1975. *Psychological Man.* New York: Harper and Row.

Carnegie Forum Task Force on Teaching as a Profession. 1986. *A Nation Prepared: Teachers for the 21st Century.* New York: Carnegie Forum on Education and the Economy.

Carnine, D. W., J. Silbert, and E. J. Kameenui 1997. *Direct Instruction Reading*, 3rd ed. Upper Saddle River, NJ: Merrill/Prentice-Hall.

Ehri, L. 1991. "Development of the ability to read words." Pp. 383-417 in R. Barr, M. L. Kamil, P. Mosenthal, and P. D. Pearson (eds.), *Handbook of Reading Research.* New York: Longman.

Fletcher, Jack M., and G. Reid Lyon. 1998. "Reading: A Research-Based Approach." Pp. 40-90 in Williamson M. Evers (ed.), *What's Gone Wrong in America's Classrooms?* Stanford, CA: Hoover Institution Press.

Foorman, B. R., D. J. Francis, S. E. Shaywitz, B. A. Shaywitz, and J. M. Fletcher 1997. *The Case for Early Reading Intervention.* Hillsdale, NJ: Erlbaum.

Frank, Jerome. 1966. *Persuasion and Healing.* New York: Schocken.

Geertz, Clifford. 1973. *The Interpretation of Cultures.* New York: Basic Books.

Gehlen, Arnold. 1980. *Man in the Age of Technology.* New York: Oxford University Press.

Glasser, William. 1969. *Schools Without Failure.* New York: Harper and Row.

_____. 1992. *The Quality School: Managing Students Without Coercion*, 2nd ed. New York: Harper Perennial.

Goodman, Kenneth S. 1967. "Reading: A Psycholinguistic Guessing Game." *Journal of the Reading Specialist* 6: 126-135.

_____. 1986. *What's Whole in Whole Language?* Portsmouth, NH: Heinemann.

Gross, Martin. 1978. *The Psychological Society.* New York: Random House.

Grossen, Bonnie. 1998. "Child-Directed Teaching Methods: A Discriminatory Practice of Western Education." http://www.darkwing.uoregon.edu/~bgrossen/cdp.htm

Hasbrouck, L.1998. "Reading Fluency: Principles for Instruction and Progress Monitoring." *Professional Development Guide.* Austin: Texas Center for Reading and Language Arts, University of Texas at Austin.

Hedges, William D. and Marian L. Martinello. 1977. "What the Schools Might Do: Some Alternatives for the Here and Now." Pp. 229-248 in Louise A. Berman and Jessie A. Roderick (eds.), *Feeling, Valuing, and the Art of Growing: Insights into the Affective.* Washington, DC: Association for Supervision and Curriculum Development.

Holmes Group. 1986. *Tomorrow's Teachers: A Report of the Holmes Group.* East Lansing, MI: Holmes Group, Inc.

Inglehart. Ron. 1977. *The Silent Revolution: Changing Political Styles Among Western Publics.* Princeton, NJ: Princeton University Press.

——. 1990. *Culture Shift in Advanced Industrial Societies*. Princeton, NJ: Princeton University Press.

Juel, C. 1988. "Learning to Read and Write: A Longitudinal Study of 54 Children from First through Fourth Grades." *Journal of Educational Psychology*, 80, 437-447.

Kramer, Rita. 1991. *Ed School Follies*. New York: St. Martin's.

Lerner, Barbara. 1985 [1996]. "Self-Esteem and Excellence: the Choice and the Paradox." *American Educator* (Summer): 9-13, 41-42.

Liberman, I. Y., and A. M. Liberman. 1990. "Whole Language vs. Code Emphasis: Underlying Assumptions and Their Implications for Reading Instruction." *Annals of Dyslexia*, 40, 51-76.

Martin, Bernice. 1981. *A Sociology of Contemporary Cultural Change*. New York: St. Martin's.

Maslow, Abraham. 1964. *Religions, Values, and Peak-Experiences*. Columbus: Ohio State University Press.

——. 1968. *Toward a Psychology of Being*. Princeton, NJ: Van Nostrand Reinhold.

Mitchell, Richard. 1981. *The Graves of Academe*. Boston: Little, Brown.

Moats, L. C. 1999. *Teaching Reading is Rocket Science: What Expert Teachers of Reading Should Know and Be Able to Do*. Washington, DC: American Federation of Teachers.

——. 2000. "Whole Language Lives On: The Illusion of 'Balanced' Reading Instruction."http://www.edexcellence.net/library/wholelang/moats.html#foreword Thomas B. Fordham Foundation.

National Commission on Excellence in Education. 1983. *A Nation at Risk: The Imperative for Educational Reform*. Washington, DC: Government Printing Office.

National Institute of Child Health and Human Development. 2000. *Report of the National Reading Panel*: Teaching Children to Read, An Evidence-Based Assessment of the Scientific Research Literature on Reading and Its Implications for Reading *Instruction*. Washington, DC: Government Printing Office. Available: http://www.nichd.nih.gov/publications/nrp/smallbook.htm.

Nolan, James. 1998. *The Therapeutic State: Justifying Government at Century's End*. New York: New York University Press.

Patterson, Cecil H. 1977. "Insights about Persons: Psychological Foundations of Humanistic and Affective Education." Pp. 145-180 in Louise A. Berman and Jessie A. Roderick (eds.), *Feeling, Valuing, and the Art of Growing: Insights into the Affective*. Washington, DC: Association for Supervision and Curriculum Development.

Rice, John Steadman. 1996. *A Disease of One's Own: Addiction, Psychotherapy and the Emergence of Co-Dependency*. New Brunswick, NJ: Transaction Publishers.

Rieff, Philip. 1966 [1987]. *The Triumph of the Therapeutic: Uses of Faith After Freud*. Chicago: University of Chicago Press.

Rogers, Carl. 1961. *On Becoming a Person: A Therapist's View of Psychotherapy*. Boston: Houghton Mifflin.

Russell, Cheryl. 1992. *The Master Trend: How the Baby Boom Generation is Remaking America*. New York: Plenum.

Sennett, Richard. 1978. *The Fall of Public Man: On the Social Psychology of Capitalism*. New York: Random House.

Smith, Frank. 1977. "Making Sense of Reading—And of Reading Instruction." *Harvard Educational Review* 47: 386-395.

——.1978. *Understanding Reading: A Psycholinguistic Analysis of Reading and Learning to Read*, 2nd ed. New York: Holt, Rinehart, and Winston.

Stewart, Jill. 2001. "Blackboard Bungle: Why California Kids Can't Read." Available: http://www.kidsource.com/kidscourse/content/whole.1.html

Sykes, Gerald. 1995. *Dumbing Down Our Kids: Why American Children Feel Good About Themselves But Can't Read, Write or Add*. New York: St. Martin's.

Texas Center for Reading and Language Arts. 1998. *Professional Development Guide*. Austin: Texas Center for Reading and Language Arts, University of Texas at Austin.

Tucker, James. 1999. *The Therapeutic Corporation*. New York: Oxford University Press.

Weber, Max. 1958. *The Protestant Ethic and the Spirit of Capitalism*, trans. Talcott Parsons. New York: Macmillan.

Yamamoto, Kaoru. 1977. "Humankind: Shadows and Images." Pp. 11-28 in *Feeling, Valuing, and Growing: Insights Into the Affective*.

Yopp, H. K. 1992. Developing Phonemic Awareness in Young Children. *Reading Teacher*, 45, 9, 696-703.

7

Online Communities in a Therapeutic Age

Felicia Wu Song

Amidst all the excitement and speculation over the Internet, hopes have been staked on technology's capacity to revitalize civic and community life in America. The proliferation of online communities, in particular, has been regarded as a possible counterbalance to the trends of declining social capital observed by Robert Putnam in his book, *Bowling Alone*. While Putnam may have aptly noted a significant cultural change in the decreasing membership of local associations, many scholars suggest that the main lesson to learn from Putnam's work is simply that it is time to locate civic duty and social connectivity in new institutions. As Francis Fukuyama (2000) commented: "For every bridge club or Masonic temple that has folded, there are countless AIDS advocacy groups or Usenet discussion groups to take their place....The Internet by itself clearly constitutes a major revolution in many-to-many communications, one that by itself could easily overwhelm all the other downward trends cited in *Bowling Alone*."

Fukuyama has not been alone in his optimism. While many early observers of the Internet recognized the important qualitative differences between face-to-face and computer-mediated communities, they nevertheless maintained that online groups are genuine communities, and thus valid substitutes for the local communities now in decline. Several key characteristics have been commonly noted as evidence that online communities are indeed "communities." For example, in his book *The Virtual Community* (1993), Howard Rheingold set the stage by offering a compelling account of how computer-mediated communication often supports earnest, intimate and affective ties between people. Others claimed that online communities can be as effective as their offline counterparts in matters

137

of social and political action (Brint, 2001; Smelser and Alexander 1999). Online groups also often possess shared standards of conduct, a common attribute of face-to-face communities (McLaughlin, Osbourne, Smith, 1995; Baym, 1995; Watson, 1997). As such, many perceived the online community as a new form of sociability that essentially operates as any previous community has in the past. Considering the likelihood that many Americans' primary social ties are sustained through non-local social networks, online communities may actually improve people's ability to communicate and participate in each other's lives, giving individuals the means to combat the atomizing tendencies of contemporary America's economic, cultural and social realities (Wellman, 1999).

There are, however, good reasons to question whether online communities can function as a viable alternative to communities of place and local associations. While acknowledging that the Internet is still in a stage of relative infancy, several features of online communities strongly suggest that it is unlikely for these communities to cultivate the types of social bonds and associated norms of reciprocity often understood to be the building blocks of a stable and vibrant democracy. Because of the particular ways that computer technology mediates the relationship between an individual and a community, the Internet may lead to an increase in the *quantity* of social connectedness, but the *quality* of that connectedness will be very different from that which Putnam and Alexis de Tocqueville rested their democratic hopes. Put another way, while online communities may boost the number and breadth of social networks, they may not be conducive to fostering the norms of mutual obligation needed for achieving communal ends.

Instead, the type of social connectedness that online communities may tend to cultivate bears a greater similarity to Philip Rieff's vision of the therapeutic culture—that is, they may tend to enhance the well-being of the individual at the expense of the community. Historically, liberals and communitarians have conceptualized the problem of community in terms of a delicate balance between the individual and the communal good. However, this crucial dynamic is apt to become undone in an online community, resulting in a community whose therapeutic function has become its sole purpose for being. That is to say, beyond asserting individual rights as being prior to the communal good, an online community has the potential to become a community in which individual rights *are* the communal good. As its institutional and technical features enhance the power of private control, an online community runs the risk of being reduced to what Michel Foucault (1988) referred to as "a technology of the self," that which permits individuals to "transform themselves in order to attain a certain state of happiness, purity, wisdom, [and] perfection" (p. 18). In this way, the dynamic between an individual and the collective in online communities begins to share a strong resemblance with Rieff's vision of the therapeutic culture.

The Therapeutic Nature of Online Communities

Are online communities a reliable sources of new social capital? Rieff's notion of the therapeutic is helpful in addressing this question because it directs the focus of analysis to the changing character of the individual, rather than that of the community. For regardless of how one might characterize the changes that American communities have experienced historically, Rieff's account of the fundamental shift in the way that people participate in social institutions still radically alters the terrain on which any discussions about contemporary public life take place.

The shift that Rieff calls "the triumph of the therapeutic" describes an inversion of the relationship between an individual and a collective, or social institution. Where the relationship between individuals and institutions was formerly characterized by the priority of external communal goods over individual ends, in contemporary therapeutic culture, personal well-being supersedes communal goods. The external communal purposes, which had formerly been sources of personal identity and meaning, are now viewed as causes of neuroses. Formerly considered first principles, they are now nothing but binding demands that ought to be abandoned. The pursuit of personal well-being is the end and justification of all our actions. Yet, Rieff's therapeutic individual is not someone who recklessly spurns social institutions altogether. Rather, the therapeutic individual is someone who *does* participate in social institutions, but participates in a newly detached and strategic manner that may not be easily discerned at first glance. Consequently, though social institutions may appear to have retained their original form in society, they are now regarded as technologies of the self. Therapeutic individuals approach them as savvy consumers seeking to invest only in that which serves "the enrichment of their own experience." As Rieff (1990) eloquently described:

...psychological man cannot completely shake off his past. He has in fact the nervous habits of his father, economic man: he is anti-heroic, shrewd, studying unprofitable commitments as the sins most to be avoided, carefully keeping a balance of his satisfactions and dissatisfactions, but without the genial confidence of his immediate ancestor that the sum will mount to something meaningful and justify his entire life. He lives by the ideal of insight—practical, experimental, and leading to the mastery of his own personality. (p. 4)

Since the impact of the "triumph of the therapeutic" is mainly located in the individual, any form of community—whether local or non-local, face-to-face or computer-mediated—becomes equally subject to appropriation as a technology of the self by a therapeutic individual. How then can online communities be viewed as being particularly therapeutic?

Because of their unique features, online communities are particularly well suited to enacting and reinforcing the doctrines that constitute the therapeutic culture, making the therapeutic ideal tangible, plausible and compelling. For the medium of the computer and the organization of the Internet's many-to-many communication have the capacity to make ordinary socially binding expectations and demands powerless, and thus, predispose individuals towards prioritizing the pursuit of personal satisfaction at the expense of communal ends. Consequently, it may be with great irony that enthusiasts place their hopes in online communities for renewed social trust and mutual obligation. For if Rieff is right in his assessment of therapeutic culture, at best, online communities will fail to revitalize American community life; at worst, they will institutionalize the therapeutic sensibility in its extreme form.

Let us now consider how the particular constitution of online communities serves to structurally reinforce the therapeutic sensibility. By looking at the ways that computer mediation impacts four major aspects of communal experience: (1) a collective sense of belonging; (2) the authority of socially binding demands; (3) the character of social interaction; and (4) the nature of trust, we will see how online communities are not merely extended versions of communities as they have been historically conceptualized and understood, but actually *inversions* of them.

Belonging Redefined

A brief survey of online communities reveals that there are many different types of groups. Some groups "meet" both face-to-face and virtually; others groups exist exclusively online. The purposes and missions of the groups vary greatly. Some merely act as a clearinghouse for information on a particular topic, others are geared towards providing emotional support and cultivating a sense of belonging. Imaginary text-based environments known as multi-user domains (MUDs) are primarily used for recreational social interaction, while the most common online groups are specifically intended as forums for discussions. These groups span a wide range of topics from the most mundane (discussion groups for crock-pot cooking) to the serious (support groups for men with prostate cancer), and from the promising "Anti-Racism" group where "racists and non racists come...to debate" to the eyebrow-raising "People Having an Affair" group.

The online communities assessed for this chapter are mainly newsgroups, discussion forums, and electronic bulletin boards that exist solely online. (Analyses and observations were made during February-March 2001.) These types of online communities range in size from a handful of individuals to groups such as the Yahoo! "Islamic Community" Club which claims a membership of over 10,000 people. These groups are often accessed through World Wide Web search engines, service providers (such as America Online) or individual websites. Online communities can also be found on Usenet, one of the largest discussion group systems. In 1997, studies showed that Usenet averaged 20,000 people per day, posting 300,000 messages on over 14,000 newsgroups (Smith, 1999). It is estimated that there are 130 million Usenet users per year, with approximately over 13.1 million individuals posting messages in 2002 (Festa, 2003). Taking into consideration that Usenet is a group system that is not easily accessible or in mainstream use as Yahoo! Clubs or AOL groups are, one can only begin to imagine the level of email traffic and sociability occurring on the Internet as a whole.

While online groups may vary by size and purpose, technically speaking, all online communities are essentially electronic and digital communication systems. As such, one of their most celebrated features is their capacity to overcome spatial limitations. In this way, the online community is the latest development in a long trend of technology and media that have altered the basis for conceptualizing community by diminishing the relevance of geography and place, and increasing the salience of communication. What we find in online groups then is an understanding of *community as communication* taken to new extremes. For when an online community is materially wired and culturally imagined as a communication network, there is a strong sense in which belonging to one means posting and reading messages either on the group's home page or through one's email account. For all the various social interactions that take place within an online community are recorded in these threads of messages (except for the contents of real-time chat sessions or private email exchanges.) As a result, these archives are not merely a chronicle of what members have said, *but actually represent the substance of the community itself.*

Because such a community essentially would not exist if the messages did not exist, an individual's understanding of his/her relation to the community is apt to become subtly inverted. Communications scholar Steven Jones (1997) points to evidence of Usenet newsgroup members who feel that the group and its messages "belong" to them. He writes, "No longer do *we*, as members of the group, belong to the community, rather the community belongs to *us*" (p.16). This phenomenological difference between online communities as an immaterial log of messages and "offline" communities as people inhabiting a particular place, turns the very notion of belonging on its head, so that the individual is now the agent to whom a community belongs. This inversion of belonging, though abstract and subtle, provides an opening for individuals to view online communities as institutions that they "possess" and appropriate according to their private sense of well-being.

The Evasion of Social Authority

Furthering this tendency towards viewing communities as mere technologies of the self is the capacity for computer technology to facilitate the act of *choosing* one's community. For implicit in this choice is the assumption that individuals will choose to associate with people who share common characteristics, status or preferences. Indeed, the very organization of online communities on the World Wide Web is divided up according to categories that mirror the target groups of niche marketing. From hobbies to hair color, eccentricities to addictions, individuals are expected to choose to associate with others like themselves. Under the Yahoo! Club category "Cultures and Communities," Baby Boomers alone have eighteen groups, women have 443, and teenagers have the most options with over 17,000 possible groups to join. On iVillage.com, a commercial website voted by Yahoo! Internet Life as the best community website for women in 2001 and 2002, the home page encourages new members to scroll down a menu labeled, "Women Like Me," providing a wide array of options varying from age, religion, ethnicity to marital and familial status. Sociologist Barry Wellman (1999) sharply observed that "in online communities, the market metaphor of shopping around for support in specialized ties is even more exaggerated than in real life" (p.186).

However, many enthusiasts of online communities believe that communities are simply *better* when people choose them. Over thirty years ago, it was imagined that "life will be happier for the on-line individual because the people with whom one interacts most strongly will be selected more by commonality of interests and goals than by accidents of proximity....communication will be more effective and productive, and therefore more enjoyable" (Licklider and Taylor, 1968, p. 31). Set free from the "accidents of proximity," communities would be less burdened by free-riders and less troubled by instances in which a coercive power must force community members into their share of mutual obligations.

Many scholars have criticized such communities, viewing them as "lifestyle enclaves" and questioning their capacity to generate the kind of mutual obligation necessary for the pursuit of communal ends (Bellah, 1985; Levine, 2000; Sunstein, 2000). In *Habits of the Heart,* Robert Bellah has argued that collectives formed out of common interests alone are rarely robust enough to be called "communities" because such groups exist solely to fulfill individual needs. These critiques point to the therapeutic tendencies of most online communities. Yet, while these groups may be too narrow in scope for cultivating thick community bases, there are signs of how online communities do seem to serve an important, perhaps even necessary, social function.

Consider the Usenet newsgroup: soc.support.youth.gay-lesbian-bi. It is self-described as existing to "offer support, understanding, and friendship to young people who are coming to terms with their sexuality, which may differ from the heterosexual norm." Their mission statement explains how the group exists explicitly for the purpose of meeting a need in contemporary American society:

> These people often suffer from unimaginable shame and guilt because they feel attracted to members of the same sex, or to both sexes; should these feelings become publicly known, these young people may become outcasts in their communities.... The intent of this newsgroup is to let these people know that they are not alone, and that there are people they can turn to for friendship and comfort.

For minors who live under parental supervision and struggle with a stigmatized status, an online community such as this one is not only a source of advice, but also a life-line that affirms their personal struggles and fledgling sexual identities. The extent to which contemporary Americans desire to be in a community where "there are people like me" or where an individual can be reassured that "I am not alone" is apparent by the unusually large number of online groups oriented around particular identities or needs that usually receive little institutional support.

The ubiquity of these groups reminds us of the fact that most communities do in fact have some therapeutic function, for there undoubtedly is value to having one's identity and framework of meaning reinforced. However, where communities had once functioned as the source of these identities and moral frameworks, there is now a tendency to emphasize how individuals can choose and construct communities that share and affirm their pre-established, self-derived identities. As a result, there is little to keep online communities from being reduced to communities of therapeutic function alone, again at the expense of external communal ends.

One striking example of where this intensification of the therapeutic culture can lead is the Yahoo! club called "People Having an Affair" which offers its visitors and potential members:

> a refuge for those of us who are having affairs, or are contemplating having one. We all have two basic things in common...the need to be happy, and to fulfill our desires. Come share your thoughts, your joys, your worries, and your sorrows. We're here to listen, and help each other. Experience the energy, excitement and compassion that has made our club unique.

While this online community may be deeply rewarding for an individual's personal sense of well-being, the uncomfortable fact remains: through computer technology, it becomes quite easy to offer support to those conducting sexual relations that the current moral order deems illicit or inappropriate. Because these types of social interactions have been conducted online, the socially binding consequences, which normally uphold the existing moral order, have been evaded and rendered powerless. Undermining the social and moral demands of the institutions of marriage and family in order to enhance individual well-being, this online community is a crystallized form of how therapeutic institutions are ultimately anti-communal in their tendency to release its members from socially-binding expectations and consequences.

Freedom from Embodied Interactions

As computer mediation functions to release or distance individuals from the pressure of normative demands, it not only guides the types of online groups that can exist, but also shapes the nature of social interactions within online communities. It is common for skeptics of online communities to point to the inferiority of computer-mediated communication when compared to face-to-face communication. Computer-mediated communication is often noted for its relative inadequacy in communicating emotions that normally are expressed through facial expressions, voice inflection or other non-verbal cues in face-to-face encounters (Walther and Burgoon, 1992; Reid, 1991). As a result, computer-mediated communication does not lend itself to expressing humor or irony, with attempts often resulting in misunderstandings.

This lack of physical embodiment in computer-mediated communication also releases people from particular social demands that have traditionally guided how people treat each other. One result is that the social inhibitions that keep incivility and hostility in check during face-to-face interactions are no longer felt (Kiesler, 1984; Rice and Love, 1987; Schmitz, 1997). Long extended tirades in response to other people's messages, known as "rants" or "flames," can end up creating more difficult and contentious environments than that of the usual face-to-face interactions.

Yet, because computer-mediated communication conveys far less information than face-to-face interactions, it has been known to empower certain people groups who finally can interact with others without the usual hindrances of their stigmatized physical appearance or social status (Baron, 1984; Hiltz and Turoff, 1978; Van Gelder, 1984). While many scholars regard this phenomenon as evidence of increased egalitarianism online, it seems necessary to confront the fact that the egalitarian environment is not a product of diminished prejudice or true understanding, but a result of computer mediation's capacity to free individuals from existing social norms by offering almost complete control over the management of their identities. Individuals are accepted as equals only because they can hide their true conditions under carefully constructed personas. Online communities can become useful spaces for individuals to experiment with multiple personas whether it be through gender swapping, or exploring new degrees of vulnerability or promiscuity (Turkle, 1995).

Thus, for better or for worse, computer mediation offers individuals unprecedented control over the management of their identities and behaviors. They can hide their actual conditions under constructed personas or act out without any socially binding consequences.

Because computer-mediated communication can equally lead to a more hostile or congenial social environment, many online communities attempt to manage this new and uncertain social terrain with rules or charters. On the iVillage website, a "Community Covenant" establishes the boundaries of communication, and in doing so, implicitly shapes the purposes of the community itself. iVillage explains to its members :

> iVillage is a place where it's okay to be yourself—be that harried, jovial, silly or sad— as long as you always act with respect for your fellow iVillagers....The real objective of community is to understand each other, not to attack others and convince them that you're right.....Agree to disagree respectfully.

Representative of many other online communities, iVillage frames itself as a community that is centrally concerned with letting its members "be themselves" within a judgment-free environment. While these goals are well intended, such objectives tend to reveal a rather thin notion of communal ends. When the impetus of any form of reciprocity or obligation is solely the protection of each individual's sense of self, it becomes apparent that these online communities are actually inversions of accepted notions of communities, for the preservation and enhancement of personal well-being have essentially *become* the communal purpose.

Instant Intimacy Among Strangers

Lastly, what kind of trust is fostered in a community that has released individuals from external social demands and pressures, enabled them to control their projected identities, and perhaps most importantly, given them anonymity amidst social interaction? Some of the social consequences that result from allowing people to hide their offline identities have already been discussed. Through cryptic usernames or aliases, people are granted a degree of psychological disinhibition, which, in one instance, frees them to attack each other, and in another, curiously stimulates an "instant intimacy" among them. In these circumstances, it is worth noting that, instead of being suspicious of strangers, people find themselves discussing their lives and opinions more openly with those who they probably have not met and will *never* meet in person.

To a significant degree, the club for "People Having an Affair" rests on this very premise as members mutually confess their respective affairs and exchange emotional support in their activities, without the complications of public disclosure. One member's message captured a common sentiment when she wrote:

> Thanks all for being here!! We certainly do need a place to let the WHOLE truth come out...I spend so much time 'editing' the truth to present it to various friends....that it's crazy making at times.

This type of trust in strangers found frequently in online communities seems to be qualitatively different from the sort of trust that Putnam and other social scientists have sought to measure. This is the kind of trust that Georg Simmel discussed in his famous essay "The Stranger." In it, he describes a unique type of trust in the archetypal stranger who is not "...the wanderer who comes today and goes tomorrow, but rather...the man who comes today and stays tomorrow— the potential wanderer, so to speak, who, although he has gone no further, has not quite got over the freedom of coming and going" (p. 143). For Simmel observed that when "the one who is remote is near," people easily divulge their kept secrets, problems and confessions. In the same way, any time a member of a online community logs on, they can pour out their hearts in the privacy of their bedroom or office to the multitude of online readers who are "out there," but, like any good friend, are "always there for you."

Simmel suggested that the appeal of the stranger as confidante is a function of the stranger's possession of (1) an apparent objectivity and (2) a potential for mobility. First, as someone who is not directly involved in the confessor's life, the stranger lacks personal ties that can prejudice perception. Online, individuals frequently make a plea for input from those who have "an open mind" (that is, implicitly, in contrast to the closed or narrow minds of their family members and friends). As one member of "People Having an Affair" explained in her message:

> I KNOW that what I am DOING is not right, but, I need to face what I am FEELING. Knowing it is wrong does not make the feelings go away. I need to talk about it with someone who has an open mind and is not going to just tell me how wrong it is! I already know that part!!!

Interestingly, in this instance, the possession of an open mind does not even seem to mean having objectivity about the issue of extramarital relations. Rather, open-mindedness here refers to having a therapeutic appreciation for the individual's personal desires and pursuit of self-fulfillment over and against the existing social and moral order.

Second, the potential for mobility is, in one sense, present in all members of a online community. Since the geographic component of a community has already been made irrelevant, members can leave or "disappear" at any moment. Online communities have such low entry and exit costs that becoming a member often only requires registering with a user name and email address. Since maintaining membership is only contingent upon posting messages, it is practically impossible for a community to know the cause of a person's absence or failure to post more messages (unless the information is volunteered). Because online communities have unusually low entry and exit costs, there is a sense in which even the most intimate of personal self-revelations are framed within a structure of loose ties, low expectations and weak means of accountability. The less binding the ties, the more people trust each other with a peculiar blend of quick compassion and selective indifference. As such, the community of intimate strangers becomes a normative ideal for online communities, an ideal that has turned traditional notions of community inside out on many different levels.

The Reality of Unintended Consequences

In all, the structural and technical features of online communities have the effect of releasing individuals from the usual socially binding demands that guide our everyday lives. With an increase in personal autonomy over controlling one's identity, social interactions, and degree of communal participation, the online communities usually function as therapeutic communities, existing primarily to serve the personal ends of its members.

It is interesting to note that even as Internet use and experience changes through the years—becoming more fully integrated within people's everyday offline practices and routines, rather than remaining a separate realm of activity—its cumulative effect has continued to reinforce the cultural and social shift away from all-encompassing socially-authoritative communities to individually-fragmented personal communities (Wellman and Haythornthwaite, 2002). The significant turn towards living in multiple, specialized, partial communities where limited commitment is given to each, as network theorists have argued, is a process further instantiated by the technological capacities of the Internet. Wellman and Haythornthwaite claim that Internet technology has developed to cultivate "networked individualism" where "it is the individual, and neither the household nor the group that is becoming the primary unit of connectivity: gleaning support, sociability, information, and a sense of belonging....People remain connected, but as individuals rather than being rooted in the home bases of work unity and household" (p. 33, 34). Therefore, even as some speak of the Internet as a technology that does not replace, but supplements and augments social interactions, it is a medium that structurally places the individual at the center of social and communal experience.

As scholars continue to puzzle over the feasibility (and desirability) of renewing local communities and civic associations amidst today's economic and cultural conditions, there is no question that online communities have an incredible potential to be the safe and convenient havens of support and advice that people are seeking. But to claim that they can simply replace local communities and their associations as the building blocks of democracy is to fail to appreciate how the medium and configuration of online communities are predisposed to encourage and institutionalize a therapeutic understanding of communities. To presume that social bonds in an embodied local community would retain its character and quality in a virtual and "place"-less one, is to neglect the dynamic ways in which our environments of social interaction provide limitations and supply possibilities for particular behaviors, perceptions, and thoughts, impacting what we think is possible and good in a community.

It is unfortunate that many of the benefits online communities bring to the individual are the very factors that may undermine the cultivation of particular sensibilities necessary for citizens of a vibrant democracy. For the strength of online communities is ultimately their capacity to subvert embodied social authority. This, however, effectively weakens the community's ability to prioritize external communal ends over personal well-being. When there is an absence of anything socially binding, individuality and freedom can flourish as we desire. But, the cost is a loss of effective sanctions that can encourage the pursuit of larger communal purposes. This is not to dismiss the reality of specific individuals and particular online communities who do indeed pursue and achieve larger communal goals that reach beyond their personal sense of self-fulfillment. Rather, it is to say that the structures of these communities simply lack the resources to consistently resist being appropriated by a culture that most prizes an individual's sense of well-being. As a result, online communities will probably fail to meaningfully revitalize American communal life and may even bear the unintended consequence of furthering its decline.

References

Baron, N.S. 1984. "Computer Mediated Communication as a Force in Language Change." *Visible Language,* Vol. 18, No. 2, 118-141.

Baym, Nancy. 1995. "The Emergence of Community in Computer-mediated Communication." In *CyberSociety: Computer-Mediated Communication and Community*, ed. Steven G. Jones. Thousand Oaks, CA: Sage Publications.

Bellah, Robert, Richard Madsen, William M. Sullivan, Ann Swidler, and Steven M. Tipton. 1985. *Habits of the Heart: Individualism and Commitment in American Life.* Berkeley: University of California Press.

Brint, Steven. 2001. "Gemeinschaft Revisited: A Critique and Reconstruction of the Community Concept." *Sociological Theory,* Vol. 19, No. 1 (March).

Festa, Paul. 2003. "Microsoft's In-House Sociologist." *CNET News*, August 19. Available at *http://news.com.com/2008-1082_3-5065298.html*

Foucault, Michel. 1988. *Technologies of the Self.* Amherst: University of Massachusetts Press.

Fukuyama, Francis. 2000. "Community Matters." *Washington Post,* May 28.

Jones, Steven G. 1997. "The Internet and its Social Landscape." In *Virtual Culture.* Ed. Steven G. Jones. London: Sage.

Kiesler, S.B., J. Siegal, and T.W. McGuire. 1984. "Social psychological aspects of Computer-mediated Communication." *American Psychologist,* Vol. 39, 1123-1134.

Levine, Peter. 2000. "The Internet and Civil Society." *Report from the Institute for Philosophy and Public Policy,* Vol. 20, No. 4, Fall, 1-8.

Licklider, J.C.R. and R.W. Taylor. 1968. "The Computer as a Communication Device." *Science & Technology,* April, 21-31.

MacKinnon, Richard C. 1995. "Searching for the Leviathan in Usenet." In *CyberSociety: Computer-Mediated Communication and Community,* ed. Steven G. Jones. Thousand Oaks, CA: Sage Publications.

McLaughlin, Margaret L., Kerry K. Osborne, and Christine B. Smith. 1995. "Standards of Conduct on Usenet." In *CyberSociety: Computer-Mediated Communication and Community,* ed. Steven G. Jones. Thousand Oaks, CA: Sage Publications.

Putnam, Robert D. 2000. *Bowling Alone: The Collapse and Revival of American Community.* New York: Simon & Schuster.

Reid, Elizabeth. 1991. *Electropolis: Communication and Community on Internet Relay Chat.* Unpublished master's thesis, University of Melbourne.

Rheingold, Howard. 1993. *The Virtual Community.* New York: Harper.

Rice, R.E., and Love, G. 1987. "Electronic Emotion: Socioemotional Content in a Computer-Mediated Communication Network." *Communication Research,* Vol. 14, 85-108.

Rieff, Philip. 1990. *The Feeling Intellect: Selected Writings of Philip Rieff,* ed. Jonathan B. Imber. Chicago: University of Chicago Press.

Rieff, Philip. 1966. *The Triumph of the Therapeutic.* Chicago: University of Chicago Press.

Schmitz, Joseph. 1997. "Structural Relations, Electronic Media, and Social Change: The Public Electronic Network and the Homeless." In *Virtual Culture,* ed. Steven G. Jones. London: Sage.

Simmel, Georg. 1971. "The Stranger." In *George Simmel on Individuality and Social Forms,* ed. Donald N. Levine. Chicago: University of Chicago Press.

Smelser, Neil J., and Jeffrey C. Alexander, eds. 1999. *Diversity and Its Discontents.* Princeton, NJ: Princeton University Press.

Smith, Marc A., and Peter Kollock, eds. 1999. *Communities in Cyberspace.* London: Routledge.

Smith, Marc A. 1999. "Invisible Crowds in Cyberspace." In *Communities in Cyberspace,* eds. Marc A. Smith and Peter Kollock. London: Routledge.

Sunstein, Cass. 2001. *Republic.com.* Princeton, NJ: Princeton University Press.

Turkle, Sherry. 1995. *Life on the Screen.* New York: Simon & Schuster.

Van Gelder, Lindsey. 1985. "The Strange Case of the Electronic Lover." *Ms Magazine,* October, 98-124.

Walther, J.B., and Burgoon, J. 1992. "Relational Communication in Computer-mediated Interaction. *Human Communication Research,* Vol. 19, No. 1, 50-88.

Watson, Nessim. 1997. "Why We Argue About Virtual Community: A Case Study of the Phish.Net Fan Community." In *Virtual Culture,* ed. Steven G. Jones. London: Sage.

Wellman, Barry and Milena Gulia. 1999. "Virtual Communities as Communities: Net Surfers Don't Ride Alone." In *Communities in Cyberspace,* eds. Marc A. Smith and Peter Kollock.. London: Routledge.

Wellman, Barry and Caroline Haythornthwaite. 2002. "The Internet in Everyday Life: An Introduction." In *The Internet in Everyday Life,* eds. Barry Wellman and Caroline Haythornthwaite. Malden, MA: Blackwell.

8

New Age Healers and the Therapeutic Culture

James Tucker

The therapeutic culture has spread throughout much of modern American society. We find it in the schools, the workplace, the legal system, and even the political sphere.[1] But what about religion? Religious life would seem to be the one area where therapy is largely absent. After all, most religious institutions promote ideas that are antithetical to a therapeutic worldview: self-sacrifice, moral absolutism, enduring truths. But therapeutic and religious worldviews are not incompatible. In fact, much of Western religion now incorporates at least some elements of a therapeutic ideology. Many American Protestants, for example, now define God more like a counselor who responds to individual needs and feelings than a judge who condemns sinners and blesses the faithful.[2] The synthesis of therapy and religion is most clearly evident, however, among the many so-called New Age spiritual activities that have become popular during the past few decades.

Below I present some of my observations on the therapeutic nature of New Age religion. These observations are based on several years of research in northern New England where I interviewed more than a hundred New Age healers, including individuals who claim to manipulate unseen psychic energies, channel spirits of the dead, and explore past-life experiences. To many readers of this book, these individuals may seem rather amusing and perhaps foolish yet hardly consequential. I discovered, however, that New Age healing is more than just a fad. It represents a noteworthy, albeit extreme in some instances, manifestation of the contemporary therapeutic culture. In particular, New Age healers embrace a "therapeutic theology," which, among other things, exalts the self above all else, discourages judgment of any kind, and rejects the concept of absolute truth. In the pages that follow, I describe this theology, relying on the words of healers themselves as much as possible. I conclude this paper by examining the social conditions that promote this increasingly noteworthy part of the therapeutic culture.

The Divine Self

The self is at the center of therapeutic theology. Most notably, the self is considered to be divine yet incomplete and in need of help. Hence, healers repeatedly talk about the importance of a "connected" self, an "integrated" self, a "total" self, an "expanded" self, a "true" self, and so on. The comments of Celeste (all of the names are pseudonyms) are typical: "I desire to help people go back together, to become whole again." For Celeste, "people" includes just about everyone: "Most people today have some serious holes." Emily puts it this way: "You hear a lot of talk of wholeness these days, but the truth is that we are not really whole. We're pretty fragmented." Ellen argues that "there is no part of ourselves that we don't have, but we need connectors to get ourselves together, to get whole, to get integrated." Along these same lines, Marcus describes his therapeutic work as a "journey where we discover who we truly are, the divinity of who we truly are. And we are divine you know." Again, "we" means most of the population. Everyone needs help.

New Age healers see it as their job to clear away all of the "stuff" that prevents people recognizing the negative consequences of a broken self. Many "clients," as healers call people who pay for their services, seek help for concrete problems, often family and work related troubles. But, as Jenny argues, such troubles are considered mere symptoms of deeper problems:

> I think people are drawn to you in some sense. They do come in with particular issues they want to deal with, but a lot of times I don't even think they know fully why they're here. And they're looking for answers to life's problems. It's just that they're at a cross roads or things aren't going as well as they want them to go and they're looking for answers. As so they are gently guided to a place where they will find out who they really are.

So while clients come to healers with a range of personal problems, all of these are ultimately traced to the problems with self. Or as Debra explains: "Everybody has specific psychological challenges, and they represent certain sorts of disconnections with the self." Sally describes these disconnections as "short circuits" that cause people to "lose a sense of self." Alison speaks about individuals "leaving chucks of themselves everywhere" and Christy claims that "the self is a complicated machine and we can run into a lot of problems when our wires get crossed." Of course, practitioners of therapeutic religion are not unique in this regard. Conventional psychotherapists claim that many mental problems stem from deep-seeded conflicts with the self[3]

Fixing the self normally entails rejecting the broader social world. As Vivian declares: "The journey here is within. You know, everybody wants to run out there and fix everything. We can do those things, but we have to take the responsibility within." In fact, most of the individuals I spoke with did not have a lot to say about social institutions such as the family or community other than to describe what they considered to be the constraining effects of these institutions on personal growth. Patricia, for example, remarks: "We have been taught by society that in order to reach our humanness we must be in relationships with others. We have not yet learned how to be in a relationship with our self." Kevin is a bit more specific, claiming that American consumerism is responsible for disconnecting people from their human potential and their "real" selves: "In this culture we have grown up buying into this notion that bigger and more is better. So we have all of this clutter and stuff around, and we pay a price, by not nurturing or supporting ourselves."

Because they have not yet been corrupted by cultural influences, children are considered to be more "pure" and more in touch with their genuine selves than adults. Cathy puts it this way: "Children are so wonderful because they are so innocent. They just came from the source. You need to think about that. If you ever want to know the truth, ask a child, because they are not programmed with the bullshit. They haven't been here long enough to forget who they are." Sharon suggests that corrupting influences appear early in life: "Newborn children breathe, really breathe. And then our growing process is a process of limiting our experiences with our bodies and ourselves." This concept of the child, put forth by most of the healers I interviewed, is like Rousseau's "noble savage," uncontaminated by civilization and therefore closer to a "natural" state of humanity.

Given their assumptions about human nature, it is not surprising that healers tend to characterize their work as a kind of de-programming. Wendy, for instance, describes what she calls "the journey" as follows: "It is about peeling away of all of the facades, the masks that society makes us wear. The more we peel them back the more we get to our natural selves." Similarly, Ben speaks about "cleaning up stuff, completing yourself and coming home in some way.

"Coming home" does not mean reconnecting with the family, and it may mean just the opposite. After all, many healers describe the family as a harmful social institution that disconnects people from their true selves. Expressing a widely shared view, Angela claims: "I grew up in a dysfunctional family, but who didn't? Show me a family that's not dysfunctional." Angela and others nonetheless rarely condemn their parents for not supporting their journeys of self-discovery. As Helen notes: "We need to honor what we have from our parents. They gave us the best they had to offer. We may not like it, but it's the best they had to offer."

With their attention focused mainly on the self, healers do not find much time to participate in civic life. For example, few of the people I spoke to care much about politics, and only a handful vote in local or national elections. As Sally told me: "What's the point. These people [elected officials] don't matter. There are more important things that make the world go 'round, things that a lot of people don't realize are important. We [healers] know what they are." Melanie goes further and claims that politicians should be avoided as much as possible because they have yet to be enlightened: "Our leaders bring too much negativity to the world. They are not where they need to be spiritually."

Healers are not necessarily unaware of current events. In fact, some closely keep up with the news and offer their unique interpretations of happenings around the world. Natural disasters and wars, for instance, may be byproducts of supernatural phenomena such as "cosmic shifts" and "energy imbalances." Katherine, for example, provides this explanation of the political unrest in Haiti during the mid-1990s, when I first interviewed her: "The energies around there, in the Carribean, are all out of whack. I can feel it all the way up here. I think the universe is trying to tell us something. These things don't happen by accident, you know." Shortly after September 11, 2001, I caught up with Katherine, who also had a supernatural explanation, with a feminist twist, of the terrorist attacks on New York and Washington, D.C.: "All of those years of male spiritual energy in that part of the world finally exploded. It was just waiting to happen. We need to move away from that and embrace the divine female energy."

The Omnipotent Self

New Age healers frequently make statements such as the following: "There are no coincidences in this world." The implication is that people's lives are not entirely of their making. Stan, for example, suggests that people have a "map laid out for their journeys." Likewise, Lori claims that "the source, or God or Goddess, or whatever, has a game plan and we are part of it." Even so, healers conclude that, in the end, people control their own lives and the world around them. In the words of Sheila: "There's a blueprint for where we are headed, but there's a lot of room for choices and decisions along the way."

A closer look reveals that healers strongly embrace a "pull yourself up by your own bootstraps" social philosophy normally associated with political conservatism. This philosophy, which healers take to the extreme and hold people responsible for virtually all of their misfortunes, is at odds with the "victimization" rhetoric often associated with the therapeutic culture.[4] It is also at odds with religious traditions that require followers to surrender to a higher power.

Irene's comments nicely elucidate this philosophy: "You try to get people to see themselves as they really are instead of blaming it on something else. 'Oh, well, you know, my life is terrible because I lost my job and blah-blah-blah.' Although these issues are viable, a lot of times these are blaming techniques. You've got to make the person take a little responsibility and move forward." In a similar vein, Jane makes the following claim: "We have chosen to disconnect with who we are. We get stuck in the construct that we put ourselves in. People are enormously in control even if they are not aware of it." Linda is more succinct: "We simply show people the reality they are creating."

Irene, Jane, Linda, and others often accept responsibility for actions that most of us would consider well beyond our control. In fact, some healers suggest that people who are physically victimized, even murdered, may have "asked for it" in a psychic sense. Kim, for instance, declares: "When someone is born into a situation where they've been abused in numerous ways, yes, there's a soul choice. I do believe there's a soul choice in that." Susan endorses a similar position and thus blames herself for the incestuous actions of her father while she growing up: "You see, I chose a tough life. I chose tough lessons. So by the time my father was molesting me, I was already half out of my body. And naturally I chose this experience. My feeling about this is that it happened because I probably molested someone in a past life. And I have to find out what the fallout of that feels like."

Many healers claim to have extraordinary godlike abilities to change the world beyond their own lives. As the examples below indicate, some of their claims might seem to outside observers to be delusions of grandeur. Celeste, for example, notes that she can use her spiritual powers to revitalize an old mill town not far from where she lives:

> This town is going through some extraordinary struggles. There is a negative energy source that's pulling negativity down to the earth and holding it. It is though it's a giant dump site of negative waste. And the town is really in the pits business-wise. So what I plan to do is reverse the flow of energy and clear it.

Lucy alleges that she has similar powers and is currently working on clearing "negative spiritual energies" over Tibet:

> If you look energetically down at the earth, you'd see like a bubbling pot and a lid that's on the pot. And the lid over Tibet is this dark energy source just holding down that energy, just weighing it down. I have one of the gateways for the positive energy in my backyard and am able to communicate with the energy through the spiritual level. Much of the dark energy has been able to move off Tibet and off the planet.

In a final example, Frank boldly proclaims: "I know how to materialize and de-materialize anything. You want to create a new earth over there. I know how to do it. You want to know how to dissolve the earth into liquid. I know how to do it."

At first, I was struck by how much confidence healers have when they make such claims. I expected them to be concerned about being taken to task for much of what they have to say. But I discovered that healers live in a social world where people are reluctant to judge and condemn others for any beliefs they may hold or actions they may take, no matter how unconventional.

A Sinless Religion

Judgment, of others and oneself, is about the only behavior that New Age healers are willing to criticize.[5] Hence, according to Steven: "We are all powerful over people, places, and things, but what we do with that power is within ourselves and we need to recognize that. We should not use it to control others. We should not stand in judgment because I feel there is a purpose for all things." Likewise, Jane claims that "almost all things that you might see going as wrong are caused by self-judgment." Carol's comments reflect a similar theme: "We have been brought up in a society that places judgment on things and people, and we think we have failed. But, you know, judgment of the self is always worse." Beth too sees judgment as harmful:

People are enormously wise, and enormously in control of the situation even if they're not consciously aware of it. But we get stuck in this conscious existence where we have chosen to disconnect with who we are, at least in consciousness. And we then we get stuck in the construct that we put ourselves in, and then we get really judgmental because we don' know all of ourselves and we think that we are really limited. So we reject ourselves and things get distorted.

Healers are accordingly not fond of what they consider to be the overly moralistic nature of conventional theologies. "Christianity and all the others," Doris says, "are too dogmatic, too judgmental. They tell you what to do, how to do it, and when to do it." Emily, likewise, claims that popular religions have too many rules: "I believe that there are spiritual laws but no rules. Besides, rules were made to be broken, we have to remain flexible. Most religions don't allow that." At the same time, however, healers tend to be tolerant of those who do follow more judgmental faiths. Speaking of mainstream religion, for instance, Nancy informs me: "There's nothing wrong with it, but it is not the only way." Or as Lisa states: "I don't care if people are into 'big R religion.' Not all of it is bad and it may be good for some people. But just don't force it on me."

Of course, traditional theologies may also discourage its followers from passing judgment on others. A well-known line in the Bible, for example, reads: "Judge not, lest ye be judged."[6] And in another Biblical passage, Jesus is quoted as saying: "He that is without sin among you, let him first cast a stone."[7] But Christianity and other religions normally have omnipotent Gods who do pass judgment. Healers recognize no such Gods, and they reject the concept of sin. More generally, right and wrong are not part of the healer vocabulary. Patricia thus declares: "I am a firm believer that there are no right or wrong choices. The main thing is that we learn. And no matter what we choose, there's always lessons to learn. So it's a matter of becoming consciously aware of the opportunities and what's in it for us to learn." Along the same lines, Brad asserts: "No experience to me is wrong or bad. It's how we interpret it to be. that. And if it is good for us, that's what matters."

Consider Mary's take on marriage and monogamy:

If I see two people who are not happy in their marriage, I find out if they've been together before in another lifetime. And I find out what the connection is and whether they need to continue. That's important because I don't believe that we are meant to be monogamous fully in this lifetime. If you are with a partner and that is your intent, great. And that's beautiful, but that's for each individual to choose. So I tell people that when they've gotten what they need out a relationship, it's time to search out more and bring new beauty to other people, and to accept the ending.

Not only can the death of a relationship be a healing experience, so can the death of a person. Vivian, for example, claims: "Dying is an awfully profound occurrence, and probably can be the thing that leads to enlightenment for a person if they let themselves have it." Carla goes so far as to say that suicide is acceptable and potentially liberating: "For some people dying can be a really healing experience, and so I don't try to talk people out of dying. I just try to support people into accepting what might be wisdom and they should be open to that." Jeremy's comments to me after a close friend killed himself are also illustrative: "I don't think it was a bad thing. He did what he needed to do. I think society is too quick to judge people who choose to end their lives."

The unwillingness of healers to pass judgment extends to large-scale social phenomena as well. This became especially apparent after the September 11, 2001 terrorist attacks. Paula's reaction was common: "Yes, what they [the terrorists] did was harmful, but we can't stand in their shoes, and it doesn't do any good to put our energies in hating or punishing them. We need to work on healing." But the healing work is not, as we might anticipate, aimed at the victims or their families. Instead, as Kim explains: "We are all hurt by this and we need to focus on healing ourselves." Other healers shared this sentiment, and so did the organizers of an interfaith service at a local state university the week after the attacks. Ostensibly an event where people could come together and mourn the dead and pray for the injured, the service focused almost entirely on those in attendance. Among other things, the host of the event had audience members hold a long purple ribbon and recite phrases about "self love" and "inner healing."

The "sinless" aspect of therapeutic theology represents an extreme version of what philosophers call moral or cultural relativism. This philosophical position holds that we cannot and should not claim that the moral code of one culture is superior to another. Healers apply this philosophy at the individual level so that each person's moral code is given the status of a culture and therefore something that needs to be understood and accepted on its own terms.

Postmodern Faith

Like their position on morality, New Age healers hold that truth is in the eye of the beholder. Carrie sums it up best: "If it is true to you, that's all that matters." This position sounds somewhat like the "postmodernist" position on truth. Postmodernism, as most readers are probably aware, is an intellectual movement that gained popularity among some academics in the humanities and social sciences during the late twentieth century. Among other things, postmodernists are skeptical of modernist assumptions about the nature of reality, in particular, that there are universal truths that can be discovered through research and reason.

Because they embrace a postmodernist position on truth, healers can make assertions about the world without having to provide proof of any kind or to adhere to conventional standards of logic. Marsha, for example, insists the United States has two governments operating out of Washington, D.C. One is the federal government that we all know. The other government operates in secrecy: "The government is wise to the metaphysical and they've developed a second government that 'picks the brains' of healers. All of it is underground, and they have secret bases throughout the country. They even have a second Pentagon to work with extraterrestrials." This alleged conspiracy is widespread. Doris claims that extraterrestrials already live among us, telling me: "I'm from another planet, you know."

Some healers do make reference to scientific ideas and language when espousing their views, but few scientists would take seriously their claims about the natural world. Consider, for example, how Michelle draws on science to make a point about how the "separation" that so many people experience is an illusion:

> Part of healing is to heal the belief that there is separation. There is an appearance of separation all over the place. But science is beginning to understand that the separation is not real. Even science knows that the molecules that are now in your body will, in a very short period of time, move out of your body. Those molecules may end up in India in the body of another person. Or they may end up in Alaska in dog, or as part of a tree in the redwood forest.

Nick also turns to science, once again molecular biology, when I pose a question about the future. He claims that a "critical mass of people" will lead the way toward spiritual enlightenment:

This group of people have in their DNA, in their cellular membranes, pieces of the puzzle that it is going to take to complete their ascension from the earth, from the three-dimensional to the fifth and into higher dimensions of reality. It's happening right now and it will be complete soon. We're each having to bring these pieces together because no one of us has all of the answers. It's because of the oneness of all things. We're needing to learn to co-create and bring all of these pieces together with the loving intention to complete whatever it is we need to do at that moment in that time. It's not clear what humans will choose in that process. It has to work in a perfect harmonic balance, to be in the middle because there is a natural contraction and expansion of all things. But I am very optimistic.

Although they speak with conviction, healers seem not to care whether others accept or even understand what they have to say. And for the most part, they have little interest in convincing people that their vision of the world is the correct one. In other words, healers are not particularly evangelical. Consequently, they are skeptical of followers of traditional faiths who make universal truth claims and, in the words of Charlotte, "try to impose their truth on the rest of us." "The beauty of not being affiliated with a particular church," Sharon notes, "is that you can write your own messages, define your own truth."[8]

Healers are unwilling to question the truth claims of other healers and in that sense are rather ecumenical. Consider, for example, how Betsy describes her fellow healers: "Each of us has a different talent. It's not that one is a true healer and another is not, or that one healer is a better healer than another. They each have different skills. They each have different focus. They are supporting change is different ways, each of them." Irene goes a bit further and offers mild criticism of healers who claim to know "the absolute truth": "I must say that sometimes I get impatient with healers who have it all laid out, who have an explanation for everything. I think we do a disservice when we do that." Nick sees the larger culture as part of the problem: "We come from a society that wants to label everything and put it into neat little boxes. I don't like to label and define things in that manner. The information that I share is not black and white."

Healers can appear rather gullible, accepting ideas that many of us might consider farfetched to say the least. But their gullibility rarely leads them to blindly accept the word of God, a cult leader, or any other authoritative figure. Healers are also unlikely to be strongly committed to a particular set of ideas about how the world works, and they regularly embrace new ideas and drop those that no longer meet their needs. Truth and morality are therefore not only personal, they are subject to change, much like everything else in their lives.

Spiritual Crisis

New Age healers constantly talk about change. "Everything," Sonya insists, "is continuously evolving and unfolding." Max agrees: "The only thing that is constant is change. Just look around. It's everywhere." Most healers claim that now is especially significant period for change. "This is a special time in the universe," Jenny argues, "It is a time of transition." Or as Tammy explains: "There's chaos in so many areas of life today. So many people are in crisis, change, and transition."

Change is not always visible. "It may be very subtle, and it may affect some people more than others" says Gabriel. Nicki contends that individuals simply need to "open their eyes" and "get in touch with themselves" and then "they can see how their lives, their souls are changing." According to Wendy, many people seek stability because it is more comfortable: "Change is hard. People just don't want to deal with it. So they bury their heads in the sand. That can work for a while, and I don't blame them for doing it because dealing with any crisis is painful. And they may even be happy, or seem happy."

The theme of change comes through clearly whenever healers meet with clients. Almost without exception, everybody who visits a healer is, in the words of Mitchell, "going through a period of transition, whether they know it or not." Along these lines, Angela describes her clients as follows: "They have a lot of things going on. They are at a crisis time and aren't sure what to do." Similarly, for Jessica, clients are at a "crossroads in their lives" and come to her "sometimes in desperation looking to figure out what's going on."

For some healers, the "crisis" extends to the earth itself. Yet, unlike mainstream environmentalists, they rarely point to industrial pollution or global climate change when describing the ecological challenges facing humankind. Instead, healers offer their own unique predictions about the future of the natural world. Debra told me: "The planet is in trouble. A shift is coming, a shift in poles and what this is going to do is to cause the plant to tip on its side. I'm sure you heard about that." Stuart describes what he sees as the problem: "The earth is way out of balance. We've been abusing it for so long that one of its breaking points could be triggered any moment." Similarly, Theresa predicted that a major natural disaster might occur in the near future: "Some people know about this. It should happen in six years or less. It's coming right up." Lucy suggests this possible fate for the planet and its inhabitants: "The earth is getting frustrated with us. It might just take a giant heave and swallow us all up."

Despite their concerns about the future, few healers can be described as apocalyptic. In the end, most are optimistic, even Pollyannaish, about what lies ahead. This distinguishes healers from Christian fundamentalist preachers and "doomsday" cult leaders who claim that the end is near and that non-believers face a future of eternal damnation. Healers insist that we can and will make this world a better place, and they do not believe in heaven or hell. Helen puts it like this: "I don't believe in living your life so that you can get into heaven, which I don't think exists, at least in the way people think it exists. And I don't believe that there is a hell down there, that you're going to get punished if God doesn't like you. That blows my mind when people get into that."

Spiritual Evolution

Religions tend to be resistant to change. The major contemporary denominations, for example, embrace ideas that are thousands of years old. And although some are more open to change than others, most religions have belief systems that are meant to endure over time. Moreover, these beliefs systems normally encourage followers to become part of stable communities, where they can come together and worship immortal gods and accept moralities and truths that are not subject to change.

New Age healers, by contrast, regard stability as a barrier to spiritual enlightenment. Change, even radical change, is considered both inevitable and desirable. Stacy's declaration is illustrative: "We face lots of changes and an uncertain future, but we are in control of it. We should not fear it. We need to embrace it. It is part of our spiritual evolution." Carrie also captures a common sentiment among healers: "I love where I am today. I know what I believe and what I want. But that's how I feel today. I will change. Who knows, next time you see me you might not even recognize me." Barbara, too, told me that she is unlikely to stand still. After meeting with her, I asked if we could meet again. Barbara explained: "I'll keep your card because I never know where I'll be." I then asked her: "Are you thinking of moving?" Her response: "I'm always thinking of moving."

Healers not only seek change themselves, they encourage clients to do the same. Frank thus makes this point when describing his work: "I want to use what I know to help people the courage to move into a new relationship, move into a new job." Similarly, Dana tells her clients: "We are in a constant process of death and rebirth. As that process continues, we grow in enlightenment and understanding. Don't be afraid to give up things and people that don't work for you."

Although healers claim that everyone is capable of change, they see themselves at the forefront of a broader spiritual transformation. Again, they are not alone here. Many evangelical Christians, for example, see themselves as the vanguard of religious change. But healers are not trying to convert people to a particular belief system or particular organization. Nor do they expect to people to make any sacrifices. The only commitment people need to make is to the self.

Explaining the New Age

Of course, not everyone has become a healer and relatively few Americans embrace New Age ideas to the same degree as those people whose words appear above. Even so, therapeutic theology has expanded its presence in modern America and is found in some otherwise conventional settings. The university where I teach, for instance, offers courses on "feminist spirituality" and "earth-centered religions" which give students an opportunity to "experience different spiritual practices and healing ceremonies." My university also sponsors workshops for faculty and staff on topics such as "guided mediation" and "finding inner peace." Some American corporations provide similar programs through "employee assistance plans," or EAPs as they are commonly known. We can even find evidence of the U.S. government promoting New Age ideology. The Department of Housing and Urban Development, for example, recently provided financial support to a private organization in Washington, D.C. to implement "creative wellness" programs for public housing residents. As reported in the Washington Post last year, these programs include "healing affirmations" and the use of goddess imagery to improve "mind, body, and soul."[9]

At the same time, we should not overestimate the scope of therapeutic theology. It is expanding, but it is much more active among some people than others. Who are the most active participants in

New Age religion? We know that they are not a representative cross-section of the American population. Committed healers, including those in my study, are disproportionately white, middle-class, and female. Most are single, having been married at least once in the past, and between thirty and fifty years old. Although healers are at any one time likely to have a small group of close friends who are much like themselves, they tend to have few long-term relationships of any kind. A significant portion, in fact, have severed ties completely with their parents and siblings. Among those who are currently married, most reject the traditional model of marriage for a more egalitarian and open partnership. Few derive their economic livelihoods solely from New Age activity. Instead, New Age healers often support themselves financially through other means. Many work in the helping professions in occupations such as teaching and nursing, but like they do with romantic partners and other friends, they also change jobs and residences with some regularity.

These individual demographic characteristics reflect a distinct *social* environment in which the most active healers are likely to inhabit. This environment, or what sociologist Donald Black would call a social field, has three significant features—atomization, equality, and fluidity.[10] In other words, New Age healers spend much of their time alone, and when they do interact with others, they normally do so for short periods of time as relative equals, without being subjected to the authority of others or having authority over others. As sociologist M.P. Baumgartner notes, American suburbanites are especially likely to live in such an environment.[11]

Why is therapeutic theology so popular in this social environment? Most sociologists of religion would answer this question by focusing on the social and psychological benefits that New Age religion allegedly provides people in the modern world who are detached from traditional social institutions. The argument goes something like this: Modernity fosters individualism and a gradual weakening of traditional social institutions, including, most importantly, religion. As religion weakens, people increasingly have no overarching spiritual framework to help them make sense of the world. As a result, many individuals turn to New Age religion to fill the spiritual void left by secularization.

When addressing the New Age in these terms, social scientists often sound like cultural critics or religious leaders defending their faiths. Some years ago, for example, Daniel Bell claimed that New

Age "exotic consciousness-raising movements are not religions. They
are an illustration of the confusions of authenticity, the search in the
multiple discordant world for the authentic 'I.'"[12] More recently,
anthropologist Michael Brown, who studied spirit channeling among
middle-class Americans, criticizes New Age spiritual practices for
their failure to support "the creation of moral communities, without
which meaningful spirituality is impossible."[13]

In my view, whether New Age religion is a barrier to genuine
spiritual enlightenment is a question appropriate for theologians rather
than social scientists. After all, social science is incapable of determining the authentic spiritual needs of human beings. The critics are
right, however, in one regard. New Age religion, therapeutic theology, or whatever we call it, does not do the things that traditional
religion does. It does not bind people to a larger group or society
nor require them to submit themselves to a higher authority. Indeed,
it does just the opposite. As I describe above, New Age healers mostly
reject the social world and any kind of authority beyond the self.

Despite appearing to be the antithesis of religion, New Age ideology is similar to conventional religious ideology in one important
sociological sense: It mirrors its social environment. This means that
we can see the central features of the healers' social environment—
individuality, equality, and mobility—*directly reflected* in the content of the theology itself. Thus, it is the inner life of the *individual*
that is defined as sacred and considered to be at the center of the
spiritual universe. The *egalitarian* character of therapeutic theology
is evident in its treatment of right and wrong. As we learned earlier,
all ideas and behavior are equally valid. Change is also important.
According to therapeutic theology, everything is in a constant state
of *motion*, and people are encouraged to embrace this change by
ending old relationships and developing new ones (including, most
importantly, new relationships with the self).[14]

The isomorphic relationship between religious ideology and the
social environment, where it appears was first suggested by Emile
Durkheim over a century ago. Durkheim, as most sociologists know,
proposed that "religious representations are collective representations
that reflect collective realities."[15] My research indicates that this general relationship holds not only for older, communal religions studied
by Durkheim and those following in the Durkheimian tradition such
as Guy Swanson and Mary Douglas,[16] but also for new religions
that are emerging in our more individualistic therapeutic culture.

Notes

1. See Nolan (1999), Rice (1998), and Tucker (1999).
2. Hunter (1980) finds that even American Evangelicals, who are among the most conservative Protestants, have embraced elements of a therapeutic world view. Hunter notes that "God has been ascribed psychiatric capabilities" (Hunter, 1980:124) and is increasingly preoccupied with people's emotional and mental health. The new Evangelical God is defined as the "Great Counselor" who "understands our every need," and He is closer and more informal than the old God: "The image of the imminence of God has translated from Divine Protector to Best Friend" (Hunter, 1980:124).
3. On therapy as a response to conflicts with the self, see Black (1995:835).
4. See Sykes (1993) and Nolan (1998).
5. Brown (1997:42) notes that the spirit channels he interviewed have a similar aversion to judgment: "Attainment of holism requires a suspension of 'judgment,' a term that for them carries only negative connotations."
6. Matthew 7:1.
7. John 8:3.
8. Similarly, Brown (1997: 42-43) finds that "the sovereignty sought by most channels makes them wary of religious orthodoxy of any kind. Although a few channels have authored best-selling works that are considered authoritative in some respects, even admirers are careful to stipulate that no single message is appropriate for everyone. . . . [T]ruth is ultimately personal and situational."
9. Funding for these programs was approved in October 2000, near the end of Clinton administration. In June 2001, the Bush administration cut the funding (*Washington Post*, June 1, 2001: A29).
10. Black (1993).
11. Baumgartner (1991).
12. Bell (1977:443).
13. Brown (1997:187).
14. Horwitz (1982) finds that "individualistic" therapies such as psychoanalysis, which stress individual autonomy, appear in settings where people have few social ties. By contrast, he shows how "communal" therapies such as healing rituals in small-scale societies, which focus on social reintegration, occur in settings where people have strong social ties.
15. Durkheim (1915:22).
16. Douglas (1970), Swanson (1970, 1974).

References

Baumgartner, M.P. 1991. *The Moral Order of a Suburb*. New York, NY: Oxford University Press.
Bell, Daniel. 1977. "The Return of the Sacred? The Argument on the Future of Religion." *British Journal of Sociology* 28:419-449.
Black, Donald. 1993. The Social Structure of Right and Wrong. San Diego, CA: Academic Press.
——. 1995. "The Epistemology of Pure Sociology." *Law and Social Inquiry* 20:829-870.
Brown, Michael F. 1997. *The Channeling Zone: American Spirituality in an Anxious Age*. Cambridge, MA: Harvard University Press.
Douglas, Mary. 1970. *Natural Symbols: Explorations in Cosmology*. New York: Pantheon.
Durkheim, Emile. 1915 [1965]. *The Elementary Forms of Religious Life*. London: George Allen and Unwin Ltd.

Horwitz, Allan V. 1982. *The Social Control of Mental Illness*. San Diego, CA: Academic Press.

Hunter, James Davison. 1980. *American Evangelicalism: Conservative Religion and the Quandary of Modernity*. New Brunswick, NJ: Rutgers University Press.

Nolan, James L., Jr. 1998. *The Therapeutic State: Justifying Government at Century's End*. New York: New York University Press.

Rice, John Steadman. 1996. *A Disease of One's Own: Psychotherapy, Addiction, and the Emergence of Co-Dependency*. New Brunswick, NJ: Transaction Publishers.

Swanson, Guy E. 1970. *Religion and Regime: A Sociological Account of the Reformation*. Ann Arbor: University of Michigan Press.

——. 1974. *The Birth of the Gods: The Origin of Primitive Beliefs*. Ann Arbor: University of Michigan Press.

Sykes, Charles J. 1993. *A Nation of Victims*. New York: St. Martin's.

Tucker, James. 1999. *The Therapeutic Corporation*. New York: Oxford University Press.

Part 3

Therapeutic Culture
in Contemporary Life

9

Spoiled for Choice

Digby Anderson

A preoccupation with myself, a wish, even a need to talk about myself and my problems, a predisposition to think such problems happen to me and an aversion to assume responsibility for them, perhaps a view of myself as a victim with rights denied, and a belief that talking is the first stage to curing the problems together with a government and a range of policies which endorse such tendencies: this sort of culture is what might be termed therapeutic. And it is, of course, reasonable to ask if this is what modern society is like.

I shall take a different tack and ask whether "therapeutic" is the best term to describe modern society. No, I shan't quite get that far. All I can manage is to explain and illustrate four other ways of describing modern society that overlap with "therapeutic," and largely leave it to others to judge which pejorative—and they are all pejorative—is best. The four competing views are that: there has been a loss of virtue; that there has been a weakening of negative sanctions; that there has been a loss of manners; and that modern society has become sentimentalized. Hence my title. But as an aside, a word of caution. I have always been very struck by a paper the sociologist Harvey Sacks wrote on "Sociological Description." He pointed out that unlike the case of natural phenomena, sociological descriptions can always be added to; they are incomplete and uncompleteable. He also and elsewhere, with Harold Garfinkel noted that they failed one test of the good description; you could not remotely construct the object described from the description. Indeed all its most prominent characteristics would be missing. So how on earth one would rank competing descriptions of a society, I really don't know. Anyway here are four of them.

The Loss of Virtue

One might assert a loss of virtue in at least three senses.[1] Our behavior might be less virtuous; for instance there might be more sexual promiscuity and less courage. Second the role of virtue in the maintenance of social order (right) and social justice (left) might be less acknowledged than in previous societies. Instead other "causes" might be substituted such as social structural factors, loss of self-esteem or political factors. Third, loss of virtue might be understood as a loss of articulateness about moral matters.

To illustrate the first; Christie Davies points both to the surge of crime, self-destructive behavior and social disorder in the last seventy odd years and to the reduction in crime in Britain, in the nineteenth and early twentieth century. The experience of the last 150 years is a U curve. The Victorians inherited what they considered high rates of crime and illegitimacy (8 percent) and more than halved them. The explanation for the subsequent rise in crime and illegitimacy cannot be convincingly sought in structural factors such as poverty or poor housing since both were worse in the low crime and disorder period than they were in the high crime and disorder period. The explanation lies in a change of national moral character, an increase in the number of aggressive, self-destructive people, the reduction of conscience and self-control, and the provision of moral excuses. This anti-moral movement has been promoted by progressive intellectuals.

For the second case that virtue has declined in that its role is no longer acknowledged in the maintenance of order and justice, I merely refer to the corpus of sociology and social policy textbooks of the last half-century. For a particular instance, consider the contemporary analysis of poverty. I have argued that domestic poverty is not simply the result of low incomes but is affected by competence in saving and expenditure, by family budgeting and the management of debt. Often it is poor domestic economy or imprudence that turns temporary low income into long-term poverty. Low-income families that get out of poverty do so through a range of characterological virtues including meticulous stewardship, self-denial, and especially in the wife's case, self-sacrifice. In all the poverty literature I have encountered this virtue aspect is conspicuously and, I think deliberately avoided.

This refusal to acknowledge the role of virtue is bound up with the third loss, which also needs more specific illustration, the loss of articulateness about the virtues. Simon Green has argued that two important quasi-virtues, manliness and civility are both misunderstood today. The first is seen as male aggression, the second because it is seen as insufficiently virtuous, a mere formal accommodation of others. In fact the two go together. Manliness makes civility possible. Manliness is not maleness; women can be manly. It is the opposite of animality. It is the control of the innate, the modest cultivation and improvement of the common sum of man's attributes, the best of what is human. It is not heroic or saintly, still less priestly. Nor is civility, which does not sacrifice to others but quietly recognizes their rights and the importance of each going his own way. It is the bourgeois virtue of privacy and limited publicness. Both manliness and civility rely on a self-control and ordinariness which therapy's dislike of "repression" and fondness for the dramatic would find unacceptable.

John Gray has argued that modern society misunderstands toleration as moral neutrality. True toleration is unfashionable because it assumes human imperfectability and because it assumes evils to be tolerated and thus is inherently judgmental. It also offends against equality and implicitly elevates a basic culture embodying the virtue of toleration itself. Neutrality wants to abolish prejudice and incorrect thinking, that is, non-neutral thinking. Toleration leaves people alone and in peace. Toleration is at odds with the therapeutic ideal in its acceptance of imperfection and its judgmentalism.

It is sometimes said that modern thinking dwells on rights rather than duties. Patricia Morgan suggests that even when it talks about duty, its conception of it is unsophisticated. In marital break-up for instance if fault in admitted at all it is legalistic fault, a default of contract. Whereas what used to be pointed to was infidelity. The obligation of fidelity is unconditional. It comes with the status of being a husband or wife and is not reduced by the other's faults. It is not re-negotiable. Fidelity is perhaps the most obvious case in which we can see the old language of the virtues has been lost.

But even more offensive to therapy is the old idea of fortitude. The troubles of the modern age, natural disasters, cancer, and discrimination have this in common: they are adversities to be endured. The virtue of enduring adversity was fortitude. It has all but disap-

peared because the work ethic in which it was anchored has been replaced by a leisure, welfare, and therapy ethic and a victim culture.

We might continue our tour of old ideas by inspecting the way
honor, honesty and trust helped society to police itself, how diligence was central to the understanding of education and schooling,
how respect protected valuable institutions from unrestrained criticism, how discretion made fine distinctions between, for instance,
the deserving and undeserving. But enough has been said to show
the argument. It is that there was once a sophisticated and elaborate
list of virtues, perhaps some twenty of them, certainly not the care
and compassion duet which monopolizes the field today. These virtues were applied by an equally fine casuistry. Both the list and the
science of its application to social problems are not understood today. Insofar as the virtues were morality, we may talk of modern
society being morally illiterate, a loss of virtue in deed and in thought
and culture.

The Loss of Sanctions

There has been a little grudging acceptance over the last decade
that virtue has a role to play in both the good society and the analysis of the good society. What is much less accepted is a focus of
analysis on the sanctions that enforce virtue, especially the negative
sanctions.[2] Older societies took it for granted that men had bad,
selfish appetites and that these had to be restrained by a long menu
of sanctions including shame, stigma, conscience, ridicule, exile,
physical pain, and ostracism. The maintenance of order is painful
because these sanctions are painful but also because the fear of them
is painful. A yet further way in which these sanctions are painful is
that they work informally and thus with limited tidiness and accountability. More, they require a measure of hypocrisy and secrecy. If
you want to have the social order produced by such sanctions, the
price may be giving up at least some of other cherished values such
as openness, accountability, tidiness, self-authentication, and lack
of inhibition.

Consider ridicule. It may not have the high moral tone of shame.
But it is, in fact, one of the chief defensive weapons of an orderly
society secure in its values and assumptions. If a robust and sophisticated sense of the ridiculous were here today, the acceptance and
endorsement of deviant sub-cultures and the idiocies of political
correctness would not last a moment. A number of Britain's and

America's social ills, the growth of one-parent families, crime, AIDS, have not entered society on their own but have been accompanied by ideas and ideologies justifying, excusing, or asking for acceptance of the lifestyles that give rise to them. In this sense we may speak of dangerous ideas. The ideas were also, at the time of their introduction, outlandish. The idea that voluntary single parenthood was as valid as married family life was laughable. The idea that male sodomy was as normal as heterosexual intercourse was once dismissed outright. Indeed homosexual practice was regarded and listed as a perversion.

There is, then, a process by which ideas once outlandish and the behaviors they justify become accepted. The ideas and behaviors— and the social problems associated with them—spread and become mainstream. That process depends on the idea of debate, the modern notion that all ideas, however outlandish, have a right to be debated and that the debate should be conducted on grounds of the consequences of the behavior associated with them. For instance, should a really outlandish idea and behavior such as necrophilia be proposed for toleration it would typically be debated along the lines of who was hurt by the practice, were innocent others damaged, were there dangers to public health, or the un-wisdom of using law to hound private behavior. In short, the willingness to debate everything and the consequentialist and utilitarian rules by which such debates are conducted could find little reason for not permitting something as outlandish as necrophilia.

Older societies would not have let necrophilia get as far as debate. They would have ridiculed it, dismissed it out of hand. This capacity to ridicule and dismiss protected them better than rational debate protects modern society. These older societies had a more complex topography in which some ideas remained in the shadows, others were tolerated in the mainstream, and yet others were protected as public doctrine. They also had a respect for traditional learning and a readiness to practice its short-cut application in what are now denigrated as prejudices. If modern society is to be protected from outlandish ideas and behavior, and all the problems they bring, it must recover its confidence to rule ideas out of court, its acceptance of the necessity of prejudice, and its sense of proportion and the humor which depends on it: the sense of the ridiculous.

Or consider public punishment: If modern societies are unwilling to use the informal sanctions, such as ridicule, which served former societies so well, they are similarly unwilling to use the more formal punishments associated with those societies. There is an absolute confusion among contemporary penologists about what to do with criminals. This is not because they have lots of competing suggestions; quite the reverse. No new suggestions have emerged since the extended use of prison in the nineteenth century. Indeed, today's penologists effectively rule out the wide range of punishments their forebears could choose from, punishments which inflicted physical pain, punishments which removed the criminal from the community geographically (banishment) or socially (ostracism), punishments which left a stigma or mark (branding), punishments which mobilized public scorn (pillory, stocks, the dunce's cap in the corner), and especially punishments in public: what separates many of these from today's punishment is that these were morally based while today the justifications for punishment are political. Even "treatment," now largely abandoned, was a moral justification.

Graeme Newman has suggested why punishment has been demoralized. Because of two forces: first, the intrusion of science into social questions-social science that has driven out value in the pursuit of an amoral "objectivity." Science replaces value with probability. It, unlike faith, is built on uncertainty. In the end, without value and morality, penology reaches a stage where it can see nothing to distinguish the criminal from the law abiding; nothing in his character, except his having been convicted as criminal. The other force is socialism, or rather socialism re-applied from classes to other groups and individuals. This too collapses distinctions between, say, criminals and law abiders in the name of equality. The murderer is no different from you and me except in his circumstances. But, just as morality needs punishment, so punishment needs morality. A moral punishment, unlike a utilitarian punishment, involves criminal and punisher and society taking responsibility respectively for the criminal act and the punishment. This sort of punishment is the very opposite of prison, which hides punishment away. It is public at least in the sense that it is seen to be done, publicly willed, and taken responsibility for. It involves all parties recognizing the crime and punishment for what they are.

Then consider ostracism and stigma. Rabbi Daniel Lapin has analyzed the painful process for building authority and civilized order. Faced with soaring illegitimacy rates, rising violent crime, obscenity, and public disorder, both social scientists and lay people ask what the cause is. It is the wrong question. These things, a state of disorganization and degradation, entropy, are natural. Ask instead what miracle it was that once kept society safe, prosperous, well mannered, and stable. For this is not a natural state at all. And since it is not a natural state, ask what special intelligence or energy initiated and maintained it. What did we do to produce such a state out of chaos? The stable, safe, and courteous society had a whole armory for maintaining itself, for fighting entropy. As the word suggests they were weapons. They hurt. Order depended on being willing to inflict pain. And not only physical pain but shame, disgrace, ostracism, and stigma. It was prepared too to inflict them on children, for example on illegitimate children.

There was a justification for this readiness to hurt in the cause of order. In the case of children, "civilization depends upon maintaining a community of the generations." Everything we do affects the generations to come, and either honors or dishonors our ancestors.... We know that our positive achievements and our monetary success benefit our children. Why should we expect that our sins will not harm them?' Moreover, the stigma is a deterrent weapon. When the stigma of illegitimacy was stronger, fewer suffered it for there were fewer illegitimate births.

Ostracism need not always be harsh. Social sanctions can be applied in varying degrees of intensity. Banishment is ostracism. So is the exclusion of a sloppy dresser from a prestigious business luncheon. The allocation of offices, desks, perks, and promotions, who is consulted about what, are testimony to the fine workings of sanctions in the corporation.

Last and most significant for the therapeutic ideal, consider repression and inhibition. For over half a century repression has been thought to be damaging. In popular culture men and women are depicted as having needs, the denial of which is dangerous. The popular phrases are coming to terms with oneself, coming out, being happy with oneself, being true to oneself. Denying and blocking such needs is unhealthy. Yet, as Joseph Rychlak has argued, repression, under its nineteenth century name, self-control, was once thought a good thing. It was once thought not only desirable, but necessary for social order. This change in reputation has come about largely from the influence of two psychological schools, Freudianism and behaviorism.

Both base themselves on a Newtonian view of science, the behaviorists enthusiastically, Freud in response to the urgings of his colleagues and more ambivalently. This view of science defines cause, and therefore the explanations that science may seek, in ways which do not admit of human agency, intention, or purpose. They thus demoralize action. Freudianism therefore presents individuals as being repressed or blocked by internal dynamics over which they have little understanding or control. Behaviorism presents the individual as being controlled by external stimuli. Yet a considered look at the Freudian thinking on repression shows a role for understanding and purpose is possible and hence an admission of responsibility. "What we call 'character' [is not just the result of internal or external forces but] is germinated in the graceful acceptance of life's negative reinforcements, as well as overcoming them though personal effort. [Human] agents also reap the benefits of praise and satisfaction when decisions are successful. Finally, agents know that for an orderly and satisfying personal life, as well as promoting tranquillity in social affairs, a degree of self-suppression (conscious 'repression') is not only inevitable but highly desirable."

The Rise of Sentimentality

A third focus is through the concept of sentimentality.[3] There is an old dispute about whether ideas or interests determine the state of a society. But what if it were not an idea or an interest but a feeling? Sentimentality is a feeling, or rather the distortion of a feeling, deep in the psyche of western civilization. And this same corruption of feeling is the key to threats to religion and morals, to music and literature, to the relief of pain and suffering by medicine and charity and to the sensible conservation of the earth. A sentimentalism can capture an entire nation. Writing about the funeral of Diana, Princess of Wales, Diana, childlike in her self-centeredness, Professor Anthony O'Hear finds that funeral the very definition of sentimentality, the elevation of feelings, image, spontaneity over reason, reality and restraint.

In a recent analysis of sentimentality, the authors found the sentimentalist refusing sound judgement in medicine, chasing miracle cures, defying cancers, indulging himself in revelatory counseling. He is there in the medical commentator undermining the necessity for doctors to make judgements. He is a peddler of utopias. The sentimental environmentalist is determined that his utopia shall not be prevented by equivocal or even hostile scientific evidence, or by cost. The sentimentalist bestrides gigantic social engineering projects such as affirmative action impatient that numerical quotas of income be met and contemptuous of the discrepant natures of those he regards as a homogeneous group. Sentimentality is in music, literature, and food. In modern music the sentimentalist indulges himself with no sense of humor. In the modern novel he fakes feelings and he even fakes having no feelings. At the dinner table he disguises his childish whims as he rejects good food under modish "isms." All through, he is a poseur affecting compassion and emotion to the point of self-deception. He conjures illusions in front of the looking glass. His aim is not understanding, sociability, truth, social betterment or even genuine feeling, though that is its superficial appearance. It is self-image.

When sentimentalists have their way with an education policy or a welfare policy, with literature or music, with religion and even with pleasures such as eating and drinking, they drain them of substance, cut them off from reality and leave only a corpse pleasantly scented but rotting within.

Let's consider just one domain, health. Bruce Charlton points to the threat posed by sentimentality to good medical practice. When people are ill, getting old or dying, there are obvious temptations for them, their doctors and their friends to indulge in wishful thinking and related forms of sentimentality. If the temptation is given in to, the consequences can be serious for the simple reason that sickness and death are realities of a very prominent sort: they are biological realities. To deny biological facts in medicine is to undermine the practice of medicine. Spectators of disease, viewers watching distant famine victims on television can be excused their indulgence in a little sentimental sympathy. It may even be natural to exercise this sympathy. But the doctor is not a passive spectator. He is the one who has the power to help or harm.

Here sentimentality is a corruption of good medical practice, since it evades the facts. Patients are tempted to sentimental reactions, one of which may be to deny a diagnosis of, say, cancer. This reaction masquerades as courage. But denial is not the same as courage. Denial turns away from the facts. Courage faces them. Plucky resistance and the refusal to despair are all well and good, but willful self-deception is not. The result of denial has been a sentimental culture in which it is asserted that every health problem must have a cure if only we fight hard enough or spend lavishly enough. Such evasion plays havoc with any attempt to ration scarce money and resources sensibly. Quack doctors and journalists who praise denial as courage thereby incite denial and are engaged in ethically questionable behavior. Denial of medical facts becomes especially dangerous when it is collective. It creates pressure to join with other relatives or friends in forms of denial, which create a histrionic world of pretence.

Green philosophies of health are another fertile source of sentimental nonsense. For nature is not harmonious: it is a continuous state of trench warfare. The idea that health is natural and sickness unnatural is mistaken. Belief in natural cures arises out of sentimentality. Disease and death are natural. Fringe medicine is a triumph of public relations over scientific and rational evidence. It is a form of wishful thinking. People would like fringe medicine to be true in the way they would like *The Wind in the Willows* to be true: because it's nice. When there is a serious breakdown in health, people usually abandon their sentimental attachment to fringe medicine and return to orthodox practice, which may at least be able to do something. Vulnerable sick people and those sentimentally prevented from facing harsh medical truths easily become the prey of con artists and cranks.

Sentimentality ousts a stoicism necessary where disease is concerned By contrast, stoicism is a neglected virtue. People used to have an unfussy attitude towards their health, but the media culture has encouraged self-pampering until this has become endemic. This is especially revealed in the phony occupations of psychotherapy and counseling. Psychotherapists and counselors are self-selected and in effectiveness worse than amateurs. Therapists are required first to undergo therapy: this is in order that they may be effectively brainwashed into the superstitions and lingo of the cult. But friendship cannot be acquired through a technique. Professional help is a sentimental concept: it is a private shirking of responsibility combined with a public display of cheap compassion. Confessional psychotherapy has no proven effectiveness. What it provides is an excuse for indulgent personal reverie. Moreover, professional counseling undermines the truly caring network of family and friends. Confessional counseling damages both individuals and society.

Sentimentality in medicine undermines the need to make tough decisions. It is the opposite of proper medical practice. It is a cloak for evasive waffle and covert exploitation. Realism in medicine is the antidote to sentimentality.

The Loss of Manners

The loss of manners resembles the loss of virtue in several ways and differs from it in one very important way.[4] The loss could be, as with virtue, a loss not only of behavior but vocabulary. We may be worse mannered and we may no longer understand the role of manners very well. However, one reason manners are dismissed by some today is that, unlike virtue, they are seen as small matters or surface phenomena, mere outward show, form. In fact bad manners, though often individually "trivial" may together make a neighborhood unlivable in and may coarsen and degrade public space and life. Some manners are the outward manifestation of internal morals. Even when they are not, when they are simply mechanical, it may be that the lack of trivial manners causes more social damage and unhappiness than the lack of heroic morals. This is difficult for contemporary wisdom to accept. Long before the 1960s, the triviality of manners had been derided by those who prided themselves on thinking big. There was only one term of abuse stronger than bourgeois and that was petit-bourgeois with its connotations, in English use, of the trite and unimaginative. The decadent 1890s, Freud (or rather his disciples), Bloomsbury, the Marxists, and the flowering of them all in the 1960s, could at least agree on this: their contempt for little men and their mindless daily habits, their manners. Some of them did not have overmuch time for morals either, but at least morals were about big things.

In the 1960s, manners were condemned for being artificial as opposed to natural, restrictive as opposed to liberating, habitual as opposed to thoughtful or critical, mechanical as opposed to existentially committed, hierarchical as opposed to open or equal, hypocritical as opposed to genuine or straightforward, traditional as opposed to progressive. There were counter voices. Perhaps surprisingly, one of the strongest came from within social science and reached a peak in those same 1960s. Anthropologists, in particular, brought massive evidence of the role of the daily, repeated, tiny acts of culture in maintaining social order. Sociologists started to study much smaller fragments of social interaction, conversations, dress, body language, in order to show how order was achieved from second to second. It did not last. Or rather it had little impact on the wider understanding of society. The analysts of ritual, gesture and conversation were dismissed as irrelevant: irrelevant to the major themes of class struggle,

anti-racism and the new revolution against bourgeois cultural hegemony. In an age when not to be political was to be politically reaction-
ary, these micro social scientists were not joining the barricades. What
had body language to do with liberating the poor?

Perhaps quite a lot. That is what we can now see. A society that
takes its manners seriously may not change the big aspects of any
one group of people: it may not make the poor rich. But it does
make society easier and better for everyone. And if that sounds too
strong, consider the opposite. A society which does not value the
quality of the millions of daily acts that happen between its members, but only the grand themes of policies and politics, will leave all
its members worse off in their daily lives.

Manners were not examined and argued against in the 1960s.
There was no sustained attempt to improve manners by weeding out
the silly or outdated and retaining the sensible. They were dismissed
as manners because they were manners. Life was to be individual
and experimental, constructed with the dawn of each new day to fit
the newly pondered needs of authentic self-expression. The onslaught
did not, of course, mean that manners obediently disappeared. If
they are indeed essential for orderly society, then their disappearance would mean not just the coarseness of current Britain and
America, but chaos. We still stick by rules of common language and
gesture. How could we do otherwise and survive as a society?

Indeed, one could argue that most manners have survived. But
not all, and the ones which have do not exert the same force. With
manners, small shifts can have enormous consequences. This is
largely because manners are to do with predictability. Citizens who
can count on manners can feel secure and at ease. Once familiarly
safe territory has been violated, once safe times to go here or there,
to do this or that with predictable consequences, have been cast into
doubt or thrown into confusion, then citizens become apprehensive,
circumspect, nervous or afraid. They have to think about making
journeys, saying things, doing things they never thought about before. The criminologists are correct in that most people do not suffer
grievous assault or rape. But the truth is that one does not have to
reach for the extremity of rape to demonstrate the roughness on the
streets, or to total family collapse to show the day-to-day rudeness
of young to older people. Citizens who have never been raped or
robbed are still treated daily to countless small incidents which make
them fearful.

The crisis in order is a crisis in manners. Respectable, middle-class people going about their normal routines in the street, the train station, the shop or the park, increasingly feel that these are not their streets, stations and parks, but occupied territory. Or just territory that may be hostile, where you have to look around, hold your bag, or be out of by dusk. Small inconveniences are, because frequent, the largest aspect of civic breakdown So, the actual incidence of crime is not the sole, nor perhaps even the principal element of the sense of collapse of civic order which many feel. Despite the mammoth public expenditure on local government, streets strewn with litter help to foster the impression that there is a physical decay in our towns and cities. The fear of an elderly and frail person living alone that neighbors cannot be relied upon to summon help in the event of an accident is all too understandable at a time when many inhabitants of cities can hardly name another individual in their neighborhood. And the breakdown of relationships is clearly indicated by the spectacle of supposedly sophisticated societies which require legal agreements between couples during progressive stages of courtship, allow children to divorce their parents, and require cumbersome legislation to divide in public places those who smoke from those who do not.

This small thing, manners, is no small thing. Without the expectation of fairly predictable responses when dealing with fellow-citizens, incomprehension, inarticulateness and offence quickly characterize discourse. Businessmen (who might carefully study the customs of their counterparts in foreign countries) without basic skills of courtesy may find that they cannot communicate with those with whom they wish to do business at home. Banks and shops find that their customers are reluctant to deal with incompetent and impertinent staff; people of different generations find that they cannot talk together easily. The rediscovery and habitual adoption of manners one solution to these large-scale problems Manners, suggest the authors of the book, oil the wheels when these different groups interact. They provide a shared and understood pattern of behavior in social intercourse, and allow, through a recognition of the differences which might otherwise separate individuals, spontaneous and productive exchanges.

Part of the strength of manners is precisely the informality and flexibility that they allow when they are automatic, instinctive and ingrained. Simply, they make everything very much easier.

Prejudice can, or course, be an unpleasant and dangerous thing. But the useful prejudices which manners instill allow a stability and spontaneity in discourse and encounters between people who may be from different or unequal backgrounds or, indeed, competing interests. This easiness is precisely what is missing from the cumbersome codes of behavior, which have sprung up in an attempt to replace manners. Only when courteous behavior is as ingrained as manners can be, when the process of opening doors, deferring to the infirm or elderly, remembering to say please and thank you is automatic, unthinking, is there the possibility of ease of this sort in encounters between people. The legalistic codes of political correctness and charters drawn up by civil servants and governments can never supply the same instinctive readiness.

But the correctness codes are a useful piece of evidence in the manners debate. What they do is to admit that some regulation of, for example, relationships between men and women, is needed. Several of the targets of PC codes are activities in which one person's pleasure may be another's pain. Two are sex-relations and smoking. The codes give guidance on how to behave. So did manners. Mannerly societies recognize that their members will seek pleasure and that in so doing they may hurt others. They also realize that general injunctions not to hurt others are insufficient. So, in such societies manners are evolved which govern courting habits or the relations between smokers and non-smokers. Another example is with the consumption of alcohol. Essentially manners are ways of making potentially harmful pleasures and even vices, harmless or less harmful. They do this not only by setting controls of time and place and sequence but by socializing young people into such behavior. Sensible societies do not, for instance, forbid young people to drink alcohol until they are adults but socialize them into drinking from an early age. They also acquire social institutions for drinking, such as pubs, which themselves have their own codes that informally regulate drinking. The achievement of manners is to control behavior without the use of law or government and through custom and informal community sanctions. In contrast with the evolving, sophisticated control by manners, control by political correctness committee is clumsy and, because it often involves explicit legalistic rules and monitoring, oppressive.

It has been argued that manners are almost the epitome of repression and inauthenticity, two concepts that earned the scorn of progressive academics and politicians, especially in the 1960s. In the rush for self-expression, many of the manners that prevented unchecked gratification and allowed easy social relations were abandoned. Manners were also spurned as relics of an outmoded class system, rather than seen as the means by which people of different backgrounds could meet within a code of behavior based on shared values. The behavior of and between gentlemen and ladies was an early target of radical feminists, those who were keen to remove not only inequality, but all realistic distinctions between the sexes. Some of these distinctions were indeed small. But the assault on the manners of the sexes has gone far beyond castigating what was once thought solicitous—offering a bus seat to a lady—as patronizing. Crusading against patriarchy and Eurocentrism and in the name of feminism and multi-culturalism, progressives have effectively voted to annihilate the understanding of what it is to be a man or a woman, especially a gentleman or a lady in everyday life. The manners, the codes, the rules once covered everything.

They gave men and women ways to behave, virtues and appearances to take on, ways of relating to each other, conduct for this, that and every occasion. That understanding was built up over years. It was wisdom. It is now derided and in its place are put slogans, charters, and politically initiated directives on behavior. Manners have always had to change in history. What is happening now is not gradual organic change but ideologically driven political correctness, much of it based on a poor understanding of past sex role manners.

Characterizing Modern Society

What are the relations between these four ways of characterizing modern society and between the four of them and the therapeutic characterization? For the most part I leave that to the reader. As mentioned at the outset, I know of no methodology to rate descriptions. But a few comments might be made. Clearly "virtue" has some claim to include all the others. Sanctions are a way of enforcing or promoting virtue. Sentimentalization is a way virtue is corrupted. Manners are virtues ritualized and externalized. The therapeutic ideal can be seen as the result of the loss of virtue and as a partial replacement of it, even as one of the developments responsible for the loss. But it is only one of them.

Clearly too the loss of virtue, manners and sanctions and the rise of sentimentality and therapy have something to do with the passing or rejection of a traditional order. Curiously the replacement is not a simply a rational order. The enlightenment project appeals to reason but has also spawned sentimentality and the therapeutic cult, not to mention several political "religions."

Yet another way to link our five views might be to ask what concept of man, what anthropology lies behind them?

Finally, perhaps we should resist the temptation to systematize the five views and the social processes they describe into one. For they seem bigger left as five. And they ought to seem big. For what we have lost in modern society is no one thing but a wealth of understanding and civilization. We need more pejoratives not fewer.

Notes

1. The references in this section are all to chapters by the authors cited in *The Loss of Virtue: Social Disorder and Moral Confusion in Britain and America*, edited by Digby Anderson, The Social Affairs Unit & National Review, 1992.
2. The references in this section are to *This Will Hurt: The Restoration of Virtue and Civic Order*, edited by Digby Anderson, The Social Affairs Unit and National Review, 1995.
3. The references in this section are to *Faking It: The Sentimentalisation of Modern Society*, edited by Digby Anderson, The Social Affairs Unit/Penguin Books, 1998.
4. The references in this section are to *Gentility Recalled: Mere Manners and the Making of Social Order*, edited by Digby Anderson, 1996.

10

Rules for Realness: Child Adoption in a Therapeutic Culture

Ellen Herman

During the twentieth century, policies and practices related to child adoption changed enormously in the United States. Even as one adoption revolution reversed the most cherished achievements of the last, new theories and approaches were invariably announced with great fanfare and high hopes that scientific research, policy innovation, and humanitarian progress were synonymous. Few revolutions have been more consequential and less considered in the history of modern adoption than the novel association of helping professionals and practices with the process of making families and then managing them once "biological strangers" are turned into kin.[1] When, how, and why did the exchange of children–an ancient transaction traditionally tied to concerns about property and charity— become a process requiring intensive scrutiny, information management, psychological sensitivity, and instruction and guidance by professionals? What have been the consequences of making adoption into a therapeutic operation, as well as a legal and social one?

This chapter consists of two parts. The first considers an issue that has preoccupied students of therapeutic culture and is also central to adoption's modern history: authenticity. The second offers examples of how two particular authenticity problems in adoption–telling children about their adoptive status and probing the motivations of infertile couples–were addressed. The documentary basis for this survey consists of a large number of child placement manuals and how-to books, published between 1915 and 1965, as well as unpublished materials such as case records and agency minutes.

It was during this period that adoption got a psychology of its own, a psychology taken for granted in the adoption world today. Therapeutic ideals and practices in adoption are traceable to historical developments early in the twentieth century, including the female reform tradition, the movement from child welfare to child science, the popularization of Freudian ideas, and the professionalization of human understanding and aid (in social work especially) during the first half of the twentieth century. But "therapeutic adoption" was especially prominent and concentrated in the period around mid-century, a chronology that corresponds to the emergence and consolidation of therapeutic culture in general.

Like other examples of therapeutic culture, the case of adoption provides an opportunity to document the shifting meaning of authenticity and explore the many practices that have been invented and reinvented to stabilize, manufacture, and ensure its survival in difficult modern and post-modern times. Therapeutic practices proliferated with the disenchantment of the world famously described by Max Weber, and scholars have explored their historical correlation with a voracious culture of consumption and increasingly global capitalism that draws more and more experience into the nexus of market relations. Whatever its causes and consequences, therapeutic culture has inspired vigilant efforts to recapture authenticity, the sense of *being, becoming, and experiencing the really real.*

Authenticity Problems and Therapeutic Solutions

In adoption, the therapeutic revolution aimed to confer authenticity on a type of kinship widely understood as artificial and second-rate. The struggle to make adoptive kinship look and feel as real as the "real thing" has been a virtual obsession in law, language, and literary representation as well as in the social practices that make families up. This is perfectly understandable in a society where the dominant measure of realness in family life is blood, as in "blood is thicker than water." Because adoption is a purely social relationship created by law, lacking the biogenetic premise that underlies American kinship ideology, it has been consistently viewed as more risky (because less real) than either kinship cemented by nature alone (which even law cannot eradicate) or kinship defined at once by nature *and* law. To the extent that modern American culture has defined realness in kinship as a product of blood-based identities and ascribed affiliations, adoption illustrates the difficulties of all forms of voluntary belonging. The very acts of planning and consent that make adoption exemplary also serve to delegitimate it. Solidarities founded on social choices are construed as flimsy and superficial in comparison with fixed and unchosen natural givens. This is curious in a liberal culture whose core values include individualism, freedom, and choice.

Adoption has not come "naturally." The cultural positioning of adoption as artificial kinship has galvanized developments aimed as securing a more complete authenticity for its disadvantaged participants. These have taken the form of policies governing the eligibility, emotional profiles, demographic characteristics, and behaviors of all the parties to adoption. Such authenticity quests have relied on what we might call "rules for realness."

Over the past century, adoption's rules for realness have shifted dramatically, moving from a dominant emphasis on the *authenticity of similarity*—prevalent before the 1960s—toward a new interest in the *authenticity of difference*. Between World War I and the late 1960s, most adoption reforms stressed wholesale kinship replacement, an ideal in which authenticity was achieved through substitution and simulation of a nuclear family made biogenetically. Pluralism may have been acceptable in the public square of social life during this era, but it had few backers in the realm of private experience. Early advocates of difference in family life included New York jurist Justine Wise Polier, novelist Pearl S. Buck, and Helen Doss, whose popular memoir, *The Family Nobody Wanted* (1954), described a large family forged transracially and transnationally at the dawn of the Cold War. H. David Kirk, in *Shared Fate* (1964), was the first scholar to consider adoption as a serious theoretical issue in the sociologies of family and mental health. All of these individuals are conspicuous today as dissidents who questioned the authenticity of similarity. They were prophetic, but they departed from majority opinion at the time.

Before the 1960s, *matching* summarized the dominant rule for realness. This way of thinking about authenticity in kinship—as a byproduct of similar appearances—governed the concrete steps of family formation. Matching required that adopters be married heterosexuals who looked, felt, and behaved as if they had conceived, by themselves, children born to others. The consensus among professionals that children should be told about their adoptions nevertheless pointed to widespread awareness that adoption was a different way to make a family. Matching did not preclude sensitivity to adoption's uniqueness; excruciating awareness that adoption was artificial was precisely what made it so important to fit families together carefully. Nor did matching refer to bodily characteristics alone. Great effort was devoted to pairing children with parents whose intellects, temperaments, and personalities would be as similar as their bodies. Artifice was the paradoxical key to an authenticity based on similarity.

Since 1970, new rules for realness have emerged. Demands to open sealed adoption records, moves toward open adoption, searches and reunions, and the increasing visibility of transracial and transnational placements have contested, if not dislodged, the codes of matching and secrecy that previously governed adoption. According to this view, it is precisely the rejection of matching that promotes authenticity. Compared to the stipulation that children and adults match according to superficial appearance is the more profound love that bonds family members across borders of difference. (Some critics of matching suggest that adoption across racial, ethnic, and national lines will benefit the nation as well as its children and families by advancing diversity and civil rights where they may count most: at home [Kennedy 2003] .) Champions of difference in adoption allege that matching was a cruel hoax, incompatible with authenticity. The realness that difference promises, on the other hand, is the real thing. Such changes may tell us as much about tectonic movements in the deep structures of cultural meaning as they do about the history of adoption and family life.

Rules for realness that addressed the authenticity problem therapeutically were evident in child placement manuals and how-to books between 1915 and 1965. These materials were often addressed to professional audiences, especially social workers involved in day-to-day adoption placements. After the mid-1930s, they also reached participants in adoption, especially prospective adopters. This literature, along with case material drawn from agency files, illustrates how the adoption process itself was transformed into an operation that advanced the most significant ideals of therapeutic culture: self-scrutiny, emotional training, and the commitment to lifelong management of selfhood and social relationships.

Systematic procedures, detailed investigations, and expert clinical control from start to finish were the hallmarks of therapeutic family formation. Although agency professionals never gained a legal monopoly over the adoption process, and commercial and senti-mental adoption persisted, many of the safeguards and standards professionals favored were incorporated into state adoption laws between 1917 and mid-century (Herman 2002). These included man-datory pre-placement social investigations, post-placement supervi-sory periods of six to twelve months, confidentiality of court pro-ceedings and records related to adoption, and movement toward equalizing inheritance rights. During this era, many social workers, psychologists, and physicians advanced therapeutic approaches to family life–and to life in general. By the early 1970s, only 21 per-cent of all non-relative adoptions were privately arranged. This was the high point of professional authority in adoption. It was also the century-long numerical high point, when adoptions peaked at around 175,000 annually. The total number of adoptions has been declin-ing ever since (Stolley 1993).

Therapeutic adoption aimed, above all, to be a helping operation in which skilled professional mediators offered an indispensable asset: "interpretation." Interpretation summarized the psychological work required of all adoption participants and marked the transfor-mation of adoption into a full-fledged subject of casework and coun-seling. Even during the period when the matching paradigm domi-nated, professional emphasis on interpretation drew meaningful at-tention to the uniqueness of adoptive family formation by endowing the steps in adoption with layers of complex, often unconscious, emotional meaning that individuals did not appreciate, and certainly could not adequately negotiate, by themselves. Insight and guid-ance by experts trained in the intricacies of human motivation and behavior were just as necessary to successful adoption as meticu-lous documentation and up-to-date knowledge of state laws. Match-ing was no crude mechanical blueprint that paired like with like on the basis of superficial characteristics alone, writers took pains to point out. Making a real family was an act of the most delicate psy-chological engineering imaginable. Therapeutic skill and exper-tise were crucial during all phases of the adoption process: investi-gating children and adults, bringing together those who had the po-tential to make authentic families and rejecting those who did not, overseeing the probationary period during which (it was hoped) the potential for authenticity was realized.

So central did this therapeutic vision of adoption become over time that key legal and social operations involved in family formation were eventually discussed in terms of their emotional meaning. Termination of parental rights, placement, guardianship transfers, and adoption decrees mattered largely because of what they signified for children's sense of secure belonging and psychological development, according to *Beyond the Best Interests of the Child*, a 1973 book that marked a profound change in legal practices surrounding child placement. The challenge facing the law was to "assure for each child a chance to be a member of a family where he feels wanted and where he will have the opportunity, on a continuing basis, not only to receive and return affection, but also to express anger and to learn to manage his aggression," according to its authors (Goldstein, Freud, and Solnit 1973: 5-6). Because courtroom decisions clearly influenced human development, they argued, the ingredients of children's psychological welfare (rather than abstractions like justice or rights) should be primary legal considerations. This perspective served to prioritize continuity of nurture (preservation of the relationship to the "psychological parent"), speedy and permanent decisions, and humility about what the law itself could accomplish for children (which was not very much). In adoption as well as other decisions involving placement conflicts, therapeutic logic subordinated law to psychology.

Making families the therapeutic way involved even more than accumulating the knowledge to make families up well rather than poorly. Adoption was a growing and learning experience in itself, in which the ability of participants to demonstrate that they were growing and learning indicated the success of the process as well as the probable quality of the product. The cultivation of constructive self-consciousness was key to therapeutic adoption, and it became a credible indication of readiness for family life, whereas hostility to inspection was judged quite harshly. From early in the century, professionals warned that resistance to being investigated was an ominous sign. Would-be adopters who did not cooperate with professionals were likely to make poor parents. In contrast, willingness to ask for and use help during the course of the adoption process was among the best predictors of successful outcomes. By the late 1950s, therapeutic cooperation had itself become a quasi-legal requirement. According to the Child Welfare League of America's landmark *Standards for Adoption Service* (1958), applicants who displayed openness to personal growth "indicate their flexibility and adaptability to adoptive parenthood" (CWLA 1958: 32).

The relationship between such displays of therapeutic maturity and the growing ranks of middle-class, managerial occupations during the first half of the century is obvious. Adoption practices sustained class, race, and ethnic stratification, and religious matching had long been legally stipulated in many jurisdictions. The fact that healthy white infants were in highest demand made them the likeliest subjects of therapeutic adoption. Standards of all kinds were eventually relaxed for older, non-white, and other hard-to-place children that professional couples seldom wanted: income and insurance requirements, requirements that mothers not work, requirements that children be given bedrooms of their own, etc. After 1945, programs were organized to promote the adoption of Negro, Puerto Rican, American Indian, Oriental, and mixed-race children, as they were called at the time. The National Urban League's Foster Care and Adoptions Project, and Adopt-A-Child, the first nationally coordinated efforts to deliver adoption services to children of color, identified a host of therapeutic practices as major obstacles to recruiting minority adoptive parents. Therapeutic probing was equated with systematic prejudice against non-white, non-elite applicants. Why wouldn't such applicants avoid racist agencies that made them think they had to be rich (as well as white) to adopt?

As for the many middle- and upper-class white couples who sought assurances about children's health and educational potential, therapeutic professionals allayed anxieties about the impoverished origins of many children available for adoption by conducting detailed background studies and administering batteries of mental and physical tests (Herman 2001). For would-be adopters, however, becoming active therapeutic partners was one of the few steps they could take themselves. "You may well feel that you have experienced just about the ultimate in a complete goldfish bowl exposure of your life and private affairs," wrote Ernest and Frances Cady sympathetically in 1956. "But you may rest assured that a happy and successful adoption makes it all worthwhile" (Cady and Cady 1956: 46). "Screening yourselves as an agency would screen you" is a smart thing to do before applying for a child, Louise Raymond assured readers in a chapter, "What You Should Know About Yourselves," designed to help applicants succeed in getting the children they wanted (Raymond 1955: 8). The ability to relax and move beyond anger at having to prove one's parental fitness was a mark of emotional maturity, according to Raymond, whereas persistent discomfort betrayed "the deepest-rooted resentment of all–the fact that you and your husband *can't* have your biological children, through no fault of your own" (Raymond 1958: 8, emphasis in original).

Although birth parents and adopters were uncomfortably dependent upon mediators for help in surrendering or acquiring children, no one entered into adoptive kinship accidentally. Professionals turned this act of volition into a sign of character strength. In 1943, Dorothy Hutchinson, a leading social work educator, wrote "There is no special virtue in loving one's own child; such love is taken for granted. However, to love someone else's child requires really uncommon qualities of heart and mind" (Hutchinson 1943: 133). People who considered adopting "are people of more than ordinary emotional depth, greater than common seriousness in their relation to life and to each other, more than usual conscientiousness," added Frances Lockridge and Sophie van Senden Theis in 1947. "They are able, consciously, to examine their own feelings" (Lockridge and Theis 1947: 32-33).

One of the great paradoxes of therapeutic adoption is that the powerful emphasis on the interpretation of invisible dynamics in family formation came to prominence at the same time as the matching paradigm, which credited appearances as ultimately meaningful indicators of love and belonging. This suggests that competing recipes for authenticity in kinship coexisted in adoption practice and philosophy. While realness resided in the fact of physiological likeness between parent and child, it also resided in the intangible aspects of the relationship between them. These two conceptions of authenticity were not necessarily contradictory, of course, and adoption workers strove mightily to produce both kinds of realness on the theory that they were mutually productive and reinforcing. But it is also worth considering how the two types of authenticity could diverge.

Therapeutic professionals who trusted depths over surfaces, elevated psychological over material welfare, and insisted that the truest qualities of kinship were located in its emotional geography cast a shadow of doubt, however unintentional, over the commitment to adoption as a mirror of biogenetic nature. Wasn't it possible for kin to match physically without matching emotionally, and vice versa? The critique of the matching paradigm–so central to the direction of adoption philosophy and reform during the past several decades– has roots in both the therapeutic sensibility, with its refusal to equate feeling with appearance, and the rights revolution that sharply recast the terms of individual identity and collective belonging, in the private realm of love and intimacy as well as the public sphere of political and economic participation.

The work of interpretation mitigated preoccupations with skin color and body type by promoting careful attention to emotional currents lurking below the superficial veneer of human bodies and behaviors. Seeing beyond the tangible evidence was the raison d'être of therapeutic approaches. "Even the would-be parents themselves don't always realize just *why* they want a child," one how-to pamphlet from the Child Welfare League of America explained. "But in the course of friendly conversation, expertly guided, under-the-surface reasons are bound to come up" (Carson 1957: 9, emphasis in original). Whether the questions were about motivation to adopt or marital sex, it was presumed that the role of skilled interpreters was to extract important emotional truths that would not be voluntarily offered, even when applicants were convinced they had nothing to hide. The habit of checking applicants' own stories against independent sources of information–confidential physicians' reports documenting the cause and treatment of infertility, for instance–illustrated that truth was as much a therapeutic as an empirical quality.

Interpreting Adopted Children: "Telling"

"Telling" has been among the most persistent features of the literature on therapeutic adoption, in part because it highlights the chronic problem of making adoptive kinship real while also acknowledging its distinctiveness. Throughout most of the century, adoption professionals maintained a firm consensus that children placed as infants or toddlers should be told of their adopted status early in life. Adoptive parents did not always agree. They dreaded telling, and evidence suggests that some children were told in adolescence, on the eve of marriage, or even later in life, rather than when they were young. After the New Deal, requests for social security and unemployment benefits brought previously unknown adoptions to light because of the birth certificates that were required, and during the two world wars, many young draftees were also surprised to discover their adoptions. While the bureaucracy of warfare and welfare revealed some adoptions previously kept secret, many adoptees never heard about their adoptions at all. There is no way to know exactly how many.

Throughout the century, professionals maintained that secrecy, misinformation, and deception between parents and children had no place in adoption, although it must be noted that these same professionals frequently stopped short of full disclosure themselves when children's backgrounds included such sensitive factors as racial mixture and illegitimacy. During the 1930s, a few agencies stopped pleading with adopters and started imposing more coercive enforcement policies, refusing to place children with parents who refused to tell and routinely incorporating instructions on how-to-tell into the adoption process. By mid-century, most agencies required adopters to pledge, in writing, that they would tell, and how-to-tell conversations were routine parts of adoption investigation and supervision, along with lessons in how to answer children's inevitable, curious questions about their birth parents. The how-to literature aimed to help parents face "the dreaded job of telling their child the truth of how he came into the family" (Doss and Doss 1957: 28). Many adoptive parents resisted telling and remained very uncomfortable talking about it, and professionals viewed this as proof that adoptive parents felt insecure about their entitlement to children and needed more help and better interpretation. The difficulties of telling were bound up with the difficulties of acknowledging adoption's difference from biogenetic kinship, even within the closed circle of the family itself.

Why Tell?

If telling emphasized the difference between adoption and real kinship at a time when matching and sameness were valued, why was it mandatory? The rationale for telling had less to do with honesty than it did with therapeutics. Parents would be wise to tell children about their adoptions before they learned the truth from unfeeling relatives, nosy neighbors, or cruel classmates. (The presumption that adoptees would necessarily be penalized by their status is another indication that therapeutic ideals took white, middle-class norms as their starting point. African-American and other poor and working-class communities had histories of informal adoption that often made telling irrelevant.) "Greater dangers...lie in wait for those who beg the question," warned a 1933 *Ladies Home Journal* article (Faegre 1933: 32). "Tell them it's OK. There's nothing to worry about," declared one twelve-year-old adoptee whose parents were apparently models of rectitude (Lockridge and Theis 1947: 153).

Emotional inoculation against shock and stigma was the main reason for telling, with closeness and trust between parents and children a secondary benefit. Some parents still resisted, convinced that adopted children who did not know they were adopted were less likely to face embarrassment and more likely to be "just like our very own."

The therapeutics of telling required parents to do far more than simply tell. By telling, they navigated the precarious gap between constructively emphasizing and destructively over-emphasizing the fact of adoption. They were supposed to acknowledge that adoption was different, at least to their children, but also behave as if it were not. They were supposed to raise children who appreciated the momentousness of their adoption, but also displayed their adjustment by almost never thinking or talking about their natal backgrounds. They were supposed to carefully approach the explosive potential of adoption with an attitude of studied casualness. Benjamin Spock, to take a famous example, advised parents to accept the fact of their child's adoption "as naturally as they accept the color of the child's hair," while simultaneously suggesting that adoption was anything but a neutral fact of this kind. Adoption made children fearful and insecure. Spock warned parents that "one threat uttered in a thoughtless or angry moment might be enough to destroy the child's confidence in them forever" (Spock 1946: 507).

Adoption mattered, but it was not supposed to seem that way. Telling earned a unique place in the literature of therapeutic adoption. It linked deliberate, emotional labor to the effective management of potentially dangerous difference.

When, How, and Who to Tell?

Exactly when and how to tell were described at great length and in great detail. The most popular advice about telling capitalized on the growing trend toward parents reading to their children daily. Classic children's books about adoption like *The Chosen Baby* (1939) and *The Family That Grew* (1951) (the latter came with a separate instruction book for parents) were only two examples from a burgeoning literature recommended by agency professionals and popular media alike (Wasson 1939; Rondell and Michaels 1951). Books provided handy aids that literally made adoption go down as easily as a bedtime story and relieved parents of always having to tell in their own words. Parents who wished to move beyond pre-formulated texts were urged to individualize story-telling rituals by filling in details specific to their families or supplement them with custom-made scrapbooks including photographs of landmark events: the day you came home, the day adoption was finalized, etc. Occasionally, the strategy of allowing adoptees to "adopt" something themselves–usually pets–was advocated as an aid to telling. One fictional adoptee took in two kittens–he named one Really and the other Truly—after a neighborhood child taunted him about his adoption and explicitly challenged his authenticity as a "really truly" member of his family (Haywood 1944). As an activity with no guarantee of working out well (pets could misbehave, run away, or die), it had obvious disadvantages.

Until the past few decades, preferred telling methods stressed "chosen child" themes. Specific words, phrases, and sentences to use (and avoid) in telling were identified, underlining the power and peril of adoption as a factor in children's emotional development. Sample scripts were common. Parents were tutored to use the words "chosen" and "adopted" interchangeably and only with a happy and relaxed tone of voice. Telling was supposed to happen early and often because children would assimilate their parents' feeling about adoption long before they could talk or understand the meaning of their words. Any hint of anger of frustration could defeat the purpose of telling by betraying adoption's negative associations and substandard social status. *"Under no circumstances, ever*, should the child be reminded that he is adopted when the parent is feeling angry at him," admonished Robert Knight of the Menninger Clinic. "The adoption should *never be mentioned* except as a pleasant matter" (Knight 1941: 71, emphasis in original).

Even with infants too young to understand, verbal repetition promised to cement positive associations with phrases like "my precious adopted daughter" and "my dear little adopted son" (Gallagher 1936: 116). The aim here was not only to boost children's self-esteem, but prepare them for the inevitable encounter with adoption stigma. If a child's parents faithfully exclaimed, "How glad we are we picked you out!" then he was likely to feel carefully selected in comparison to other children, whose parents were obligated to accept whatever nature gave them. Selection made adoption special, even superior.

Constructive government of children's emotional development was inseparable from strict government of parents' emotional expression. Parents who passed the telling test advantaged their children while also proving they were real parents: mature, loving, able to prioritize their child's needs, and willing to acknowledge that adoption made their family both different and not different. Parents who failed, however, betrayed doubts about their own authenticity. The same experts who maintained that there was no formula for how to tell also maintained that there were right and wrong ways to feel about telling. Inculcating the appropriate "feeling tone" and attitude in adults was a chief goal of the telling enterprise (Louise Wise Services, Meeting of Psychiatric Consultants, 1962).

Telling children themselves was mandatory, but there was far more room for debate about whether neighbors, teachers, and health care providers also needed to be told. Occasionally, a liberal approach to "coming out" was advocated, but most advice-givers cautioned parents against exiting the adoption closet too boldly. First, confidential information conveyed in a moment of excitement might return to haunt the child. Second, adoptees had an unusual need to fit in smoothly, especially with peers. The very measures that others recommended as symbols of authentic belonging–adoption announcements, adoption day celebrations–might accentuate the child's differentness and tempt teasing. In deciding whether and what to tell others, parents faced a fundamental dilemma. How to normalize and dignify adoption without either publicizing its distinctiveness or denying that it involved any meaningful distinction at all?

What to Tell?

Sensitive information about adoptees' natal backgrounds frequently included poverty, alcoholism, mental illness, criminality, sexual immorality, incest, and other sordid characteristics. What, if anything, should be disclosed about these things? This question tortured parents and was, by their own account, the most difficult of all "telling" problems. Advice-givers emphasized that parents' love and their ease with children's backgrounds was far more important than the substance of any information conveyed. Curiosity about the people who had given them life was inevitable, and it was perfectly normal for adoptees to ask questions, typically at the point when they were old enough to understand sex and reproduction.

Talking about birth parents was not easy. The dilemma of what to say about them symbolized the threat that unembellished information posed to the adoptee's fragile personality, much as the fact of adoption did. Children needed to be comfortable with whatever they were told about their "first" parents, advisors agreed, in order to sustain trust in their "second" and "real" parents (Terminological sensitivity in adoption is nothing new.) In many cases, this involved highly censored communication, if not outright lies. A long-term follow-up of a hundred New York agency adoptions from the 1930s found that the vast majority of parents (90 percent) had told their children, scrupulously following instructions to tell early, often, and with the appropriate words and tenor. But no parents at all had given their children full and candid details about the reasons for their adoption (Jaffee and Fanshel 1970: 129). Illegitimacy remained out of bounds through the 1960s. Many parents lied to their children, "killing off" birth parents rather than saying they had been unmarried. This approach was urged by some agencies before 1940, and many parents preferred it, even after it broke the rules (Lawrence 1963). To convey certain facts would publicize the moral failings of those parents and, by association, smear the children themselves.

That so many parents withheld information that embarrassed them and menaced their children is understandable. In the interest of preventing children from realizing too early that birth parents had been unable or unwilling to raise them, they were told always to maintain that their children's original parents (particularly mothers) were good individuals who had made selfless decisions for the sake of their children. The contradictory pressures built into telling were irreconcilable on this point. The same culture that demonized women who refused to mother, or to be "good" mothers, expected adoptive parents and children to consider surrender the result of maternal devotion–rather than desperation, coercion, or, occasionally, callous disregard. If some adults "chose" to become parents through adoption and dutifully reinforced the rhetoric of "chosen children," this reflected the powerlessness of others: birth mothers too poor and frightened and dependent to be attributed with choice-making authority of their own (Solinger 2001).

Communicating something to children about birth parents was–like telling itself—important for therapeutic rather than legal or moral reasons. In theory, it put children's minds at ease. Comforting children with the thought that their birth parents had been decent human beings was hardly an invitation to search and reunion, the movement among adoptees to locate lost natal relatives that has become organized and visible since 1970. Most advocates of telling prior to 1970 were also advocates of confidentiality and anonymity. There was no contradiction, in their view, between the routine practice of telling children and the equally routine practice of keeping secrets about birthparents' identities and whereabouts. They denied that adoptees had civil rights claims to specific background information, and argued well into the 1970s that "confidentiality is essential to a child's sinking his roots deep into his adoptive home" (Sitomer 1974: 7).

Before the records wars of the 1970s, dominant views about telling emphasized that good mental and emotional development in adoptees was manifested by *lack* of interest in locating natal relatives. Even Jean Patton, founder of the first adoptee search organization in the United States, Orphan Voyage (established in 1953), formulated a "search hypothesis" in which the impulse to seek out natal relatives was calibrated to the security of the adoptive home (Paton 1954: 114). Adoptees who developed normally and felt loved, in other words, had no particular reason to search and probably would not. That a renegade early search advocate conceded such a direct relationship between insecurity and searching suggests the extent of therapeutic consensus about what mental health looked like in adoptees: "the best-adjusted adopted child is the one who almost never thinks about the facts of his natural birth" (Cady and Cady 1956: 118). Michael, a teenager in 1965, had "been preoccupied since 5 with the past and with the true identity of his parents," a situation interpreted by the agency that placed him as evidence of "emotional disturbance" and need for help "away from his blind search for his mother to the more realistic approach of psychotherapy" (Louise Wise Services, Summary of B Case, 1965). Children like Michael, who dwelled on lost relatives, talked about them incessantly, or set out to locate them as adolescents or adults needed psychiatric help. They were living proof of adoption's problems. Divided loyalties doomed authenticity.

Adoptive parents were expected to talk honestly to their children about their birth parents, but the expectation that they say nothing to upset the children's emotional equilibrium or support search fantasies put them in a terrible bind. Helen and Carl Doss, whose own transracial and transnational adoptions flouted matching, implied that the fact of having two sets of parents was a more difficult difference to handle than others in adoption. They urged adoptive parents to *"forget everything that would not be helpful to your child"* (Doss and Doss 1957: 191, emphasis in original). Forgetting was the most re-

vealing approach to the conflict between what parents knew, or suspected, about their children's natal backgrounds and what they were
told their delicate children could bear. It diminished the danger of
difference by disregarding knowledge of it.

"I don't know" was the ideal answer to children's questions–and
all the better if parents really did not. This helps to explain why a
remarkable number of parents between 1940 and 1970 did not want
background information about the children they adopted and sometimes actively declined it during the adoption process. The possibility that communicating prejudicial facts might cause anguish
prompted agencies to wonder "whether or not to inform the adoptive parents of history which might be a cause of constant concern
to them" (Free Synagogue Child Adoption Committee, Minutes, 1943:
2). One scenario in which such anxiety was probable involved mixed-
race children (or children suspected of having mixed ancestry) who
might be able to pass for white; another involved a family history of
mental illness. Agency practices varied widely on this. Some professionals maintained that agencies had moral obligations to convey
what they knew. Others went to far as to suggest that adoptive parents be given little or no information at all. "Parents should be able
to say truthfully that they do not know the reasons why the child
was given up," reasoned on psychiatrist, and "this will enable the
child to think that he comes from two loving parents who, by reason
of some catastrophic event (the nature of which will be left to his
own fantasy) could not keep him" (Louise Wise Services, Seminar,
May 9, 1957: 1).

One study of almost 500 Florida adoptions finalized between 1944
and 1947 found that only 20 percent of adopters wished to know as
much as possible about their children's birth parents and backgrounds, with a full 80 percent favoring little or no information
(Witmer et al. 1963: 93). This was a rather contorted way to preserve
children's self-confidence and their own credibility, to be sure, but if
everything worked out, children would take whatever they were told
in stride. *"If he knows in his mind he is adopted but feels in his heart
that he belongs to his family,"* the adoptee would follow a course of
normal mental and emotional development (Doss and Doss 1957:
204, emphasis in original). When telling was managed well–done
for the right reasons, in the right ways, at the right times, and with
the right information–children turned out to be real members of real
families.

Running the gauntlet of telling was as much a test of parents' authenticity as it was a method of insuring that children experienced realness in family life. Passing the telling test suggested that parents were real: mature, loving, able to prioritize their child's needs, and willing to acknowledge that adoption made their family both different and not different, all at the same time. Failure to tell well, or worse, to tell at all, indicated that parents doubted their own realness and harbored toxic fears that children born to others could never truly be their "own." Although no precise formula existed for the timing or vocabulary of telling, advisors spared no effort in conveying to parents that there were right and wrong ways to feel about adoption. "If you yourselves have fully accepted your child's adoption," one advisor concluded in 1955, "you will be able to make him accept it, fully and happily" (Raymond 1955: 85). Doing so frequently involved calculated efforts to manage the emotions associated with infertility as well as illegitimacy. In therapeutic adoption, how parents turned out was key to how children turned out.

Interpreting Adoptive Parents: Infertility and the Problem of Motivation

Children were the first parties to adoption whose need for inspection, interpretation, and assistance took a therapeutic turn. Their distinctive experience of family life, involving as it did some kind of separation and loss, made them uniquely vulnerable to special stresses and problems, as the example of "telling" suggests. But adoption's adult participants were not far behind; they were equally handicapped in their quest for authenticity. Interpretation, applied to aspirants to adoptive parenthood, identified several issues as fundamental targets of therapeutic intervention and help. Among the most important by mid-century was the question of infertility.

Infertility was a central concern of the home study, as the therapeutic determination of applicant fitness came to be called, because no other single issue was a more sensitive barometer of normal marital adjustment and parental capacity than "sterility," a term more commonly used than infertility before the 1960s. Inability to conceive had not always been a decisive qualification for adoption, but childless couples have probably always been attracted to adoption. By mid-century, infertility loomed so large that most agencies refused to even consider applications from fertile couples, even when they expressed a preference for adoption. In 1958, *Standards for*

Adoption Service noted only two valid reasons for fertile couples to adopt: "factors in heredity or serious risk to the life of the mother" (CWLA 1958: 37). The practical reason for reserving adoption for infertile couples was to limit the pool of applicants at a time when there was a growing gap between supply and demand for healthy white infants. Even couples who had experienced multiple miscarriages were sometimes denied children because their reproductive potential was theoretically intact.

Agencies typically requested confidential medical reports from physicians to verify that applicants actually were infertile, but they also used infertility workups as diagnostic tools in the course of the adoption process. By the early 1960s, infertility was so well established as a qualification that to apply for adoption was "an overt admission of biological failure," according to one Mayo Clinic psychiatrist (Barry 1961: 52). If children made families and infertile couples could not have them, it made sense to privilege infertility as a qualification. Matching, which sought to bring adults together with children they might have conceived by themselves, further cemented the association between infertility and adoption.

Translating infertility into a positive motivation for adoption curiously required that couples first work long and hard to correct their reproductive breakdown and have children of their "own." How long had they been trying to conceive? How many doctors had they seen? How much time had they devoted to treating their infertility? The more strenuously they resisted their infertility, the more they appeared to want children, but the more strenuously they resisted their infertility, the further they were from the "resolution" of infertility that therapeutic adoption mandated.

It is an ironic fact that making medically documented infertility a prerequisite for adoptive parenthood was premised on the belief that having children naturally was the universally preferred alternative. Adoption was advisable only after the normal method of biogenetic reproduction failed. That requirements for adoption were founded on its status as a last resort doomed even the best-intentioned efforts to normalize and authenticate adoptive kinship. The poignancy of this paradox was illustrated by couples who honestly admitted that they preferred to have their "own" children and wished to adopt because they hoped adoption would "cure" infertility and induce pregnancy. (This conviction, hotly debated in the medical and academic communities, was and is sustained by anecdote, desperation, eugenics, and popular belief in the psychological forces at play in human fertility.) Although couples convinced that adoption would facilitate pregnancy were merely expressing culturally sanctioned preferences for natural kinship, this motive was often dismissed as evidence of neurosis (Fradkin 1963). Couples were expected to want their own children above all else, but they were also expected to want adopted children for their own sake.

In therapeutic adoption, where nothing was taken at face value, even the fact of infertility was open to interpretation. The question was not whether couples were infertile, but why. Especially after World War II, during the golden age of psychoanalysis in the United States, the etiology of infertility was carefully probed. Psychiatrists like Viola Bernard, a Columbia University specialist in reproductive medicine who was also a trained psychoanalyst and longtime adoption agency consultant, elaborated an important theoretical distinction between "organic" and "psychogenic" infertility. The difference made all the difference in assessments of parental capacity (Bernard 1963; Frank 1956). Organic causes for infertility were medically explicable and figured infertility as a permanent state, located in the reproductive physiology of husband, wife, or both. Couples afflicted with infertility of this kind were childless against their will. They were innocent victims of reproductively uncooperative bodies, and therefore "offer the most hopeful prognosis for adoption and for adopted children" (Free Synagogue Child Adoption Committee, Report, 1942-1943: 4).

In contrast, the causes of psychogenic infertility were located in the mind, and that made childlessness mysterious and suspicious. The most serious risk was that infertility might conceal unconscious hostility toward parenthood unknown to the applicants themselves. Perhaps applicants were actually terrified of pregnancy and childbirth, or reproductively paralyzed by neurosis, or convinced they would make inadequate parents. "Psychogenic factors...may be far from evident to the casual observer," noted a one agency intake report in the mid-1940s, but they betrayed dangers "which we most desire to avoid for the adopted child" (Free Synagogue Child Adoption Committee, Report, 1942-1943: 4). "This is one of the most difficult things to get at," social worker Helen Fradkin admitted almost twenty years later, "because the woman is not, certainly, going to come to the adoption agency and say, "I am afraid to have a child of my own, I'd rather adopt one." You will never get this information by asking directly" (Fradkin 1963: 49). It is curious that professionals who expressed such mistrust of the verbal surface would simultaneously regard verbal communicativeness as a hopeful sign. Talking casually about infertility–with friends, relatives, and, of course, adoption workers–was considered a sign that the difficult emotions surrounding infertility were on the road to resolution. It could mean the difference between getting a child and living without one.

There were occasional exceptions to the rule that psychogenic infertility was impossible for clients to detect and ominous for children, and these vindicated the work of interpretation by showing that no easy-to-follow recipes for kinship existed. One thirty-four-year-old social worker with experience in the adoption field worried that she had "no maternal feeling" and sought psychiatric help over a period of years before applying for adoption, admitting that "her infertility is probably emotionally caused" (Louise Wise Services, Referral Suggestion, 1953). One agency, impressed with a young couple from Ohio whose decade-long infertility was inexplicable, allowed them to apply for adoption as a way of encouraging them to get pregnant! (Free Synagogue Child Adoption Committee, Case of Mr. and Mrs. K, 1944: 4)

The difficulty of determining the underlying meaning of infertility led some agencies to experiment with projective tests as an interpretive tool (Kuhlmann and Robinson 1951). Mr. and Mrs. W of New Jersey, for instance, were given a Rorschach test in 1947 and told that there were no right or wrong ways to respond, but Mrs. W worried anyway that the test might spoil their chance to adopt. Nothing out of the ordinary was discovered about Mrs. W, whose results suggested she was a "*'normal'* subject" (Case of Mr. and Mrs. W, 1947: 12, emphasis in original). Mr. W., however, turned out to be a "neurotic personality" whose sterility was linked to castration fears (Case of Mrs. And Mrs. W, 1947: 13). He was insecure, impulsive, and lacking in imagination, but, according to the Rorschach, without severe emotional disturbance. A decade later in New York, Mr. and Mrs. R were not so fortunate. Her test showed "many hysterical features intermingled with the obsessive tendencies" (Louise Wise Services, Mrs. R, Psychological Examination, 1958: 4). His "expresses chronically frustrated passive receptive longings," noted the psychologist who administered the tests. "Mr. R expresses concern about his masculinity with emphasized homosexual inclinations" (Louise Wise Services, Mr. R, Psychological Examination, 1958: 3).

Even without resort to projective tests, the significance of infertility might be glimpsed by careful observers of the adoption process. Viola Bernard suggested that the very first sight of a potential son or daughter could reveal all manner of unconscious reservations related to infertility. At this crucial moment, seemingly ideal couples might have qualms that disclosed how much the prospect of adoption actually disappointed and disturbed them. Confronted by the tangible evidence of their own inability to conceive, someone else's child, some couples panicked. Upon first seeing Joel in 1951, the Bs had an "extreme and unrealistic reaction": they called the child "moronic," proving only their neurotic wish for "a guarantee against abnormality...., behind which was the pain of their own infertility" (Louise Wise Services, Minutes, 1954). Such reactions proved they still harbored secret fantasies of having children of their own and remained mired in feelings of guilt and inferiority–all elements of "the unconscious rebellion against parenthood" (Bernard 1945: 236).

In one detailed early case study of psychogenic infertility, the wife's inability to conceive was attributed to gender trouble. Unable to rectify her own parents' disappointment at having a girl rather than a boy, Mrs. A. was caught in a trap of "parental transference" rooted in childhood (Orr 1941: 445). As an adult, her career symbolized the hopeless struggle to be like a man and reinforced the unconscious masculinity that sabotaged her achievement of true womanhood and motherhood through pregnancy. Even though Mrs. A had undergone more than 500 hours of psychoanalysis between 1932 and 1940, she was only dimly aware of the psychodynamic forces permeating her own reproductive life. The kind of infertility that menaced children would not announce itself. It needed interpretation.

An especially interesting how-to literature recognized interpretation as another obstacle to be overcome by sharing the professional secrets of normality and other qualifications with aspirants to adoptive parenthood. One such manual set out to be "a practical guide to a couple seeking to convince an agency that they have the capacity for parenthood" (Isaac 1965: 6). Be sure to work hard at cooperating with agency workers, instructed author Rael Jean Isaac, who detailed thirty different ways of satisfying decision-makers while also warning applicants to "be relaxed, honest, self-searching, and unguarded." Clearly, achieving a casual, therapeutic attitude took a great deal of effort. Couples needed to use "we," not "I" (tip #1) and "show they are reconciled to their infertility" (tip #5). Husbands and wives were both required to derive satisfaction from their jobs, but working wives were told never to be too satisfied lest there be doubts about their willingness to give up fulfilling careers for the drudgery of childcare (tip #8). Intimate questions about sex had to be answered without any trace of embarrassment, and Isaac suggested that "intercourse twice a week is apt to strike the social worker as an index of a good marriage—good without overdoing it" (tip #13). Couples should always have warm feelings about kids (tip #11) and wholeheartedly agree to tell the child about his or her adoption (tip #16).

Such advice was a telling measure of the triumph of the therapeutic in adoption. While it appeared to offer a way of outwitting (perhaps even ridiculing) the gatekeepers who stood between adults and the children they longed for, how-to-adopt instructions at once conceded the power of therapeutic authority, explained its logic to a wide audience, and increased the likelihood that adoption's rules for realness would be followed.

Therapeutic approaches to infertility illustrate how complicated it was for adoption to achieve authenticity. Infertile couples were expected to adopt, but preferences for adoption were neither normal nor natural, and digging below the surface of consciousness was required to protect children and make families where kinship would be "real" in the sense of being emotionally healthy. Even when couples appeared to have resolved their feelings about infertility, childlessness itself might pose ongoing problems for them and any children placed with them. It was true enough that individuals manifested more and less desirable ways of coping with reproductive insufficiency, but even the most apparently complete resolution of infertility still left people less than whole, and the hope that adoption might compensate their loss was far from assured (Kirk May-June 1963). Unlike childlessness, infertility was usually a permanent condition. Giving children to infertile couples made them parents, but adoption could not guarantee that they would be entirely normal parents. For that kind of realness, never-ending help and instruction was needed.

Therapeutic Government and the Problem of Difference

The problem of authenticity in adoptive kinship makes it a revealing case study in the history of therapeutic culture. Rules for realness that have taught the participants in adoption how to become and remain a "real family" have emerged as central features of modern child adoption. Establishing the kind of love and belonging that defined an authentic family could not be left to chance or luck. Even when faith in the matching paradigm was at its height, therapeutic practices illustrated that quests for realness sought to imbue adoptive kinship with the invisible prerequisites for intimacy even as they claimed to make up families whose authenticity resided in appearing as real as the real thing. Matching encompassed feats of psychological as well as physiological engineering because difference took both of these forms. Realness was a quality that had to be felt as well as seen.

In recent decades, the movement toward openly honoring previously concealed differences has, if anything, increased the number of therapeutic openings and interventions in adoption. Opportunities to instruct participants and govern the course of their family lives have multiplied. The spread of post-adoption services, for instance, suggests that legalization is but one step (and probably not the most important one) on the road toward authentic kinship, and that adoptive families need help over the long haul, perhaps permanently. At mid-century, casework and probationary periods from six to twelve months were common features of agency practice, but supervision ended promptly after the new family's day in court. Therapeutic intervention into the adoptive family ceased in the interest of making it as autonomous, private, and immune from interference as any other. Post-adoption services barely existed before the 1960s because differential treatment of legally equivalent families was a flagrant violation of the matching paradigm. With the emergence of the difference paradigm, post-adoption services have spread, along with their therapeutic logic.

Today, there is very little dissent from the claim that adoption is a risk factor that jeopardizes mental and emotional health. According to both public and professional opinion, adoption causes primal wounds that may require a lifetime of effort to heal, even in cases where children show no conspicuous signs of disorder or suffering. The very differences in adoption that deserve publicity have thus also been responsible for the loss, insecurity, and crimes of trust and attachment that many believe typify adoption as a kinship arrangement. In the early twenty-first century, the therapeutic consensus is even more constraining than it was decades ago, when Viola Bernard, a dedicated proponent of therapeutic adoption, pointed out that adoption meant "the gain of something" and not just the "loss of something" (Louise Wise Services, Meeting of Psychiatric Consultants, 1962: 21-22). Loss gets all the attention now. The repair of psychological damage done by adoption has become a growth industry (Princeton Survey 1997; Soll 2000).

Whether authenticity quests in adoption were founded on a paradigm of similarity or a paradigm of difference, the ultimate measure of realness–blood–hardly budged. Matching respected a singular standard of kinship to be emulated as closely as possible in the name of achieving authenticity; families were supposed to look natural and be treated as if they were. The critics of matching advanced a pluralistic standard of kinship in which openly acknowledging adoption's distinctiveness offered a new path toward authenticity; adoptive families could finally appear to be what they actually were, and might actually deserve special protection and treatment because of their difference.

In either case, the realness that biogenetic reproduction was presumed to confer served as the index against which mediators, participants, and observers gauged adoption's successes and failures. The stamina of a profound cultural equivalence between blood and belonging helps to explain two extremely important, interrelated features of adoption's modern history that point toward underlying continuities between historical eras frequently considered antithetical: the period of "secrets and lies" before the 1960s and the self-conscious period of reform since then. First is the emergence of therapeutic ideals and practices devoted to producing authenticity deliberately, such as those represented by telling children about their adoptions and probing the meaning of infertility in adoptive parents. Second is the inability of these ideals and practices to achieve full dignity and equality in the face of a realness that was necessarily ascribed rather than achieved. Child adoption consequently illustrates some of the obstacles to therapeutic authority as well as its triumph.

Note

1.   "Adoption" is used here to refer to non-relative adoption. Adoption by blood relatives was presumed to be natural and easy, whereas the difficulties associated with adoption by strangers justified public regulation and professional oversight. A majority of children adopted during the 20th century were probably placed with non-relatives, but a significant number have been adopted by natal relatives and step-parents, especially since 1970.

References

Note: Unpublished documents cited in this article are drawn from the following archives: Viola Bernard Papers: Columbia University, Long Health Sciences Library, Archives and Special Collections; Dorothy Hutchinson Papers: Columbia University, Butler Library, Rare Book and Manuscript Library.

Barry, Maurice J. 1961. "Emotional Transactions in the Pre-Adoptive Study," *Social Work in Adoption: Collected Papers*, ed. Robert Tod: 51-60, London: Longman.

Bernard, Viola W. April 1945. "First Sight of the Child by Prospective Parents as a Crucial Phase in Adoption." *American Journal of Orthopsychiatry* 15: 230-237.

Bernard, Viola W. 1963. "Application of Psychoanalytic Concepts to Adoption Agency Practice." *Readings in Adoption*, ed. I. Evelyn Smith: 395-433, New York: Philosophical Library.

Cady, Ernest, and Frances Cady. 1956. *How to Adopt a Child*. New York: Whiteside, Inc., and William Morrow & Company.

Carson, Ruth. 1957. *So You Want to Adopt a Baby*. New York: Child Welfare League of America, Public Affairs Committee.

Case of Mr. and Mrs. W. 1947. Dorothy Hutchinson Papers, Box 2, Folder 17.

Child Welfare League of America. 1958. *Standards for Adoption Service*. New York: Child Welfare League of America.

Doss, Helen. 1954. *The Family Nobody Wanted*. Boston: Little, Brown and Company.

Doss, Carl, and Helen Doss. 1957. *If You Adopt a Child: A Complete Handbook for Childless Couples*. New York: Henry Holt.

Faegre, Marion L. 1933. "Shall I Tell My Child He is Adopted?" *Ladies' Home Journal*. June, 32+.

Fradkin, Helen. 1963. *The Adoption Home Study*. Trenton, NJ: Bureau of Children's Services.

Frank, Richard. 1956. "What the Adoption Worker Should Know About Infertility." *A Study of Adoption Practice, Volume II: Selected Scientific Papers Presented at the National Conference on Adoption, January, 1955*: 113-118, New York: Child Welfare League of America.

Free Synagogue Child Adoption Committee. 1944. Case of Mr. and Mrs. K, Viola Bernard Papers, Box 160, Folder 4.

Free Synagogue Child Adoption Committee, Minutes. April 28, 1943. Viola Bernard Papers, Box 155, Folder 1.

Free Synagogue Child Adoption Committee, Report to the Board of One Year's Intake Service to Prospective Adoptive Parents. December 1, 1942—December 1, 1943. Viola Bernard Papers, Box 157, Folder 1.

Gallagher, Eleanor Garrigue. 1936. *The Adopted Child*. New York: Reynal & Hitchcock.

Goldstein, Joseph, Anna Freud, and Albert J. Solnit. 1973. *Beyond the Best Interests of the Child*. New York: Free Press.

Haywood, Carolyn. 1944. *Here's a Penny*. New York: Harcourt, Brace and Company.

Herman, Ellen. December 2001. "Families Made by Science: Arnold Gesell and the Technologies of Modern Adoption." *Isis* 92: 684-715.

Herman, Ellen. Winter 2002. "The Paradoxical Rationalization of Modern Adoption." *Journal of Social History* 36: 339-385.

Hutchinson, Dorothy. 1943. *In Quest of Foster Parents: A Point of View on Homefinding*. New York: Columbia University Press.

Isaac, Rael Jean. 1965. *Adopting a Child Today*. New York: Harper and Row.

Jaffee, Benson, and David Fanshel. 1970. *How They Fared in Adoption: A Follow-up Study*. New York: Columbia University Press.

Kennedy, Randall. 2003 *Interracial Intimacies: Sex, Marriage, Identity, and Adoption*. New York: Pantheon Books.

Kirk, H. David. May-June 1963. "Nonfecund People as Parents—Some Social and Psychological Considerations." *Fertility and Sterility* 14: 310-319.

Kirk, H. David. 1964. *Shared Fate: A Theory of Adoption and Mental Health*. New York: The Free Press.

Knight, Robert P. May 1941. "Some Problems in Selecting and Rearing Adopted Children." *Bulletin of the Menninger Clinic* 5: 65-74.

Kuhlmann, Frieda M., and Helen P. Robinson. January 1951. "Rorschach Tests as a Diagnostic Tool in Adoption Studies." *Social Casework* 32: 15-22.

Lawrence, Joan. January 1963. "The Truth Hurt Our Adopted Daughter." *Parents' Magazine*, 44-45, 105-106.

Lockridge, Frances, and Sophie van S. Theis. 1947. *Adopting a Child*. New York: Greenberg.

Louise Wise Services, Meeting of Psychiatric Consultants on Telling the Child of His Adoption. July 10, 1962. Viola Bernard Papers, Box 162, Folder 6.

Louise Wise Services, Minutes of Dr. Bernard's Seminar. April 19, 1954. Viola Bernard Papers, Box 161, Folder 6.

Louise Wise Services, Referral Suggestion. November 8, 1953. Viola Bernard Papers, Box 157, Folder 4.

Louise Wise Services, Seminar With Dr. Annamarie Weil. May 9, 1957. Summary of Discussion, Viola Bernard Papers, Box 157, Folder 6.

Louise Wise Services, Summary of B Case. July 16, 1965. Viola Bernard Papers, Box 162, Folder 5.

Louise Wise Services, Mr. R. Psychological Examination. July 2, 1958. Viola Bernard Papers, Box 160, Folder 4.

Louise Wise Services, Mrs. R. Psychological Examination. July 2, 1958. Viola Bernard Papers, Box 160, Folder 4.

Orr, Douglass W. October 1941. "Pregnancy Following the Decision to Adopt." *Psychosomatic Medicine* 3: 441-446.

Paton, Jean M. 1954. *The Adopted Break Silence*. Philadelphia, PA: Life History Study Center.

Princeton Survey Research Associates. 1997. Benchmark Adoption Survey: Report on the Findings. New York: Evan B. Donaldson Adoption Institute.

Raymond, Louise, 1955, *Adoption...And After*. New York: Harper & Brothers.

Rondell, Florence, and Ruth Michaels. 1951. *The Family That Grew*. New York: Crown Publishers, Inc.

Sitomer, Curtis J. 1974. "What to Tell an Adopted Child." *Christian Science Monitor*, July 25, 7.

Solinger, Rickie. 2001. *Beggars and Choosers: How the Politics of Choice Shapes Adoption, Abortion, and Welfare in the United States*. New York: Hill and Wang.

Soll, Joe. 2000. *Adoption Healing: A Path to Recovery*. Baltimore, MD: Gateway Press.

Spock, Benjamin. 1946. *The Common Sense Book of Baby and Child Care*. New York: Duell, Sloan and Pearce.

Stolley, Kathy S. Spring 1993. "Statistics on Adoption in the United States." *The Future of Children* 3: 26-42.

Wasson, Valentine P. 1939. *The Chosen Baby*, New York: J.B. Lippincott.

Witmer, Helen L., Elizabeth Herzog, Eugene A. Weinstein, and Mary E. Sullivan. 1963. *Independent Adoptions: A Follow-Up Study*. New York: Russell Sage Foundation.

11

Virtue—On the Cheap

James Davison Hunter

When children murder children, as they have in the spate of suburban school shootings around the country, it is impossible not to be outraged, demanding answers. Though many Americans favor tighter gun control laws, few really believe that such laws go to the root of the problem. And when the psychologist intones that children simply need to learn how to better channel their anger, this too rings hollow. Though rarely articulated, there is a sensibility, widely shared, that neither external constraints nor psychological techniques are adequate to compensate for a culture that releases those who live within it from the structure of its inherited inner restraints. It is this sensibility that has provided a favorable environment for a renewal of neo-classical thinking about moral education.

The Neo-Classical Renewal in Moral Education

The neo-classical backlash to a therapeutic liberalism in moral education has been, in some respects, an attempt to revive the character education system established in the early decades of the twentieth century; in other respects, it attempts to recover the enduring tradition of moral education of the last millennium and more. Edward Wynne and Paul Vitz call this convergence of moral teaching, "the great tradition."[1] The general moral cosmology of this strategy operates within what philosophers call "metaphysical realism." In short, the true nature of the universe exists as an objective reality. Its complexity is neither random nor aimless but ordered and purposeful, and its design can be known to us through both revelation and reason. For neo-classicists, morality is distilled from a consensus of the ages. What makes the classical virtues so enduring and inclusive, then, is that they reflect the moral order of the universe that civilizations, in all their diversity, recognize and affirm. C. S. Lewis spoke of it as the "Tao"—a moral law shared universally across competing traditions; also described as "the doctrine of objective value," something one gets when one "lumps together... the traditional moralities of East and West, the Christian, the pagan, and the Jew." He also equates the Tao with "Natural Law" or "First Principles of Practical Reason."[2] Others speak of a "core morality," a "moral canon," and of "timeless truths." Right and wrong are not, in the final analysis, matters of opinion but essential qualities that all civilizations over the ages have discerned. They are also reflected as hard realities which human experience will confirm through well-being—by conformity to the moral law; or in ruin—by resisting the moral law. Because humans are so unformed at birth, the only way that the young acquire virtue and learn to live well in everyday life is in the formation of habits through imitation and practice.

In this light it is easy to see why the main focus of the neo-classical strategy is on the development of specific moral behaviors rather than on a general framework of developing moral reflection or reasoning. To the moral injunction to honor one's parents, for example, the emphasis would be upon those behaviors that demonstrate deference and courtesy (such as appropriate dress, speech, and posture). To the moral imperative to show kindness to strangers, the emphasis would be upon acts of friendliness and respect. To the moral ideal of compassion, the emphasis would be upon expressions of sensitivity and generosity. The strategy takes a pessimistic view of human nature: people are prone to act out of self-interest. The neo-classical strategy of moral pedagogy emphasizes the need for the individual to comply with legitimate moral authority, and for individual behavior to operate within acceptable social standards. At a bare minimum, the agenda within schools is simply to "demand good behavior from students."[3] Toward the end of developing moral habits in the young, children would live with a durable and pervasive system of rewards and punishments. They are to be commended when they demonstrate virtuous behavior and criticized and disciplined when they behave badly.

The Importance of Habit

The cornerstone of the neo-classical strategy is the Aristotelian argument that virtue is acquired in much the same way as other skills and abilities—through practice. "We acquire the virtues by first acting just as we do in the case of acquiring crafts," said Aristotle, in a famous passage from his *Nicomachean Ethics*.

> For we learn a craft by making the products which we must make once we have learned the craft, for example, by building, we become builders, by playing the lyre, lyre players. And so too we become just by doing just actions, and temperate by doing temperate actions and brave by brave actions ... and in a word, states of character are formed out of corresponding acts.[4]

In the spirit of Aristotle, there is among most neo-classical figures a sense that people possess certain natural virtues—an innate tendency to be temperate, just, courageous, loyal, and the like. But without proper habituation, these capacities remain isolated and underdeveloped, leaving the person morally stunted. Thus, it is by repetition that moral actions become second nature to us. All of the proponents of the neo-classical moral pedagogy agree on this point: the first objective in moral education is to develop good "habits of the mind, habits of the heart, and habits of action."[5] Someone like James Q. Wilson merely echoes Aristotle when he argues that good character "is formed not through moral instruction or personal self-discovery but through the regular repetition of right actions."[6] Recognizing that children are not always pliant, William Kilpatrick notes that "[s]ometimes compulsion is what is needed to get a habit started."[7] In principle, this is only the beginning.

Aristotle and his heirs recognize that the formation of habits is an abbreviation of a much more complex process of socialization. More than brainless behavioral conformity, the development of character also involves a cognitive and affective process of understanding and affirming certain moral ends with discernment and judgment in the context of different situations. Habits of moral action merely prepare the ground for true moral conduct, in which moral action is intended, not listlessly conformed to. In this, persistence is never enough; proper instruction from a reliable teacher is essential. "[J]ust as in the case of the crafts," Aristotle explained, "the same causes and means that produce each virtue also destroy it. For playing the lyre produces both good and bad lyre players. ... For if this were not so there would be need of no teacher."[8] To this end, proponents of the neo-classical alternative also advocate strong mentoring by adults who are themselves well-practiced in virtuous behavior. As one educator reflected,

How can I teach civility? I can be civil. I can use good manners with my … students. Instead of giving orders, I can say 'please' and 'thank you.'… I can model these behaviors myself. … How can I teach compassion? I can be compassionate. I can put myself in another's position. I can ask my … students, to imagine how another feels in a situation of conflict or hurt feelings. I can be sensitive to other's fear and loneliness and lend a listening ear or a pat on the shoulder. …How can I teach courage? I can be courageous. Instead of gossiping about the friend who hurt my feelings, I can speak directly to that friend. This takes courage.[9]

Without this guidance, the argument goes, children are lost. They are at best "an ethical tabula rasa." It is up to "good teachers [to] draw out energy, enthusiasm, verve, and spirit—even courage—as they impart knowledge and model virtue."[10]

Literature and Moral Understanding

For all the emphasis on generating *habits* of good moral conduct, the neo-classical strategy is not a crude behaviorism, as its critics sometimes charge. Especially important to the revival of this pedagogy is the use of great literature from the past—or at least talk about its use. The legends, drama, folk tales, and stories passed down from previous generations, neo-classicists contend, are a robust body of moral instruction capable not only of reinforcing desirable behaviors and stigmatizing improper behavior but of stimulating the moral imagination and intelligence of the young and educating them into the intellectual complexities of competing moral principles.

Though long advocated by scholars such as Robert Coles, the position has become a pedagogical cause célèbre principally among conservatives and neo-conservatives. The most well-known, of course, is William J. Bennett, whose *Book of Virtues* was published in 1992.[11] Neo-classicists' enthusiasm for the potential of literature and history to accomplish what "Values Clarification" and other psychologistic approaches have not is unqualified.

The reasons for using literature and history in moral pedagogy are numerous and mostly uncontroversial. For Bennett the key reason is straightforward. "Many of the clearest moral lessons," he argues, "can be found in classic stories from literature and history."[12] Beyond this, "[t]hese stories … are interesting to children." The conservative political activist Gary Bauer made the same case as Assistant Secretary of Education in the Reagan Administration. "I have great confidence in the power of stories to teach," he declared. "…The literary device of showing instead of telling is a very effective way to convey truths to young minds."[13] Beyond this, Christina Hoff

Sommers noted that "help[ing] children become acquainted with their moral heritage in literature, in religion, and in philosophy"[14] is a universally established way to teach the virtues. Universal and therefore uncontroversial.

Advocates of the neo-classical pedagogies offer more psychologically interesting reasons as well. Psychologists, for example, have suggested that cognitive functioning operates along two tracks, the propositional and the narrative. Both order a person's experience, but they are fundamentally different in kind and consequence, and neither can be reduced to the other. The propositional mode attempts to operate within logical universals and so tends to be separated from an emotional, social, or historical context. The narrative mode, by contrast, requires imagination, an understanding of human intention, and an appreciation of the particulars of time and place. Empathy is virtually impossible to generate, much less sustain, on the basis of abstract rationalistic principles alone, but it is virtually inevitable, however, in a narrative mode of thinking. Only after empathy exists can a child begin to make sense of moral principles. It is for such reasons that William Kilpatrick argued that "[m]orality needs to be set within a storied vision if it is to remain morality."[15] As Sommers put it, "[l]iterary figures ... provide students with the moral paradigms that Aristotle thought were essential to moral education."[16] Here too the argument is hardly contentious.

What are contentious are the social and political uses of literary and historical narrative. Such stories do indeed "give children some specific common reference points," as Bennett put it, by "anchor[ing] our children in their culture, its history, and its traditions. They give children a mooring."[17] They also have the potential of reasserting a common frame of reference in a culture in which commonality is severely strained. As William Honig put it, the essential purpose of the public schools would be "to bind together a diverse and pluralistic society by disseminating the guiding morality that inheres in our best literature and history."[18] The question is, on whose terms will children be anchored? Which stories and whose history will provide the common frame of reference for society? Not long after the publication of Bennett's *Book of Virtues,* Colin Greer and Herbert Kohl produced a decidedly liberal compendium entitled *A Call to Character: A Family Treasury of Stories, Poems, Plays, Proverbs and Fables to Guide the Development of Values for You and Your Children.* Steven Barboza edited an African-American anthology entitled

The African-American Book of Values: Classic Moral Stories.[19]
Like *The Book of Virtues,* these collections seek to anchor children culturally and morally in a set of common reference points;
but the mooring points are entirely different. It is a testimony to the
power of narrative in character formation that such points are recognized and contested.

From Theory to Practical Pedagogy

Perhaps the key advocate and practitioner of character education
in this more old-fashioned sense has been Thomas Lickona. Lickona,
author of *Educating for Character: How Our Schools Can Teach
Respect and Responsibility* and other works on the topic, argues that
there is no single script for effective character education. Indeed, of
all the academic proponents of moral education, Lickona has sought
to synthesize ideas from a wide range of conceptual and instructional paradigms. Even so, he advocates a set of broad principles
that serve as criteria in the development of character education initiatives. These principles are rooted in natural law. Those, he asserts,
are objective. As one might expect at this point, the principles and
the initiatives they spawn aim toward moral inclusiveness based upon
"widely shared, pivotally important core ethical values" such as "caring, honesty, fairness, responsibility, and respect for self and others."[20] Distilled, he contends, these reduce to "two universal moral
values [that] form the core of a public, teachable morality: respect
and responsibility."[21] As Lickona puts it, "…these basic human values transcend religious and cultural differences and express our common humanity."[22] They are not merely consensual but "rationally-
grounded, non-relative objectively worthwhile moral values" that
make a claim on our conscience and behavior.[23] The objectivity of
these values is established through natural law. As Lickona writes,

> There is a natural moral law that inhibits injustice to others and that can be arrived at
> through the use of human reason. This natural moral law is consistent with revealed
> religious principles (such as 'love your neighbor' and 'Thou shalt not steal') but has its
> own independent logic that even children can grasp. The educational implication of this
> universal natural law is very important: It gives public schools the objective moral
> content—"Be just and caring toward others"—that they may legitimately teach in a
> religiously diverse society.[24]

The heart of his synthesis is a conceptual scheme that identifies
three decisive components of virtuous character: moral knowing,
moral feeling, and moral action. Moral knowing, he argues, involves

knowing moral values, perspective-taking, moral reasoning, decision-making, and self-knowledge. Moral feeling, he says, relates to conscience, self-esteem, empathy, love of the good, self-control, and humility. Finally, moral action is a critical component of a good character, involving competence, will and habit. The goal, then, is to help children understand, care about, and act upon core ethical values.[25] By beginning with a model that includes cognitive, affective, and behavioral dimensions, he is able to invoke with approval the ideas of everyone from Jean Piaget, Louis Raths, and Lawrence Kohlberg to William Bennett and Kevin Ryan; and programs as diverse as values clarification, moral dilemma discussion, role-playing, conflict-resolution, and service learning.

Out of this grab bag of moral education initiatives, Lickona does play up the neo-classical concern for the cultivation of moral habit in everyday life. "To develop good character," he has written, "[students] need many and varied opportunities to apply values such as responsibility and fairness in everyday interactions and discussions." "[T]hrough repeated moral experiences students...develop and practice the moral skills and behavioral habits that make up the action side of character." Added to this are principles that develop the institutional support for these experiences. The school itself must be "a microcosm of the civil, caring, and just society we seek to create as a nation." "... The daily life of classrooms as well as all other parts of the school environment must be imbued with core values..." Accordingly, the "school staff must become a learning and moral community in which all share responsibility for character education and attempt to adhere to the same core values that guide the education of students." Teachers and staff must not only model the core moral values but "recruit parents and community members as full partners in the character-building effort."[26] All of this translates into classroom and school-wide strategies that view the teacher as caregiver, model and mentor, and that emphasize teaching conflict resolution, using cooperative learning techniques, cultivating moral discipline and values through the curriculum and maintaining a democratic environment and moral community in the classroom.

From the late 1980s through the 1990s, the pervasive sense of urgency to provide some moral content against the thin gruel of values clarification gave rise to a flurry of character education programs in schools across the country. Many states enacted laws like Act#95-313 in Alabama in 1995.[27]

NOW, THEREFORE, BE IT RESOLVED, that the members of the Alabama State Board of Education do hereby direct local boards of education to develop and implement, at the beginning of the 1995-96 school year, a comprehensive K-12 program for character education to consist of at least ten minutes of instruction per day; and

BE IT FURTHER RESOLVED, that this program of character education will focus on students' development of the following character traits: courage, patriotism, citizenship, honesty, fairness, respect for others, kindness, cooperation, self-respect, self-control, courtesy, compassion, tolerance, diligence, generosity, punctuality, cleanliness, cheerfulness, school pride, respect for the environment, patience, creativity, sportsmanship, loyalty and perseverance.

Needless to say, this remarkable law says more about the cultural and political climate of our time than it does about educational vision. But such are the inducements that guide this genre of moral pedagogy. In the field itself one finds at best a patchwork of approaches that lack either philosophical or pedagogic coherence.

There have been a number of notable efforts to translate neoclassical sensibilities and ideals into actual pedagogy. The Character Education Partnership, the Community of Caring, the Jefferson Center for Character Education, the Character Education Institute, the Teel Institute for the Development of Integrity and Ethical Behavior, the Heartwood Institute, and "Learning for Life," a subsidiary of the Boy Scouts of America have all developed curricula "dedicated to developing civic virtue and moral character in our nation's youth as one means of creating a more compassionate and responsible society."[28] Perhaps the most significant effort to give the character education movement coherence, however, has been the Character Counts! Coalition. This project was initiated by the Josephson Institute of Ethics in 1992 when it brought together a group of politicians, religious, and civic leaders in Aspen, Colorado to discuss the problem of moral decline in America and the need to teach values to the young. The "Aspen Declaration," forged at that meeting, affirmed six "core ethical values rooted in democratic society" that "transcend cultural, religious, and socioeconomic differences." These "six pillars of character" were respect, responsibility, trustworthiness, justice and fairness, caring, civic virtue and citizenship.[29] The Coalition itself formed about a year later and by 1999 it was a national partnership of over 300 different organizations, including church groups, teachers' and principals' unions, youth organizations, charities, and foundations.[30] Together these organizations claim to reach "more than 40 million young people." As a coalition, they are "united in one overriding mission: strengthening the character of America's youth"[31] by "integrating character education into new and existing educational programs." "The hope is that by using a consistent language with kids, the lessons of good character will be reinforced and better understood."[32] Through its "Six Pillars," coalition members have been able to revamp their values education material to stress these "core values." Toward this end, the national office has produced a range of materials, including posters and charts, videotapes, songs and activities, a "Good Ideas" collection of lesson plans, and an "Exercising Character" curriculum, not to mention ethics and character development seminars and workshops.

What all share in common is a conviction that a society that emphasizes individual rights without a concomitant pledge to certain shared public responsibilities is not sustainable over the long haul. There is, in this, a common sensibility that the vitality of civic and political institutions cannot be sustained on their own. Any decent public order cannot be taken for granted but is something for which one must work. Thus a healthy social order requires that citizens be capable of transcending personal interests; of envisioning and committing to a larger, common good. In turn, advocates of the new and improved "character education" pedagogies end up with an unequivocal affirmation of moral content in the advocacy of values. They generally agree that young people should be required to engage these values through the habits and challenges of basic life experience, especially when these ideals and practices are integrated in the entire life of the school and in the fabric of larger community.

As I noted, the appeal of this newly revived character education has been great. The curricular innovations represented by the character education movement have become popular in many schools across the country, among many educators, and even in the major educational bureaucracies. In this there is a real sense among its advocates that something important has taken place, a sea change in the way children's moral needs are addressed. The old models of moral education have fallen out of favor; a new era in moral education aimed at recovering a more traditional moral pedagogy has dawned, one capable of reversing the moral disintegration of American society. The sense of hope among many advocates is palpable.[33]

Psychology After All

These initiatives have made their mark. "There's no doubt," one conservative claimed, "that the pendulum is swinging back from self-expression to self-discipline."[34] As these representative cases present themselves in their own words, the distinctions between the new character education and the dominant therapeutic schools of moral education are fairly pronounced. But with a closer look, the line distinguishing the newly revised character education programs and the affective and psychological strategies of moral education grows indistinct. One always finds, at the very least, deep ambivalence about the role of affective strategies within a stated commitment to "objective" theories of value. But more than this, many of the prevailing assumptions of developmental psychology and client-oriented therapy strongly influence or even frame the very terms by which character education, narrowly defined, is practiced.

The Community of Caring, for example, frames much of its moral argument within the standard affective language of psychology. For instance, the organization claims that its key text, *Growing Up Caring,* helps students "experience heightened self-esteem and self-awareness"[35] and that the way they handle their emotions has a direct effect on their sense of self-worth. "Self-worth," that text contends, "affects every aspect of your life: your performance in school, your creative talents, your energy level, your relationships with others, and your overall satisfaction with life."[36] Toward this end, it is essential that the child learn to "appropriately" express rather than to withhold or "repress" his or her emotions. As *Growing Up Caring* assures readers,

> Perhaps you have heard that you shouldn't show your emotions. Your parents may have said 'don't cry.' A teacher may have told you, 'There's nothing to be afraid of.' However, your good mental health depends on your ability to recognize your emotions and to express them appropriately.[37]

"If you don't express emotions or if you dump them on others, you feel guilty or down on yourself."[38] By contrast, "persons with a positive self-worth are also able to have good relationships with other people. When you care about yourself you are in a better position to care for others."[39] In one exercise, students are encouraged to write a letter to themselves describing how special they are.

Imagine that you need to be convinced of your worth as a person. Write a letter to yourself. Tell why you are special. Include all your good points. Think of the talents you have that could be developed. Mention your values. End the letter. 'Love,' and sign your name.[40]

The point is reinforced in the guidelines for creating a Community of Caring school, in which teachers are encouraged to consult such resources as the book *101 Ways to Develop Student Self-Esteem and Responsibility*.[41] They are also pointed to *Values and Teaching*, by Raths, Harmin, and Simon—the designers of values clarification.

In framing the moral problem of cheating, *Growing Up Caring* shows a picture of a girl looking over the shoulder of another while taking a test. The caption reads, "Cheating, in any form, is bad for your self-esteem."[42] The moral argument is not that cheating is objectively wrong because it violates a universal value or principle, but that it lowers one's self-esteem. Elsewhere, the same text shows a young woman stealing something out of a store. An adjacent picture shows two people watching the robbery via a hidden camera. The caption under the photograph says, "One way to test the impact a decision will have on your feelings of self-worth is to imagine a picture being taken of you implementing your decision and that picture being shown to your parents."[43]

The Character Education Institute, to take another example, makes a point of disavowing values clarification. Instead its literature argues that "traditional family values form a framework for conducting...discussions, role playing and other activities that emphasize the consequences of the students' behavior."[44] Even so, its *Character Education Curriculum* features an exercise where teachers are instructed to help students "recognize their need for having standards."

1. Recognize our present values. What is important to us? Are our values evident by the physical and mental activities with which we choose to spend our leisure time, the people we choose to admire and emulate, the material goods on which we choose to spend our money, and most important, our willingness and ability to stand by our values?
2. Examine our present values for any conflicts that might exist. Is what we say what we do? Our credibility with others will be strengthened by the consistency between what we 'say' and what we 'do.'
3. Observe the differences between our values and the values of others. Our values should be strong enough that we can allow others to hold different values.

4.   Recognize the consequences of our actions. Decision-making and problem-solving require that we recognize our alternatives, gather as much information as possible about each alternative, and make our decision or try to resolve our problems.[45]

Though no reference is made to values clarification, that is in essence what this exercise asks for. It makes no reference to "objective values" that might inform the child about what the substance of his values should be. Values are arrived at through internal reflection and, once recognized, acted upon. Affect is not one of many factors but rather central if not paramount to self-understanding and moral engagement. As an instructional manual for teachers explains, "[l]earning to express themselves freely yet being careful to consider the feelings of others, too, may well be the most important social skill developed in students."[46]

Elsewhere, the Character Education Institute does affirm enduring values to the point of encouraging teachers to correct children when they come to the wrong conclusion about what is moral and what is not. In its own words, "The lessons have been designed to logically guide the students to the right answer... ."[47] But how are these values taught to children? The moral logic they promote encourages children to follow the consequences of their actions. Significantly, this cost-benefit logic is filtered through the child's sentiments. Why should one be good, say by caring for another? Because "it will make you feel better." Why should one not be bad, say through stealing or cheating? The reply: "how would it make you feel if someone did that to you?"

Here too, a child's moral behavior is linked directly to self-esteem. As CEI contends, "The lack of self-esteem is the most common factor found among persons who engage in student alcoholism, drug abuse, crime and even suicide."[48] It also notes that self-esteem is closely related to academic performance.[49] At the same time, constructive virtues such as responsibility derive from positive self-regard.

> Students who are most likely to become responsible citizens are those who have a good self-esteem; hence, those students who accept responsibility, increase their own self-esteem. Have you ever thought less of yourself when you did what you were supposed to do? You may not like having to fulfill your duties and obligations, but when you do, you realize that you are responsible and your respect for yourself increases.[50]

Precisely because "self-concept" is "the most significant factor in a student's personality,"[51] self-esteem "is totally underlying everything [the Institute] does."[52] To encourage the development of positive self-concept, the Institute offers exercises like "The Me Activity."[53]

The Jefferson Center also teaches core values such as politeness, friendliness, punctuality, goal setting, and the like. Yet its mission includes the mandate to "write, promote and disseminate curriculum and training programs for schools and families to teach...self-esteem."[54] The reason is that "feeling good about myself" is one of the ingredients of success,[55] a point reiterated in its *Responsibility Skills: Lessons for Success* curriculum. "Try to stress," the manual advises,

> that success is not just having money or possessions, but also knowing one's self, feeling good about what you do and being able to help others. For example, a painter may not sell many paintings, but she may feel happy and fulfilled in her work.[56]

Like the Community of Caring and the Character Education Institute, the Jefferson Center provides exercises to help students develop higher levels of self-esteem. An entire unit in the *How to Be Successful* curriculum is devoted to the techniques of "Self-Talk," where students are encouraged, on the one hand, to see how negative statements make a person fail, and on the other, to learn to write affirmations and to use positive statements daily, not least after making mistakes. Students write in their notebooks that it is "my daily responsibility to TALK POSITIVELY to myself because I want to T—Take care of myself, A —Accept myself, L—Like myself, K—Know myself."[57] The reason for this is that "successful people continue to talk positively to themselves."[58] Other exercises encourage students to "accept their likes and dislikes...to accept their strengths and weaknesses...to like themselves...to take care of themselves" and to "think of ways to reward themselves."[59]

The same ambivalence is found in the Teen-Aid abstinence-based sex education curriculum. Consider, for example, the following advice, offered to help students evaluate the moral decision of engaging in premarital sexual activity.

> Sexual activity outside of marriage can make you feel anxious and worried about getting caught, about becoming pregnant. It can also create a sense of disappointment by not living up to the standards you and/or your parents set for you. You could also feel dishonest knowing that you don't really feel what you know intercourse is saying to your partner. If pregnancy does result, the emotional trauma of abortion, adoption, or raising a child at this time in your life would be truly painful and long-lasting.[60]

The focal point for this moral decision is an emotional calculus defined by one's emotional and subjective well-being. At every level it is the child's feelings that are to be understood and consulted. It is not that engaging in sex outside of marriage is foolish or morally wrong, but that it may make the child "feel anxious and worried." Even the value of honesty is emotionally laden—"you may feel dishonest." And the basis for this feeling of dishonesty is not that the student defrauded, used, or lied to his sexual partner, but that he didn't "really feel" what he knew intercourse to be saying to his partner. This is consistent with the notion of honesty discussed earlier in the curriculum, that is, that "real" honesty is being in touch with and expressing one's feelings. Throughout, the student is encouraged to evaluate the risks of premarital sex in terms of the "emotional trauma" that may result.

In the curriculum, students are encouraged to take up activities like sports and camping as alternatives to drug use. The reason for choosing these options is the anticipation of good feelings. Participating in sports and the like "can lead to a discovery of personal talents, skills, and interests. It is that process of discovery that generates excitement and creates a positive, uplifting feeling."[61]

In the chapter "Caring," students are told that "[l]istening to our own feelings and trying to meet our own emotional needs can help us meet the needs of others. Becoming a caring person takes practice, and caring for ourselves can become an ongoing lesson in how to care for others."[62]

> Taking good care of ourselves helps keep us healthy, of course, and we can then have the energy to care in some way for others. Caring for ourselves also teaches us how to care for others. If we value and respect ourselves, we are better able to appreciate and respect others.[63]

A sense of personal well-being is also seen as an ingredient for successful living generally. Teen-Aid's material instructs students that "when you talk about ways to feel good about yourself, you are also describing the ingredients for success."[64] To this end, the program encourages students who are feeling down to talk to themselves in order to build themselves up. "When you talk to yourself, say positive things that help you believe you can succeed. 'Negative messages' will only result in self-doubt and a lack of confidence. Positive 'self-messages' could be, 'I know I can do this, I did well on that exam, I have what it takes to succeed!'[65] Elsewhere students are encouraged to seek affirmation from those around them. If this is not forthcoming they are told to give themselves "positive feedback." They are told, "Concentrate more on building yourself up—or sending yourself frequent positive messages and noting the many good things that you do. Maybe set a weekly goal for yourself and when you achieve that goal 'pat yourself on the back' with a snack, extra TV time, or a phone call to a friend."[66]

The Teel Institute also endorses self-esteem as "one of the most fundamental needs of every human being."[67] Indeed, the four "universal and inviolable principles" on which the Institute bases its curriculum are elsewhere described as "four principles of self-esteem." The Institute does make the explicit caveat that "...self-esteem cannot be given; it must be earned...Neither can genuine self-esteem be developed by focusing on unconditional self-affirmation. ...Rather, self-esteem is based on the knowledge that one is trying one's best to become more capable and more worthy—the best that one can be."[68] Self-esteem must be "an earned outcome of behavior, attitudes, and values held...." It is the effect, not the cause, of moral behavior—a point often made by conservative advocates of character education. Yet at the level of practical pedagogy this distinction is often blurred. Self-esteem, after all, is *based on the knowledge* that one is trying one's best..."[69] As Institute literature puts it, "if a student practices the skills and behaviors taught by Project ESSENTIAL, then she/he *cannot help but feel* both capable of achievement and worthy as a person. *Feeling both capable and worthy*, the student will theoretically begin to evaluate himself or herself more positively, resulting in a high self-esteem score on a Self-Report inventory... ."[70] In this, the student's emotional sensibilities provide the very framework within which competence and worthiness are measured and the means by which self-esteem is defined. In short, whether cause or effect or both, affect defines the moral language and the horizons within which character development is to take place.

Not least are the Boy Scouts of America. Unlike the Girl Scouts, the Boy Scouts have a reputation as a holdout against certain elements of cultural progressivism. The reputation is certainly justified by its efforts to resist the inclusion of atheists and homosexuals in its ranks. Yet in educational practice, one finds the strong influence of affective psychology. Its Learning for Life curriculum makes the theme of ethics explicit in the sixth grade. Here, the moral logic of "making good decisions" is very simple: "we feel good about ourselves, others feel good about us, and we don't have to worry about negative consequences."[71]

Even in a movement as visible as the Character Counts! Coalition, one finds the same ambivalence. In testifying before the National Commission on Civic Renewal in 1997, Nancy Van Gulick, a trainer in the movement, spoke fervently for the objectivity of values and the need to communicate solid moral content to children. "We have to make them conscious of right and wrong," she insisted. In the same breath, however, she declared that "[w]e have to make them committed to doing right, meaning it feels good to do right. Teach them that it feels good to do right. When you help the little old lady across the street, that feels good. You know, when you do the right thing, it feels good. When you do the wrong thing, it feels bad. Teach them to be committed. Make them feel committed is doing the right thing."[72] The founder of the Coalition, Michael Josephson, expresses much the same ambivalence. As a practical ethicist, he is as articulate a person as one can find on the moral foundations of good character. He has knowledge of different and complimentary philosophical paradigms which compel one toward ethical living. At the same time he suggests that the question, "why be ethical?" is not really important because we already know "the virtue of virtue."[73] That "inherent sense of right and wrong...tells us it's better to be a good person. I just know that I feel better when I'm doing the right thing."[74]

On Its Own Terms

While the political visibility and social organization of this neo-classical renewal has been politically and educationally assertive, a closer look at the popular pedagogy of character education raises serious questions about whether there has been any substantive challenge to the prevailing therapeutic paradigm of moral education. The assumptions, vocabulary, and techniques of secular psychology are ubiquitous. Rather than provide a challenge and an alternative, the new character education would seem to simply rework the psychological strategy within a traditional format of moral education. In this there is an implicit ambivalence that goes beyond a desire merely to include an affective dimension in moral instruction. Traditional moral values are explicitly affirmed but they are taught through programs interwoven with precisely the same therapeutic premises and techniques their political proponents deride. At the end of the day, the dominant strategy of moral education is not challenged as much as it is repackaged. By the time the challenge to the dominant psychological strategies of moral education reaches the classroom, it has come to resemble what it was supposed to replace.

But let us put that rather significant problem aside for the time being. Let us imagine that this kind of syncretism has not taken place; where neoclassical strategy takes form in curricular practices untainted by prevailing psychologisms but are consistent in the transition from theory to practice. In this way these alternative strategies maintain the distinctiveness they intend and thus are genuine alternatives to the psychological regime.

The Problem of Establishing "Objective" Morality

The fundamental problem that the neo-classicist wants to address is the loss of "any sense of objective morality." As Thomas Lickona put it, objective morality has been "washed out of the culture."[75] The pedagogical tactics that he and other character educators offer are designed to redress this deficit. It is for this reason that the first order of business in the alternative strategies is always an explicit affirmation of objective moral content in the advocacy of specific "values" or virtues. As Lickona put it, "Character education reasserts the idea of objective morality ... [a] truth ... independent of the knower.... Thus, [o]bjective moral truths have a claim on our conscience and behavior."[76] They "...demand that we treat as morally wrong any action by any individual, group, or state that violates these basic moral values."[77] As we have seen, nearly every character education organization and curriculum offers its own list of approved values. Though the values vary, the important thing is that all groups explicitly affirm "values" that are external to the self.

Yet how is the validity of those moral understandings established? How do these "values" come to make "claims on our conscience and behavior"? As with the psychological strategy, the *implicit* framework of moral understanding and engagement these alternative strategies convey is far more influential than any substantive lessons to which it may be applied. It is the implicit framework that teaches children enduring lessons about the reach and limits of moral imagination.

Consider, first, the instructive case made by Lickona himself. In his view, the objectivity of morality is no different from the objectivity of historical events.

> That Lincoln was president during the Civil War is objectively true, even if someone doesn't know it. That adultery, infanticide, torture, date rape, and cheating are morally wrong is objectively true—even if many people don't realize it.[78]

But if you are one of those people who does not realize that these acts are objectively wrong, how may you come to know it? Where is the evidence or the argument to make this claim? Curiously, Lickona's argument is grounded in a rejection of subjectivism.

> The idea that there are objective moral truths is a proposition denied by the doctrine of subjectivism. About subjectivism, Boston College philosopher Peter Kreeft writes: 'Of all the symptoms of decay in our decadent civilization, subjectivism is the most disastrous of all. A mistake—be it a moral mistake or an intellectual mistake—can be discovered and corrected only if truth exists and can be known.[79]

The case, in short, is that there must be objective moral truths because without them, all we have left are subjectivism and the decadence it brings along with it. The problem, of course, is that the negative consequences of moral subjectivism do not demonstrate the existence of objective morality.

In a similar way, Lickona argues, "people must understand and be committed to the moral foundations of democracy: respect for rights of individuals, regard for the law, voluntary participation in public life, and concern for the common good."[80] But why? Because, he writes, "[d]emocratic societies have a special need" for it. Here again, the case for the existence of moral foundations to democracy is established by assertion and defended only by the argument that there are ill effects for the individual and society if they are not adhered to. While the position is defensible, it does not establish the objective character of those foundations.

So when Lickona states, for instance, that proper moral development requires that we "care about justice—be emotionally committed to it, have the capacity for appropriate guilt when I behave unjustly, and be capable of moral indignation when I see others suffer unjustly...,"[81] it is not inappropriate to ask the question, why? On what grounds do we come to care about it? It is one thing to agree with the point and quite another to live by it. What are the terms that compel us to love justice? Lickona offers a few clues.

He argues, as I noted earlier, that there is a "natural moral law that prohibits injustice to others and that can be arrived at through the use of human reason."[82] Lickona is striving, of course, for nonsectarian support for the existence of an objective morality. Yet he still provides no means for explaining *how* these truths come to have a claim on our consciences. He does state that "many theologians and philosophers" hold to natural law, but we also know that just as many do not. The authority of experts, then, gets us nowhere. In the end, within the inclusive framework Lickona insists upon, there is no appeal capable of establishing the legitimacy of his assertion. Statements of value are not like statements of fact because they cannot be validated in the same way. In a context that requires inclusiveness, statements of value are just that: statements, declarations, assertions.

This general moral logic is at play in the range of pedagogies offered by character education more broadly. Objective morality is affirmed unequivocally but with thin justification at best.

The problem is that for all the posturing about the objectivity of the virtues and their capacity to transcend the vagaries of time and subjectivity, the neo-classical position articulated by its popularizers[83] ends up beholden to a culture of subjectivity as well. Though they are confident that good books will "do their own work in their own way," the problem is that when stories are lifted out of the particularities of historical tradition, social institution, collective identity, and normative order, their meanings are contested.

This, in many respects, is the lesson found in the very existence of such vastly different anthologies of classic stories as William Bennett's *A Book of Virtues* and Colin Greer and Herbert Kohl's *A Call to Character.* On the face of it, the books cover much the same ground, so presumably we should come away with the same understanding of the virtues they espouse. But we don't. Together they represent a deeply acrimonious division over the nature of the moral life and how it can be cultivated. And so against the objectivist position of the neo-classical educators, Greer and Kohl and kindred theorists suggest a more hermeneutical approach to understanding literature. The child is to learn to "authorize his or her own moral voice" in order to be liberated from "the social and cultural repressions" of the dominant social order.[84] To this end, they counsel readers to let the stories acquire their own meaning. "Be careful," they write,

not to shape your conversation about literature in ways that demand definite conclusions for each session or lead to your children feeling manipulated. Trust is crucial for critical family reading. Children will use their own judgment, make up their own minds about the issues at stake, and often understand the messages of what they read in ways that are surprising to adults. The personal closeness provided by serious, non-judgmental discussion, based on shared stories, is as valuable as any specific conclusions.[85]

In this light, creativity is "the excitement of taking on something new and breaking old boundaries"; courage becomes commendable when it withstands pressure from "authority figures;" self-discipline gives children the confidence to "take chances challenging illegitimate authority;" idealism means "challenging our conventional ways of doing things." Stories of integrity can indeed lead children to conclude that this virtue is, as Greer and Kohl put it, "rooted in the comfort you feel within."[86] Needless to say, scholars as intelligent and well-read as Bennett and Greer and Kohl don't agree on either the meaning of texts or the ways one should read them, it is not clear why should we expect that any one else will.

But what about the justifications offered by history? To be sure, an appeal to the historical endurance of a literary canon of moral stories is perhaps the principle way in which neo-classical educators attempt to ground the validity of the virtues they espouse. But that canon remained plausible as long as it existed within a fairly stable normative culture that idealized those virtues. That stable moral culture educators now call "Judeo-Christian" has largely disintegrated. Their appeal to history may continue to convince some but in our day it will certainly convince fewer and fewer.

History is not the only appeal. All of the narrative-based pedagogies rely on empathy as well: the meaning of stories from history or the literary canon is assumed to be self-evident to anyone who can empathize with the characters portrayed. This is what makes their example inwardly compelling to the reader. But here is the rub: empathy is sentiment, and sentiments make a pulpous foundation for anything. The main point here is that advocates assume that the sentiments will be shared, so that these shared sentiments are the basis for a shared interpretation. While they can hope for this, it is by no means guaranteed.[87] Indeed, at the start of the twenty-first century, this may still be possible, but it is certainly less and less probable.

And so it is that even the neo-classical educators offer no extrinsic mechanism for resisting the subjectivity they want so much to reject. In a context where the "enduring" values of great literature are finally grounded in the authority of shared sentiment; the intersubjective capacity to empathize with others in the same ways, moral "knowledge" must inevitably give way to moral interpretation. In the final analysis, the claim to objectivity is rendered weak at the least, if not meaningless.

Virtue, Yes... but on the Cheap

"Character education," the president of the National Education Association proclaimed in 1997, "is not about left or right.

It is about right and wrong. It is about teaching core values of honesty, respect, responsibility, and more...values that are essential to citizenship... values that virtually every American recognizes as legitimate, good, even self-evident.[88]

Are such values self-evident? If they are in our time, it is only in the realm of vague generality. What is not self-evident is the meaning of those values. Implicitly, the advocates of moral education understand this. It is easier to assert "values" as abstract universals because the moment they range into anything deeper or more practical, what is "self-evident" immediately becomes contested. And so "values" are vigorously championed by the advocates of the neo-classical strategy but they too end up as little more than platitudes.

Sensing the weakness of this position, character educators do try to ground core values in an appeal to universal reason. They simply insist that "there are rationally grounded, non-relative, objectively worthwhile moral values..."[89] But as Alasdair MacIntyre famously observed, every notable attempt since the Enlightenment to construct a rational foundation for an objective morality has been built out of non-rational premises, premises that any rational person might reasonably deny.[90] There simply is no rational consensus, even among highly rational and sophisticated thinkers.

Thus when moral educators speak of the ideals and virtues that "reasonable people of good will" possess, what is "reasonable" cannot be established.[91] In our day there is no shared or fixed reference point for establishing the objective meaning of certain moral positions. What moral positions are proposed tend to be lifted out of the particular cultural and linguistic contexts, the social practices by which they are communally reinforced, and the historical narratives that give them weight and significance. It is no wonder that these moral positions lose the qualities by which they are made rational and coherent to people. The advocacy of virtues or consensual values then becomes little more than a mechanism for the assertion of personal preferences. Their validity depends upon little more than the sentiments of individuals who, by choice, accept them.

In the history of modern philosophy, every attempt to establish good reasons for believing that there are objective characteristics to the moral life have failed. The proponents of character education fare no better. We speak to each other as though our moral choices had a rational foundation, but that rational foundation turns out to be certain preferred and shared assumptions. Without a coherent moral philosophy, rooted in social institutions and reflected in a communally shared narrative, moral codes can only deteriorate into arbitrary personal preferences whose only sanction is the emotional weight of subjective experience.

Sentiment, to be sure, can awaken individual moral sensibilities, but to be compelling and consistent, as well as socially coherent, the moral life requires an argument. Justice requires an argument; tolerance requires an argument; altruism requires an argument. These arguments must be based on something other than self-interest; in ways that go beyond personal choice and subjective experience. Moreover, these arguments have to be embedded in the taken for granted structures of everyday life experience.

In the final analysis, what the advocates of the neo-classical alternative want are the forms and outcomes of traditional morality without the substance of particular religious sanctions. A morality conceptualized without basic links to a living creed and a lived community means that the morality they espouse entails few if any psychic costs; it lacks, in any case, the social and spiritual sanctions that can make morality "binding on our conscience and behavior." What is more, without the grounding of particular creeds and communities, morality in public life can be advocated only as yawning platitudes— variations of the emotivism that now prevails everywhere. Critics who point to the absolutist quality of this moral pedagogy are not far off the point. Outside the bounds of moral community, morality cannot be authoritative, only authoritarian. In the end, tpropenents of neoclassical education do advocate virtue, but at best it is virtue on the cheap. Thus, while the neo-classical strategy of moral education disparages the subjectivism and individualism of our time, it is neither able to transcend nor escape them. In this way, the current renewal of neo-classical ideals in character education may seem like a welcome and substantive response to such problems as school shootings, but it too is inadequate to the challenge.

Notes

1. See Edward Wynne and Paul Vitz, "The Major Models of Moral Education: An Evaluation," section 2: part 2, National Institute of Education, *Equity in Values Education*, final report (Washington, D.C.: National Institute of Education, Department of Education, July 1985).
2. See C. S. Lewis, *The Abolition of Man* (New York: Macmillan, 1947), pp. 29, 56-57.
3. Kevin Ryan, "Character and Coffee Mugs," *Education Week*, 17 May 1995, p. 48.

4.   Aristotle, *Nicomachean Ethics*, quoted in Nancy Sherman, *The Fabric of Character* (Oxford: Clarendon Press, 1989), p. 177.
5.   Thomas Lickona, *Educating for Character: How Our Schools Can Teach Respect and Responsibility* (New York: Bantam, 1992), p. 51.
6.   James Q. Wilson, *On Character* (Washington, DC: AEI Press, 1991), p. 108.
7.   William Kilpatrick, *Why Johnny Can't Tell Right from Wrong* (New York: Simon and Schuster, 1992), p. 231.
8.   Aristotle, *Nicomachean Ethics*, quoted in Sherman, *The Fabric of Character*, pp. 179-180.
9.   Mary Riser, "Uncovering the Hidden Curriculum," *Perspectives* (Charlottesville, VA: St. Anne's Belfield, May 1996), p. 13.
10.   Denis P. Doyle, "Education and Character," *Phi Delta Kappan* 78 (February 1997), p. 442.
11.   In the same genre is *Books That Build Character: A Guide to Teaching Your Child Moral Values Through Stories*, edited by William Kilpatrick, Gregory Wolfe, and Suzanne Wolfe (New York: Simon and Schuster, 1994).
12.   William J. Bennett, *American Education: Making It Work* excerpted in "Educators Must Teach Morality," *Focus on the Family Citizen* 2, no. 9 (September 1988), p. 16. See too, Lynne Cheney, in "The Importance of Stories," *Academic Questions* 4 (Spring 1991).
13.   Gary Bauer, "The Moral of the Story," *Policy Review* 38 (Fall 1986), p. 26.
14.   Christina Hoff Sommers, "Teaching the Virtues," *Imprints*, vol. 20, No. 11, Hillsdale College, 1991, p. 13.
15.   Kilpatrick, *Why Johnny Can't Tell Right from Wrong*, p. 197. Kilpatrick has gone so far as to say that "[s]chools can learn a lot from the army," and acknowledge, with approval, the ways in which schools in the past were "unapologetically authoritarian" (p. 228).
16.   Sommers, "Teaching the Virtues," p. 13.
17.   William J. Bennett, "Moral Literacy and the Formation of Character," *USA Today* 117, no. 2518 (July 1988), p. 86. Indeed, moral educator, Kevin Ryan, of Boston University put the matter explicitly when he stated that "[o]ur history and our literature contain our moral wisdom and serve as the moral compass that is passed from one generation to the next" (Kevin Ryan, "The New Moral Education," *Phi Delta Kappan* 68, no. 2 [October 1986], p. 170).
18.   Bill Honig, *Last Chance for Our Children: How You Can Help Save Our Schools* (Reading, MA: Addison-Wesley, 1985).
19.   Colin Greer and Herbert Kohl, eds., *A Call to Character* (New York: Harper Collins, 1995); Steven Barboza, ed., *The African-American Book of Values: Classic Moral Stories* (New York: Doubleday, 1998).
20.   Tom Lickona, Eric Schaps, and Catherine Lewis, "Principles of Effective Character Education," Character Education Partnership, pamphlet, undated, p. 1.
21.   Lickona, *Educating for Character,* p. 67. Emphasis added.
22.   Lickona, Schaps, and Lewis, "Principles of Effective Character Education," p. 1. Emphasis added.
23.   Lickona, *Educating for Character*, p. 230; Thomas Lickona, "The Case for Character Education," *Tikkun* 12, no. 1 (January/February 1997), p. 23.
24.   Lickona, *Educating for Character*, pp. 42-43.
25.   Lickona, Schaps, and Lewis, "Principles of Effective Character Education," p. 1.
26.   All of these quotations are taken from Lickona, Schaps, and Lewis, "Principles of Effective Character Education," pp. 2-4.

27.   Utah, North Dakota, Nebraska, Oregon, Iowa, Indiana, Georgia, and New Hampshire all created or revised existing laws dealing with character education between 1988 and 1999.

28.   Character Education Partnership, "Mission Statement," *Character Educator* 6, no. 2 (Spring 1998), p. 3.

29.   Character Counts!, "Character Counts! Information," Character Counts! home page, 1 April 1997, <http://www.charactercounts.org>.

30.   For instance, the National Education Association, YMCA of the USA, National Association of Professional Educators, American Association of School Administrators, American Federation of Teachers, 4-H, Future Homemakers of America, National Association of Secondary School Principals, National Federation for Catholic Youth Ministry, Boys and Girls Clubs of America, Big Brothers Big Sisters of America, Camp Fire Boys and Girls, American Youth Soccer Organization, National Catholic Educational Association, United Way of America, USA Police Athletic League, and the Jefferson Center for Character Education.

31.   This statement is made on an information sheet attached to the "1998 Report Card on the Ethics of American Youth" (Marina del Rey, CA: Josephson Institute of Ethics, 1998), p. 47.

32.   These quotations are taken from the Character Counts! Coalition home page, 19 February 1999, <http://www.charactercounts.org>.

33.   See, for example, Don Eberly, *America's Promise: Civil Society and the Renewal of American Culture* (Lanham, Md: Rowman & Littlefield, 1998). In chapter 8, Eberly speaks of the character education movement as "one of the most dynamic movements to strengthen civil society in the United States" (p. 125). See as well the deliberations of the National Commission on Civic Renewal.

34.   Michael Horowitz of the Manhattan Institute quoted in Howard Fineman, "The Virtuecrats," *Newsweek*, 13 June 1994, p. 36.

35.   Community of Caring, "What is the Community of Caring?" (Washington, DC: Community of Caring, 1990), p. 1.

36.   Frances Schoonmaker Bolin, *Growing Up Caring: Exploring Values and Decision Making* (Lake Forest, IL: Glencoe, Macmillan/McGraw-Hill, 1990), p. 109.

37.   Ibid., p. 117.

38.   Ibid., p. 116.

39.   Ibid., p. 123.

40.   Ibid.

41.   Jack Canfield and Frank Siccone, *101 Ways to Develop Student Self-Esteem and Responsibility* (Needham Heights, MA: Allyn & Bacon, Inc., 1992).

42.   Bolin, *Growing Up Caring*, p. 34.

43.   Ibid., p. 51.

44.   Character Education Institute, "Questions and Answers," information pamphlet on the Character Education Curriculum (San Antonio, Texas: Character Education Institute, undated), p. 9.

45.   Character Education Institute, "Character Education and the Teacher," pp. 1-2.

46.   Ibid., p. 2.

47.   Character Education Institute, brochure, undated, p. 14.

48.   Young Jay Mulkey, "Why Character Education? An Editorial" (San Antonio, TX: Character Education Institute, undated).

49.   "Research," Mulkey's institute explains, "has shown that the degree of students' self-esteem is directly related to their academic performance as well as instrumental in determining how well they are able to work and play with others" (Character Education Institute, "Character Education and the Teacher," p. 2).

50.   Character Education Institute, "Character Education and the Teacher," p. 1. In an editorial by Y.J. Mulkey entitled "Why Character Education?" he provides a concise statement of the moral reasoning they inculcate within children: "to develop responsible citizens by raising students' self-esteem, showing them the benefits of determining the consequences of their behavior to themselves and to others before acting upon their decisions to solve their problems."

51.   Character Education Institute, "Character Education and the Teacher," p. 2.

52.   Y. J. Mulkey, Director of the Character Education Institute, interview with author, 11 April 1991, San Antonio, Texas.

53.   Designed to give children a "better understanding of themselves" and raise their self-esteem, the activity involves cutting out magazine pictures that symbolize their own individual character traits and paste these on construction paper cut to form the word ME. *Character Education Curriculum News* 3, no. 1 (February 1991), p. 1.

54.   Thomas Jefferson Center, *The Year in Review: Annual Report 1989* (Pasadena, CA: Thomas Jefferson Center, 1989), p. i.

55.   Jefferson Center for Character Education, "Year I, Unit I" in *How to Be Successful in Less than Ten Minutes a Day* (Monrovia, Calif.: Jefferson Center for Character Education, 1991), p. 2.

56.   Thomas Jefferson Center, *Responsibility Skills: Lessons for Success*, elementary school curriculum (Pasadena, CAif.: Jefferson Center for Character Education, 1987), p. 1.

57.   Jefferson Center for Character Education, "Year I, Unit VI" in *How to Be Successful in Less than Ten Minutes a Day,* p. 3.

58.   Ibid., p. 12.

59.   B. David Brooks and Robert C. Paull, *How to Be Successful in Less than Ten Minutes a Day* (Pasadena, CA: Thomas Jefferson Center, 1986), pp. 9, 14.

60.   Teen-Aid, *Me, My World, My Future* (Spokane, WA: Teen-Aid, Inc.), p. 128.

61.   Ibid., pp. 165-166.

62.   Ibid., p. 91.

63.   Ibid.

64.   Ibid., p. 18. At the center of the self are the sentiments. It is for this reason that the text encourages "Coming to a better understanding and appreciation of ourselves [by] look[ing] at our emotions or feelings." "Identifying feelings, dealing with them and acting appropriately is," as they say, "very helpful in building self-awareness." Ibid., p. 11.

65.   Ibid., p. 19.

66.   Ibid., p. 21.

67.   The Teel Institute, "Moral Classrooms: The Development of Character and Integrity in the Elementary School," research report, undated.

68.   Sue Teel quoted ibid.

70.   Ibid. Emphasis added.

71.   Learning for Life, Sample Lesson Plans: Grade 6, "Code of Ethics," Learning for Life Home Page, 19 February 1999, <http://www.learning-for-life.org>.

72.   The National Commission on Civic Renewal, transcript of the second plenary session, Washington, D.C., 19 May 1997, p. 23.

73.   Michael Josephson, "Ethics: Easier Said Than Done," pre-course reading materials, Character Counts Seminars (Marina del Ray, CA: Josephson Institute, 1997), p. 212.

74.   Bill Moyers, "Our Changing American Values: An Interview with Michael Josephson," in *A World of Ideas: Conversations with Thoughtful Men and Women About Life Today and the Ideas Shaping Our Future*, edited by Betty Sue Flowers (New York: Doubleday, 1989), p. 18.

75. Quoted in Tim Stafford, "Helping Johnny be Good," *Christianity Today*, 11 September 1995, p. 39.

76. Thomas Lickona, "The Case for Character Education," *Tikkun* 12, no. 1 (Jan. - Feb. 1997), p. 23.

77. Thomas Lickona, *Educating for Character* (New York: Bantam, 1991), p. 42. Here he writes, "There are rationally grounded, nonrelative, objectively worthwhile moral values: respect for human life, liberty, the inherent value of every individual person, and the consequent responsibility to care for each other and carry out our basic obligations" (p. 230).

78. Lickona, "The Case for Character Education," p. 23.

79. Ibid.

80. Ibid., p. 24.

81. Ibid., p. 23. See also Lickona, *Educating for Character*, pp. 56-61.

82. Lickona, *Educating for Character*, p. 42.

83. This is an important qualification. The neo-classical position can be formulated in a way that is grounded in specific traditions.

84. See, for example, Mark B. Tappan and Lyn Mikel Brown, "Stories Told and Lessons Learned: Toward a Narrative Approach to Moral Development and Moral Education," *Harvard Educational Review* 59, no. 2 (May 1989), pp. 182-205.

85. Colin Greer and Herbert Kohl, eds., *A Call to Character* (New York: Harper Collins, 1995), p. 8

86. Greer and Kohl, *A Call to Character*, pp. 14, 15, 45, 293, 68.

87. As Bernard Williams put it, "There simply is no direct route from considerations of human nature to a unique morality and a unique moral ideal." 87 Bernard Williams, *Morality: An Introduction to Ethics* (New York: Harper and Row, 1972), p. 66.

88. Remarks made by Robert Chase, National Educational Association president, at the Fourth Annual Character Counts! Coalition Meeting, Washington, DC, 11 April 1997, NEA home page, 3 January 1999, <http:www.nea.org/>.

89. These include: "respect for human life, liberty, the inherent value of every individual person, and the consequent responsibility to care for each other and carry out our basic obligations" (Lickona, *Educating for Character*, p. 230).

90. Alasdair MacIntyre, *After Virtue* (South Bend, IN: University of Notre Dame Press, 1981), pp. 52-54. MacIntyre made this point earlier in his book, *A Short History of Ethics* (New York: The Macmillan Company, 1966) in his discussion of Kierkegaard's work.

> Suppose that one believes that one's moral position can be rationally justified, that it is a conclusion which can be validly derived from certain premises. Then these premises in turn must be vindicated, and if their vindication consists in deriving them from conclusions based on more fundamental premises, the same problem will arise. But the chain of reasons must have an ending, and we must reach a point where we simply choose to stand by certain premises. At this point decision has replaced argument; and in all arguments on human existence there will be some such point. p. 216.

91. William J. Bennett and Edwin Delattre, "A Moral Education," *American Educator* 3, no. 4 (Winter 1979), p. 7.

12

Se offendendo

Philip Rieff

Clown [and gravedigger]: It must be se offendendo, *it cannot be else for here lies the point .... Argal, he that is not guilty of his own death shortens not his own life.*
Other [second gravedigger]: But is this law?
Clown: Ay, marry, is't—crowner's quest law.
—Hamlet, *V.i.9-24.*

A Gloss on '*se offendendo*'

Everywhere and always, human beings, whether they know it or not, live so freely in what I shall call sacred order, the vertical in authority, that they can offend against it, shuffling and sidling as they will in the remissive middle of that eternal vertical, between the interdicts above and the transgressions below. Every move humans may make may be foreseen, but freedom of will is given in the living reality to which the clowns refer. Only the dead are incapable of giving self-offense. But the self to which that offense may be given is not one that the offender can recognize easily. Being the most essential of selves, that self is most subject to repression and even to clowning as a way of release from the limits of that self.

Shakespeare's clowns were not on the Judiciary Committee. Would the first clown, at least, were. He would have added the missing grave note. By *se offendendo,* self-offense, the first clown means to say *se defendendo,* self-defense, a then common legal phrase reversed by the clown for our darkest illuminations of our temporary self-releases from the constraints of being in sacred order. Those releases, as they occurred during the Thomas hearings, may describe those hearings best in their success as comedy and failure as tragedy. Comedy is the effort at release from any acute sense of sacred order. Failing such releases, the comic effort may easily become tragic. In this stipulation, both protagonists in the Thomas hearings have become immortal characters of comedy. Neither has suffered a mortal blow from their own or others' efforts at release. Clarence Thomas has taken his seat. Anita Hill is a world celebrity who may, if her Christian modesty permits, cash in that celebrity. Both retained sense enough of their sacred selves to raise the question of the self-offense that may occur in self-defense against the offense each gave the other and both took from the clowns that were on the Committee.

Because comedy is constituted as a complex of releases from what may be called the command structure complicit in all sacred orders, the elements of release during the hearings, rightly read, would suggest how frequently the struggle against being in such orders occurs. The shadow of those struggles flickered on tens of millions of television screens. In those shadows, the war against sacred order of any sort was being conducted. Television is a cultural artifact. All cultural artifacts are instruments of mediation between sacred orders and social. At least so they were until that time, scarcely more than a century ago, when cultural artifacts began to be considered as referring to themselves merely. Yet even as that cultural artifact called the "Thomas hearing" took on a life of its own, the hidden reality remained the relation between self-offense and self-defense. Those relations can remain only where there is a sacred self to be offended and defended. The very existence of the sacred self was the major question raised, unspoken, during the hearing. I shall turn first to the imputation of a sacred self offended and defended by Professor Hill.

The moment of Professor Hill's self-showing was the public relation of a largely hidden, ten-year-old truth of an offense both given and taken. Delivering that moment of truth turned out to be beyond the combat capabilities of Professor Hill and her advocates. Such a moment of delivery, if the truth is to have its fatal effect, must disclose itself as from sacred self to sacred self. Moreover, that delivery must be not only to the accused but also to the audience constituted as an assembly of accusers and accused. Mutual incomprehension, as in "They just don't get it," suggests at best a fighting version of the reciprocal incommunicability known to the Scholastics as the *individuum ineffabile* and to therapeutics as *identity*. There is a world of difference between the two. The Scholastics referred to the sacred self. Therapeutics refer to a radically social self constituted by identifications with some authoritative Other; or other in an indefinite series of others after the parental other in which the parent question of humanity—*Am I Thy Master or art Thou Mine?*—is reduced to the Freudian parent question. Not only animate but inanimate objects are understood, within Scholastic doctrine, as self-possessed in such a mystery that only the rarest artist or otherwise gifted mind can pluck that mystery of self from the stone-hard resistance by which it is protected. The prophet Samuel knew how to pluck the mystery from a supremely resistant figure, King David: "Thou art the man." Moreover, the mystery thus plucked had as its occasion a secret sexual desire. From Genesis to Montesquieu, if not from Plato to Freud, it was held that the sacred self is most sensibly moved by whatever relates to the drive toward union between the sexes. Neither the *Genesis* truth of creation, 1:27, nor *Genesis* 2:21-25, permits a reading of the sexual as primordial. The truth of the one flesh, spiritual union in the sexual, does not suggest a primordial bisexuality now implicit in the gay liberation movement. Self-offense can be taken by such suggestions of sexuality as the god-term of humanity. For adamant Christians such as Judge Thomas and Professor Hill both appear to be, the god-term that excludes all primordialities—of sex or class or race—is God. Clarence Thomas stated this adamancy in his remark that God, not the senators, is his judge. In the second culture story, even inanimate objects, being artifacts of godly creation, protect their mystery.

Even inanimate objects protect their mystery. The time and depth of preparation necessary to pluck that mystery was imagined by a great artist of such pluckings, more often than not comic as releases of the sacred self from the order of commanding truths in which it is contained. James Joyce expressed his admiration for the Scholastic doctrine of the *individuum ineffabile* and its disclosures early as Stephen Hero. In that draft of *Portrait*, Joyce performed the transferable exercise in reading what then became, at his moment of truth in that reading, the resolved mystery of the Ballast Office clock in Dublin. That clock, at its moment of self-disclosure, became something other than an item in the catalogue of Dublin's street furniture. All at once, after long preparation, the reader Joyce demonstrated the success of his spiritual eye. That eye seeks to sharpen its readings more and more exactly upon the hidden reality behind some more obvious reality. Just such a sharpening exercise, rather than prurience, kept millions of eyes focused sharply on the television screen as an artifact of mediation between the truth hidden in an unseen sacred order and the truth shown in that profane chamber of social order. That moment of focus, the hidden reality reached and disclosing itself behind the flicker of appearance, even of a clock face, Joyce called an "epiphany." The structure of this narrative, never to be written, seeks what the mass audience sought and some may have found: an epiphany, the self-disclosure of a reality otherwise hidden in the comic futilities of readings that disclose the readers rather than that which is there to be read.

What comic futility there was among the senators, all of whom may be named, perhaps at national MLA meetings, Honorary Deconstructionists. Deconstructionists have turned all readings into disclosures of the reader rather than the read. In the traditions out of Jerusalem, which I shall call second culture, the reader finds himself, in the mediation of his reading, somewhere in the vertical in authority. Where the reader is, somewhere in the vertical, will tell him what he is. Every reader is somewhere in that vertical that is interdictory, remissive and transgressive. By such readings, sacred orders have been discovered as the hidden predicates of moral orders. Cultures are then larger meditations by which those readings of the sacred self in its movement are transubstantiated, across the distances between intention and consequence, into the messy condition we call social order. Treated typologically, in the perspectives given within their predicative sacred orders, the mess by which social orders are constituted can achieve a certain clean, heuristic outline.

In such a typology, there need be no more than three cultures mediating or not between sacred order and social. "First" cultures, all pagan mediation of primordialities variously named, from which all things and social orders derive, scarcely exist nowadays. They have been too deeply invaded by "second" cultures of commanding truths, incorporating myth characteristic of first cultures. By "third" cultures, I mean a type unprecedented in human history. Third cultures, recycling first culture myths as negations, of second world commanding truths, mediate between themselves and such selves as are invented for their promise of a future different from the past in the most essential way: that there will be in that future nothing sacred by which any self need measure the limit on self-invention. Both Clarence Thomas and Anita Hill appear to be members in good standing of second culture. Around them circled, as hunters may circle the hunted, those who were not on screen, except as occasional expert commentators hired to explain the hidden realities behind the shown realities, meager as those latter were. The hunters represented movements generally called feminist, gay and other names that may serve as banners for third culture movements that aim to end the age of moralities and religions. Yet Professor Hill's accusation of sexual harassment makes sense best within the context of blasphemy secularized and yet not secularized in the hearing of a sensibility self-announced as Christian.

It was in 1882 that Nietzsche first published his summative comment on movements not yet fully conscious of their purpose: to abolish all sacred orders and their interdictory moralities so to liberate every self from its predicate in the *imago Dei*.[1] More than a century later, by the self-defeating serendipity of Professor Hill's appearance as a woman of a certain piety, abolitionist movements appear not yet fully conscious of their purpose. An implicit doctrine of blasphemy, speech-acts that violated a pious sensibility, can scarcely provide a point of reference for movements totally antisacral in their purpose.

The speech-act of gravest offense, giving some secular analogue to blasphemy, appears to be the question: "Who put pubic hair in my Coke?" For such an offense, "Coke," the surrogate of the sacred American blood blasphemed by Judge Thomas' sexualization of it, the American voter was expected to believe that ten years before Professor Hill's sacred self had been almost mortally offended. Can second culture offenses be projected into third culture accusations of offense? The shadow of blasphemy is the substance of the sexual harassment of which Judge Thomas was accused. Being there, to be heard with horror, the polluting question of "pubic hair" cannot be read as of any import outside the shadow of blasphemy. The shadow of blasphemy appeared to call for the shadow of stoning, for which the functional equivalent was to be a recycled, pagan plebiscitarian turning of thumbs down upon the nomination of such a blasphemer.

The justice of such a punishment can be assessed best in historical context: as a radically secular exploitation of meanings that belong residually to a culture upon which radically secular vanguards are not entitled to trade. No entitlement can justify such trading upon doctrines and sentiments the traders would abolish. In that circumstance, any admission of a jot or tittle of guilt would have rendered Judge Thomas guilty of *se offendendo*. In parallel, Professor Hill would have been guilty of *se offendendo* if she had not told the truth, however the context of the telling distorted that truth. Yet the greater self-offense may have been committed by Professor Hill.

She must know that charity is the greatest protection against
self-offense. Yet spiritual heroics may demand such profundity of
insight that, in the circumstance, Professor Hill may be forgiven her
inapposite truth telling. Like self-defense, self-offense carries unintended consequence into the world of experience.

The Deadly Nature of Self-Offense

It is only as sacred selves that humans differ in kind and quality
from the animal—or vegetable, or mineral for that matter. In that
otherwise incommunicable identity, sexuality is tempered and given
its meaning by such an intensity beyond friendship as may be delivered in the word 'love'. Judge Thomas' reference to his wife as his
"best friend" echoes the predicative friendship of all lasting love
affairs: that between the sacred self and its Creator.

What kind of love affair once occurred, and at what distance in
the then and there, between Judge Thomas and Professor Hill is not
for us to know; nor for them to know at such a remove in the here
and now. That it did occur we may know from the something different into which that love turned. And we may know so much, and yet
nothing at all, despite the self-defenses that now guard the difference between love and hatred. So it is that they themselves may not
know, by now, the true story of that turning. Such stories lie somewhere between the two. Both conducted their self-defenses with
masterly prudence. Christian charity would call for far less prudence
on both their parts. But that is to ask for a spiritual heroism that no
one has the right to demand and even less right to demand on camera. If Professor Hill is ardent for the right to abortion, then her absence of charity carries with it, in the amplifications supplied by the
mass media, an instrumental rationality. Judge Thomas was to be
destroyed on behalf of some higher cause. The shape that casts the
shadows in which the comedy of self-offense and self-defense was
played out has a constitutional case name: *Roe v. Wade*. Read *Hill v.
Thomas* as a major skirmish in the world *kulturkampf* codified as
Roe v. Wade. If sacred selves may be considered a universal, then
Roe v. Wade cannot be considered the higher cause to which Professor Hill sacrificed her sense of charity.

In ritual moments, higher causes can become scarcely audible.
The silence that surrounded *Roe v. Wade* resounded in the great courtroom incantation of our second culture: "Do you swear to tell the
truth, the whole truth, and nothing but the truth, so help you God?"

That ritual answer given, the words themselves, "I do," become an action. In that action, the spirit of truth meets the flesh of politics. Senator Bill Bradley, of Princeton, Oxford, the Knicks and New Jersey, made the salient remark of third culture in face of truths beyond politics: "Everything is politics." In her confessional radiance and wonderfully saving appearance of both chastity and charity is a tremendous irony of the Professor Hill image: that image was performing a deathwork. A cognitive and spiritual dissonance bound the American public to what might have been a tragic death watch, but stopped short at a temporary release from a decorum, official or not, inseparable from civilized expressions of our sacred order.

Nothing political mars Professor Hill's opening and closing references to her spirituality, which had been offended by Judge Thomas to the point of this massive public relation.

> I was raised in a religious atmosphere in the Baptists faith, and I have been a member of the Antioch Baptist Church in Tulsa, Oklahoma, since 1983. It is a very warm part of my life at the present time.
>
> I have no personal vendetta against Clarence Thomas.... It would have been more comfortable to remain silent. I took no initiative to inform anyone. But when I was asked by a representative of this committee to report my experience, I felt that I had to tell the truth. I could not keep it silent.[2]

These are not the remarks of a disenchanted veteran of sexual skirmishes in the Chairman's office. A formidable piety stands implicit in Professor Hill's words. Judge Thomas is accused of a formidable hypocrisy, the more formidable for the office he occupied. Senator Simpson intuited what may have been the inner, even unconscious, logic of Professor Hill. Did she not know that she was "killing" Judge Thomas? But there are justified killings, even as sinners may be justified. If her purity were so sullied that for five days in February, 1983, she had to be hospitalized for acute stomach pain, and assuming, as religious minds do, the connection between microcosm and macrocosm, what would such a sullying character wreak in his office as a Justice of the Supreme Court? Whatever Professor Hill's third culture handlers may have calculated, to her spiritual eye and remembrance the hypocrisy of Justice Thomas would take on a macrocosmic cast. No other logic would warrant such a deathwork as Professor Hill offered for use to the political forces representing congeries of third world abolitionist movements.

In the appalled memory of this pure, perhaps even virgin, woman, Judge Thomas' words, in his office as her superior, are tantamount to sacrilege; his verbal efforts at seduction a fraud upon his office. The multiple meanings of his offense become clear only in the Christian world of Professor Hill and not in the post-Christian world of, say Edward Cardinal Kennedy. It was in his office, at once secular and sacred according to the traditions in which both he and his antagonist say they lived that Judge Thomas uttered what was tantamount to blasphemy. Those shows of his impurity must have robbed her, ten years later, of her charity. It must have been the constitutional crisis, the present historic expression of the *kulturkampf*, that lured her out of anonymity into a world fame that will now test the radiance of her modesty. Despite the criticisms of Anita Hill by Miss Alvarez, one of Judge Thomas' most impressive character witnesses, the sense of a self far superior to the occasion did give Professor Hill an aura, the authority of radiance, upon which there was much confused yet impressed comment.

There is an impressiveness about objects, even as about selves, that is less confusing, their authority better apprehended, if seen through the Thomist gloss on the meaning of light in the second world canon of creation. Trained as he was in the Thomist tradition of personal knowledge, Joyce refers, in a great passage of *Ulysses*, to the authorititaive "whatness of things," that divest themselves of the vestments of their appearance, in the same way that the sacred self emerges from the structure of speech-acts, and other appearances into that quality of beauty and goodness and truth that Aquinas brought under a Latinate word for light in a sacramental sense, "radiance." To be perfectly honest is a great spiritual achievement, the more so in the circumstance created by televised world theater. A great actress or actor can mimic radiance to the point of disbelief suspended. Whether Professor Hill achieved the radiance of self-disclosure, with all the authority that achievement implies; whether she achieved the mimicking presence of a great actress: those questions cannot be decided by plebiscite. Such questions go to the grace that invests personal authority or, in some staged world, mimics that investment. The lesson every biography of a great actor or actress teaches is that the radiance of self-disclosure cannot be maintained offstage. That limit does not contradict the fact that a great actor—an Olivier, for example—may never be so much himself as when he is acting. Time will test the authority of Professor Hill. Cashing in that authority, with a book or with the high office in the feminist movement to which she is now entitled, will measure the difference between the grace of authority and the charm of consummate acting. The gift of grace, charisma, that sense of a presiding presence and of its messengers that has been so butchered in the transition from second culture to third, needs to be studied with a preparation rarely available to the contemporary student of such possibilities. Third culture is to be understood as the assimilation of all hidden realities, sacred order, to world theater. Moralities and religions can survive their theatrical representations only by understanding what it is that theater reveals even as it conceals.

Nietzsche presents the reader with a largely unused, but supremely useable, conceptual alternative to the present butchered concept of charisma. He refers to what we should now call 'glitz', the shine put on things as a wax-works version of radiance. Glitz, the vulgar celebration of *"role faith,"* succeeds the sacred self as show biz succeeds liturgy. In that third culture condition, the self *"really became,"* as Nietzsche emphasized, an *actor's* self. The substance is in the performance. To give this "odd metamorphosis," of self into actor, a classical source, Nietzsche attributes it to the Greeks of the Periclean age. At the same time, he reads that same condition as "the faith of the Americans today that is more and more becoming the European faith as well: The individual becomes convinced that he can do just about everything and can *manage almost any role,* and everybody experiments with himself, improvises, makes new experiments, enjoys his experiments; and all nature ceases and becomes art." No prophecy has been more accurate. "It is thus that the maddest and most interesting ages of history always emerge, when the 'actors,' *all* kinds of actors, become the real masters." Moreover, where the actors become masters of a fictive world—the world I call, typologically, third—there another type, called by Nietzsche the "architects," are "disadvantaged to the point of disappearance."[3]

To trace the distance between the founding architects of our second world and the distance from them among their descendants, Nietzsche remarks that the best actors in Europe in his own time are Jews. Among such post-Jews, far from the formal stage, Howard Metzenbaum can serve as a character in contemporary American political theater. But I see no reason to limit the character type actor to the post-Jewish condition. President Kennedy was the most consummate actor in American political theater and is revered for his successful playing out of the role faith inseparable from the fiction of Camelot. On the problem of the actor, both as third culture Jew

and more generally as the artist, of whom the "teller of lies, the buf-
foon, fool, clown at first" is the forerunner the reader can find no
better text than in Nietzsche's remarks on the type in section 361 of
book 5 of *The Gay Science* (pp. 316-7).

Even among consummate actors, the relentless role-players prophesied by Nietzsche as the character type of third culture, there does
occur the inner struggle which parallels the outer. Whether there is a
gender difference in the expression of inner struggle is a great question Nietzsche addressed in his reflection on women as actresses.
The most radical feminists can have a field day with Nietzsche's
declaration that "they put on something even when they take off
everything ...woman is so artistic." The question of the artistic and
compassionately permissive woman as against the inartistic and
uncompassionate masculine type has risen again in the current version of our *kulturkampf.* How the inner struggle plays out among
the constantly increasing number of women in the work place is a
subject to which much research will be devoted in the foreseeable
future, no doubt, as gender studies both express and study the
kulturkampf. In its origins, the German compound *kulturkampf* referred only to the outer struggle, as, in the latter quarter of the nineteenth century, between the Roman church and the Bismarckian state.
But in the age of psychological man, studies of the *kulturkampf* are
bound to include the inner struggle designated in the Greek word
psychomachia.[4] The fight for the man and woman soul will express
itself, later if not sooner, in *kulturkampf.* One focus of that expression was the Thomas hearings. But what was at stake in those hearings could not be seen nor probed in the characters of the two protagonists. The larger context was entirely hidden from the natural
eye. The question focused in the hearings was of the condition of
our culture in its received sense: as the mediating agent between
sacred order and social. Third culture forces would have cultural
artifacts and agents refer either to themselves or negationally to some
predicate in sacred order. Thus Andres Serrano's *Piss Christ.*

There is the sublime and chilling possibility that both protagonists, as actors, have achieved such a powerful integrity of good or
evil that neither the one nor the other suffers the *psychomachia.*
Human beings may aspire to the integrity of a tree, as Wittgenstein
did. But they may also aspire to the changeability of a chameleon,
as Hamlet did in one of his greatest and most theatrical outbursts of
despair at his own inner struggle with his sacred self.[5] It is not sim-

ply, as most scholarly glosses would have the reference, that Hamlet refers to the killer speed with which the Chameleon's tongue was thought to flick up his insect prey. The chameleon was most noted as the complete role player among creatures, the one that could divest itself and take on another vestment of itself most quickly and continuously. In the myth of the chameleon, change of self and vestment amount to the same thing. The integrity of the actor is entirely a matter of appearance. To achieve the appearance of integrity, as both Judge Thomas and Professor Hill did, challenges precedent in art as in life. The characters we know who have achieved such integrity, in fact as in fiction, appear more often than not to have achieved the integrity of evil while projecting good. Iago comes immediately to mind, of course; and such other integrally evil characters in Shakespeare as Richard III, Aron the Moor, and Edmund. In life, most recently, the characters of Hitler and Stalin and many of their henchmen, and more than likely Saddam Hussein, appear to have achieved that integrity of evil, which acts as an immunization against good.

Browning's version of the integrity of evil can be cited to support Nietzsche's doctrine of a culture that will be dominated by acting selves—clowns, and yet sinister in their foolery. It is in Browning's gloss on Edgar's song, "Childe Roland to the Dark Tower Came," that Browning locates the artistic fighter in the third world *kulturkampf* against second. The narrative line can be made clear. One artistic fighter, as both fighter and artist, confronts the artistry of another fighter against the boredom of a culture directed by doctrines of commanding truth. Of the new director, yet another member of that same directing elite gives his first thought, as applicable to himself as to the other. "My first thought was, he lied in every word." [6] Such a type as Browning conjures would find life easy as lying. Malice would need no motive. The doctrine of motiveless malice may be essential to our understanding of third culture in its radically politicized character.

But it is only in its typological purity that third culture may be read as if it were energized by motiveless malice. On the American scene, malice is rarely motiveless. I have referred earlier to the substance of *Roe v. Wade* behind the shadow struggle of *Hill v. Thomas*. Whatever her spiritual sensibility as a Christian, the artistic woman in Anita Hill may have acquired so passionate a sense of urgency that, seeing Judge Thomas on the verge of decisive membership on the wrong side of the Court, her hurts, then and there, a decade ago, disclosed themselves in the here and now. The truth is not in words that may or may not have been spoken years ago. Rather, the truth co-exists with the question whether the sacred self abides, immediately in the two minds that constitute the protagonists in their permanent importance. One or both, or neither, will know and yet may not know that abortion is mortal sin and yet may not be a crime. The real and ultimate self at stake in the Thomas hearings can never be made to appear on any surface, let alone on television screens. It is the sacred self that was at issue, and will remain at issue, however the Thomas hearings are remembered. The hearings may not survive in American cultural history except as an event in the larger *kulturkampf* over the existence of the sacred self. Firm belief does not establish a truth. It establishes a battle line when and wherever there are others of equally firm belief. The question of the sacred self refers to a commanding truth that may be no longer believed firmly enough by enough Americans to make abortion at once a mortal sin and a capital crime. To firm believers, a failure to oppose what is in effect abortion on demand is a self-offense of the highest order. But there is prudence in reciprocal senses of self-offense so far as they prevent both sides of the battle line from politicizing the line to the point of violence. Yet, in the degree to which the resort to physical force may be the last way to save some ineliminable element of the commanding truths, those who continue burdened by the sense of self-offense cannot let the opposing belief take hold of them. The way of clashing truths may make violence unavoidable. For this reason, the capture of statutory law must remain the aim of both sides. Not everything is politics, but politics may be the last resort for every clashing truth.

Two truths were told. In such an integral culture struggle, the struggle, by its intensity, assures both sides that whatever is on the other side is not. Such an intensity of reciprocal repression was brought on by both the total war against Judge Thomas, portrayed as a black phallic swordsman, the most racist of all images, and the eleventh hour release from the traditions of decorum that are supposed to surround inquiries into a figure so close to ascent to the functional equivalent, in our civic religion, of a sacred seat. At such a moment of the most intense and most widely observed cultural warfare in American history, it may well have been that only the accusation of such a self-offense, by so perfectly religious an accuser against so transgressive an accused, the man charged with the office of protecting women against such transgressions, would have been all that mattered. Second culture is authoritative enough still for the hope that even such an unwitnessed assertion would bring Judge Thomas quietly to withdraw. Staffers of our third culture high officers did not know their man.

Once Professor Hill's truth was spoken publicly, its use to our third culture elites rendered it more suspect than the opposing truth. As an oppressed woman, representative of the experience of a radical new source of truth, the experience of an oppressed category of humanity struggling for liberation, Professor Hill delivered, incredibly, too pat a mythological picture: of the black phallic panther, the more predatory for being secret, the more primal a power figure for being on the prowl in his office of protecting women against such prowlers. To this mythological picture, Judge Thomas' riposte was perfect. The criticism of his riposte, that it dragged in race for tactical reasons merely, fails to acknowledge the power of the mythological picture complicit in Professor Hill's drawing upon it. That phallic primal power figure is the great mythic threat to a culture of commanding truths which was once elaborate in its mastery of good manners and the safety of decorum. The decline of decorum in American society measures the disintegration of the culture from which it derives its social authority. The indecorum at the hearings was widely remarked. But the meaning of indecorum cannot be taught by politicians and mass media announcers who have no historical sense of its importance. Of all the Senators to criticize the absence of decorum, Kennedy was the character least entitled to make the criticism. His own sense of self-offense must have been weaker than usual in his shameless repetition of the word "shame" in his defense of decorum against Senator Specter's quite decorous prosecutorial way with Professor Hill.

Commanding Truth

Many lessons of modesty may be learned from the hearings. Even commanding truths must be read, in the particularity of their occasions, with a certain modesty which grants the remissiveness of the muddle through which we pass our lives. Truth in second cultures belongs to a hidden world reality to which the bridges built in order to reach them from our worlds of seeming span distances that challenge the art of cultural engineering. Distances and distortions are inseparable from the mediating functions of culture. Revelation, in the traditions of our second culture out of Jerusalem, is always in the repressive mode. Biblical images of the repressive mode are simple enough to see, if not to read. Cloud, fire, the dark—these are the concealments behind which revelation is given. All messengers of commanding truths are burdened, in their offices of direction, by the necessity of indirection. Polonius gives us a comic version of the long way a messenger must take in the course of his own directions to his messenger Reynaldo. The carp of truth is not easily taken. Few fish are caught by technicians of truth who do not know the art of indirection. Even the most unselfconscious work of art discloses itself in hidden meanings that remain inaccessible to a culture now delivered as a hostage to the higher illiteracy. There are few readers in the world of seeming who, like Hamlet, can say, flatly and with an arrogance of a messenger from the hidden world of sacred order to the sensual world of seemings incarnate in his mother: "Seems, madam? Nay, it is. I know not 'seems.'"[7] If we are modest, what we know, other than the truths by which we are commanded, are mainly seemings, a screen of fictions to legitimate the interests of some would be power or another. It is the purpose of third culture explainers away of commanding truth to say that all truths are seemings, merely. The American public wisely takes such conflaters of "seems" and "is" as translators of good worlds into bad. In such a contest as occurred in October of 1991 in Washington, inside that most unchaste of Beltways, the vast American jury would not take the remembered "is" of Professor Hill's accusations as more than yet another interest-bound "seems." The judgment was merciful to her as it was to Justice Thomas. "Words, words, words" cannot be allowed to serve as more than a parry against the violated intimacies of truth beyond the witness of mere mortals. The sheer burden of following private truth as it makes its way into the deep and dark distance between saying and showing, seems and is, demands such artistry of representation and communicable quality of the sacred self that only a saintly artist of honesty could bring it off. The publicity of the *kulturkampf*, crossed with the privacy of the two truths told by two characters great in the absence of any visible psychomachia, so renders both their truths suspect; and yet neither guilty.

The maiden figure of purity and the masculine figure of probity are left to stand, for the rest of their lives, linked to each other and yet at a tremendous reciprocal distance. If their figures are self-invented works of art, then both command the respect of those of us who admit to being lesser artists of life and less tested by such gross and intimate exposures. Both have become high officers in the culture struggle they represent. That struggle will come to no conclusion. At least since Sinai, when the immemorially established first culture of primordialities found itself challenged by the Jewish culture of commanding truths, the struggle for world creation has gone on and on. Yet it is not the same struggle. Both cultures, first and second, created worlds based upon sacred orders. It was not until the late nineteenth century that there emerged, articulately if not massively, third culture vanguards representing a world in which there was to be nothing sacred. And yet, again, in such a showdown as dominated the world picture show as *Hill v. Thomas*, the protagonists were both of religious origins and development and the issue had an unexamined but fundamentally religious cast. That religious cast may allow illuminative reference to other, more obviously artful, dark comedies.

The Radiance of Purity and the Temptation Attached to It

Suppose, on one of her exits from the room of the Chairman of the EEOC, when her ears had been offended, Anita Hill, Esq., had repeated the religious injunction uttered by one of her fictional predecessors in purity, Isabella in Shakespeare's dark comedy *Measure for Measure: [God] Save your Honor!* As the deputy of authority over her and, moreover, publicly charged with the protection of purity, the character Angelo explains in an aside, as to himself, the special temptation of purity: "from thee—even from thy virtue!" To understand the tempting character of purity, the sheer danger of it, Angelo's examination of his sacred self at the stretch may help us read the turbulent mingling of the erotic and the spiritual.

> What's this, what's this? Is this her fault or mine?
> The tempter or the tempted, who sins most, ha?
> Not she; nor doth she tempt; but it is I
> That, lying by the violet in the sun,
> Do as the carrion does, not as the flow'r,
> Corrupt with virtuous season. Can it be
> That modesty may more betray our sense
> Than woman's lightness? Having waste ground enough,
> Shall we desire her to raze the sanctuary,
> And pitch our evils there? O, fie, fie, fie!

> What dost thou, or what art thou, Angelo?
> Dost thou desire her foully for those things
> That make her good? O, let her brother live:
> Thieves for their robbery have authority
> When judges steal themselves.[8]

Post-Protestant Washington is not Catholic Vienna. Its corruption is of this time and place. Clarence is no Angelo. Anita is no Isabella. Yet there are supra-historical constants to be read in thick texts such as *Measure for Measure*. There is the official known for his probity. There is the maid radiant in her purity. Sexual license, too, is a constant in this work of art to which the shabby realities of history rise as if illustrations. The sexual license and pernicious freedom of the Communist elite in the Soviet Union is reported with devastating calm by Nadezhda Mandelstam.[9] The historical illustrates the artistic. Sexual license appears, early as Aristophanes and late as today in Washington, in comedies of release from the constraints of life in sacred order and, more affirmative in its actions, in all manner and genders of liberationist ideologies from our received cultures of commanding truths. If Justice Thomas were so overwhelmed by the purity of Professor Hill, he did not steal from his judgment anything that is unfamiliar to contemporary verbal and hyper-sexual sensibility. The guilt that would measure his own purity, were Professor Hill's accusations accurate, would be in the ineptitude of his sexual candor as a method of seduction addressed to a woman of such Christian religious sensibility. Remarks of sexual candor would be, in the early 1980s, a conventional way of proceeding in the erotic war between the sexes. Sexual candor has been long established as a convention of language among the enlightened. To the degree he had been mobilized upward and assimilated among the enlightened, Justice Thomas may have tried, with self-defeating awkwardness, that sexual candor a woman of Christian sensibility is bound to find offensive.

How the feminist movement, dedicated as it is to a freer sexuality in a third world of nothing sacred, can trade upon Professor Hill's outrage is a question that should vex strategists in that movement. Rules for the more equal conduct of the sex war, and statutes declaring work places as sanctuaries from the universality of sexual interests and initiatives, in whatever tastes, are the more difficult to establish in a world without sacred spaces. Moreover, that same third world has not celebrated the principle of decorum in any sphere of life. Decorum in sanctuaries represents an absurd doubling back upon the abolitionist animus of the feminist movement. There is no Christian feminism in any politically relevant sense. No more can there be a Christian gay liberation movement. Movements toward the abolition of all sacred orders have taken over second languages of legitimation in order to delegitimate the languages of those cultures. The effort broadcast in the *Hill v. Thomas* hearings, to legitimate an interdict upon sexual chatter in the work place as sanctuary from such chatter, may be well beyond the vaunted capacities for translating sacred language into instruments of transgressive aim as represented in all armies of our third world night. Laws against sexual harassment can work, without storms of litigation, only if those laws are expressions of renewed sacred order, that order renewed by constraints upon sexual license.

As it happens—and will continue to happen in late second and early third culture history—sexual harassment is the verso, merely, of the recto sexual license that is the primordiality, hygienically delivered via condoms and abortion pills, in third culture fancies of paradise. Paradise is that green world of prelapsarian mythology which needs no interdictory constraint upon the meaning of the flesh; so far as flesh is opposed to spirit. In second culture doctrine, the one flesh achieved in matrimony is not opposed to spirit. Here, at the ancient question of the spiritual structure in every sexual relation, the abolitionist movements, feminist and homosexual, appear, in their main thrusts, to divide what the doctrine of the one flesh has declared indivisible. Rates of divorce and degrees of legitimated promiscuity challenge those spiritual stabilities without which social stability cannot endure movements that exact a cost not only in instabilities but also in the intimacies of treacherous relations for which indifference or insouciance is too inhumane a price. The inhumanity of contemporary humanism is not a consummation devoutly to be wished upon anyone born into this struggle between advancing third cultures and retreating seconds.

Divorce and the deeper drivings of promiscuity into younger and younger age cohorts express the scarcely hidden and prohibitively high price of abolitionist feminism. The relentless secularity of that movement has come at the cost of profanations far more harassing than the talk reported by Professor Hill, as if it had shattered her sacred self. Even if her Christian sensibility were so gravely offended, such a sensibility, exquisite as it is, would have included in its cherished arsenal of responses, the greatest of all Christian responses: charity. Morally—that is, societally—the answer to sexual harassment cannot be punitive litigation. Such litigation becomes socially destructive. Sexual harassment has as its antonym a revived ethos of sexual restraint. But it is just such an ethos which has become the radically remissive equivalent in third culture of second culture abominations.

A Teleology of Sexual Desire

The relentless secularity, third world imperiousness, of feminist outrage over Judge Thomas, without touching upon the free for all safe sexuality that secular feminism more strongly sponsors, conceals the true spiritual nature of the struggle against sexism, different as it is from the war between the sexes. Sexual difference underlies gender difference. That truth remains until the time comes when, through the world transformative agency of science, women are no longer the bearers of children. Maternal roles cannot be played by the fathers. The voices of women, not to mention breasts and hips, make maternity a biospiritual condition that cannot be reduced to an invention of patriarchal power. The offspring's relation to the female body must be different phenomenologically from the relation to the male body and, indeed, to the male voice, which is part of the child's sexual and gender identity. The dogma that society determines roles ignores the profound differentiation of roles in the being of role players.

In our second world, female sexuality means motherhood. Reciprocally, male sexuality means fatherhood. Both together, the one flesh undivorceable, means family. By a contrast that has mounted to catastrophe, for the vanguards of third world feminism, sexuality means what it means to the male sexist: sexuality without motherhood—and without marriage. Feminist sexism parallels and mocks masculinist. A feminism true to its own biological spirituality would reconstitute the truths of virginity, married love and motherhood. Third world feminism—supra-humanist in its reckless secularity—does not respect the ineliminable triangle of sexual desire, married love and family responsibility. Any truly human sexual liberation must be a freedom from the imperiousness of sexual drives and an interpretative modesty in addressing the intellect within its limits of the eternal triangle of mother, father and child in which that drive must be contained if its spiritual teleology is rightly read. What sexual liberationists call "freedom" has been known for millennia as slavery to the passions. Using the state as the agent of liberation achieves that mixing of spheres, the erotic and the political, that defines totalitarian cultures and the suppression of the ineffable individual.

Politically imperious, feminist readings, in their variety, agree, nevertheless, on a sexual primordiality that teaches disrespect for *divine responsibility/secular agency* by which all earlier social orders have achieved the limiting condition of their humanity. Dynamics of disrespect for each individual's office exercising *divine responsibility/secular agency* have been the ruinous element in educational systems that now promulgate the higher illiteracy; a principled agency of pseudo-worldly irresponsibility. Primordialities of sexual desire, as both feminist and sexual credo, oppose the very sense of both the Rabbinic and Scholastic sense of the *individuum ineffabile* and the later Benedictine sense of *stabilitas* without which our second world social order grows visibly less and less humane while inventing institutions of compassion and caring that extend empires of inhumanity. Walk into any hospital and the reader will become a spectator of terrifyingly inhumane hospital theater. The imperiousness of a double assault, the trumpeting rage of feminists and the sexual self-righteous acting up of the homosexualists, has produced an ideology which bears serious and subtle resemblances to apparently opposing activisms we are now in the mock pious habit of calling "fascism." The sexual shenanigans of fascist movements render the accusation of puritanism absurd. Earlier and future fascisms share a common sense of the teleology of sexuality as the substance of a primordiality of desire.

By contrast, in second worlds creations out of Jerusalem, the teleology of sexual desires finds its purpose in marriage and family. To the extent that third world feminism treats sexuality as divorceable from marriage and children, it contributes to the very world of sexual harassment it is committed to oppose.

The writings of de Sade constitute a prolegomena to contemporary propaganda for the primacy of sexual desire. In music, as Kierkegaard rightly understood, the eroticizing of the world constitutes the mission of Don Giovanni. His is the world of The Woman. The world woman is there entirely for endless having. There is something strange about a feminism aiming to achieve gender equality that cannot but propagate the fiction of the world woman. Far out feminism, complete with world woman god-terms old as earth motherhood, is the logical end of feminist teleologies of the profane sex war. When *Don Giovanni* was first performed, in Prague, 1787, de Sade's pamphlet "One More Step" argued the doctrine that political revolution could not be realized without a predicative moral and sexual revolution. "Sexual harassment" states a vague rule of limit to be defined by each incarnation of the world woman within terms set by the feminist wing of the sexual revolution. "They just don't get it" is as esoteric a monopoly of futurist knowledge as that once enjoyed by devout Communist Party members when they consider the objectively and historically guilty bourgeois. Polarizations of knowledge, incarnations of evil, are to be expected whenever *kulturkampf* rises to a certain level of intensity. People do not fight for abstractions or hypotheticals. People fight for truths, for superordinate realties, for recycled worlds. Those who do not know the history of first culture mythologies are condemned to repeat it in moments of third culture fictive farcicalities. To fight for a farce registers the pathos of devout feminists and angry homosexualists.

From the inclination to fight for superordinate realities, the mind's eye can read the most intimate of second world traditions. In that intimate tradition, about which too little is said here and now by its staunchest fighters, there are three parties present in every procreative act: the father, the mother and that presiding presence which superadds at the moment of conception, in addition to all genetic and other variables, the constant of an identity unique through all times and places. That identity was once called the soul. I call it the sacred self, so to distinguish it from all social selves of accrual, merely. It is that sacred self that constitutes the identity of every Tom, Dick and Francis quite beyond the class of Toms and all other classes to which that identity superadds its otherwise incommunicable personality. No identity ever exists more than once. In this respect, biological history is sacred history. Sacred history never repeats itself. The sacred self is the one and only self ever created through the genetic and other structures passing from the male and female, and their ancestors, to the unprecedented identity that will be the child of that union of flesh. The second world doctrine of grace, of power divine, is inseparable from the truth canonized in Genesis 1:26—the Jewish doctrine called, in the tradition of Latin Christian culture, *imago Dei*. Superadded but not superseding that Jewish doctrine of the sacred self is its Christian stipulation in Galatians 2:20. The sacred self becomes what Kierkegaard called the god-relation, that inwardness expressed in the words uttered by the Christian sacred self to describe his or her fully self-conscious identity: "Not I but Christ in me." Along the entire front of this foundational sense of identity in our late second culture, the abolitionist movements have attacked the truth of the sacred self.

If the abolitionist movements can win for a dogmatizing number of generations in the Supreme Court, in our schools and universities, in the mass media, they may succeed in such a repression of revelation at its most critical moment—of a god-given identity at the moment of conception, no matter what the biological and social history of that identity may become—to create a world so new that abortion, infanticide for aesthetic reasons, [10] and institutionalized euthanasia of the aged will represent the logical consequences of the forces that fought the ascension of Judge Thomas to the Supreme Court through the agency of a messenger from precisely that world they aim to abolish: the world of faith from which Professor Hill announced she had come and to which she would return after Washington. Marriage and the family consequent upon marriage comprise the most widespread institutional setting and safeguard of the sacred self—that identity communicable only through social personality and mediating institutions including marriage, the family and the organizations of work, worship and play in which the sacred self, and the presiding presence over it, from its creation to any moment in its life history, has been read in works of art representing the interplay between the sacred and its surround of social selves.

The compelling drama of the Thomas hearings was in the implication that the stuff of the sacred self was somehow within reach through the sayings and showings on the television screen. The suggestion of memories of attempted seduction, awkward and self-defeating as any known in the history of comedy, pointed an implicit sociology sharpened, however unspoken, in the minds of what constituted the first spiritual congregation, the nation seated for what I shall call a public relation, in all American history. The comic turn of this public relation pointed toward a release from the constraints of sacred order in a seduction that did not take place and of a sexuality that was not enacted. Both non-events were referred to in a manner that can be considered comic because these non-events were observed as the gravest of offenses. A grave offense can only be, as the first gravedigger announced, *se offendendo* in an order that remains implicitly yet profoundly sacred. There can be no joke about those remains. The possibility of giving serious offense, the sexual against its sacred self, stuck, however unconsciously, in the minds not only of the smarter sets inside the Beltway but even more deeply among the millions outside. But the stickings were different. For the liberated classes, cultivating their faithlessness inside the Beltway, the hearings raised the specter of a limit to the doctrine that there is nothing sacred. For the millions outside the Beltway, the hearings depended upon an argument unmade: that feminism had invented a new kind of sacrality to be observed in the sanctuary of the work place.

As feminist ideology decreates the sanctified limits of sexuality, sexual harassment becomes more a matter of subtlety than substance. There are offenses given and known to be given. There are offenses not given yet taken. Without reference to objectively given commanding truths, as in the traditions out of Jerusalem, the public relation, otherwise unwitnessed and not self-evident, between an offense and an offense taken, remains undecidable. The benefit of the nation's doubt went rightly to Judge, now Justice, Thomas. For the nation to decide in favor of Professor Hill would have entailed the acceptance of the danger the nation at large recognized: the danger of a third world teleology of sexual desire divorced its purposes that, as if to confirm the doctrine of primordiality, makes the line between sexual pleasure and sexual harassment entirely dependent upon the woman's response as an offense even if it were not consciously given. That is a dangerous doctrine of *women/power*. The distance between reasonable feminists and the lunatic fringe is not so far after all. Both argue for a sexuality which is entirely primordial and contains, if any truth, a truth entirely subversive of the commanding truths. Many women are suspicious of this element in feminism, no matter how sympathetic they may be to the rational economic and status aims of the movement.

Paralleling the triune teleology of desire in our second worlds—courtship, marriage, children—is the lonely, self-referential ideology of the predator, which establishes the satisfaction of desire as his or her *solo fides*. There in the primordialism of sexual desire is the oppositional ideology rather than teleology that the feminist movement supports. Primordialism is an embedded ideology. The end of primordial sexuality is sexuality. Teleology is constituted by a dynamic of transcendence. Courtship, marriage, and children end beyond the primordiality of desire. It is not enough to want a child. To raise a child rightly requires a discipline well beyond the desire for it. An adolescent may desire a child as a mark of status, or as a piece of welfare insurance. The classical sense of having children in the traditions out of Jerusalem depends upon a continuity of service to the commanding truths, to that self which is the directive not-I of every I. Sexual egotism and child rearing do not live well together. In second cultures, the image of lover and beloved and the image of husband and wife are closely related. By contrast, in third cultures the primacy of sexuality has become the predicate for a promiscuity that has penetrated the doctrine of fidelity inseparable from marriage and moral continuity between the generations. Third culture vanguards believe, as an article of faith to be demonstrated empirically by a new kind of Kinsey Report, one that surveys the incidents of infidelity in the American family, that promiscuity is the rule and predation more subtle in the suburbs but not less frequent than in the urban underclass. Even if Professor Hill's ten-year old charges of promiscuous intentions are true, her motives come into question precisely as they play into the third culture assertion of a promiscuity nearing universality except among those held backward by the religion of fidelity Professor Hill claims embraces her warmly.

The Impossibility of the Feminist Doctrine of a Neutralized Work Place

Second world doctrines have always recognized the interpenetration, across the space between sacred orders and social, between those orders. Such symbolisms have made those recognitions canonical, as in the placing of what was probably, in its origins, Syrian erotic poetry into the canon of the Jews as the *Song of Songs*. The erotic will not be kept out of any place, work or other. Nor will the spiritual be kept out of the sexual. Third world doctrines of the autonomy of the spheres of life and, in particular, of the aesthetic as referring to the aesthetic, are defeated regularly by reality. One truth of our traditions out of Jerusalem was demonstrated powerfully yet again: the spheres of life that the vanguards of our third culture claim have achieved their self-referential autonomy—the erotic, the political, the economic, the public, the personal, the sacred totally separate and sealed on Sundays, or other appointed days, from the profane—are nothing like separate as those vanguards protest they are and must be.

Nadezhda Mandelstam understood that even the Freudian doctrine of "sublimation" as a cultural escape from the erotic is a nineteenth century avoidance of the sensuality complicit in cultural institutions. Writing of the close connection between love in all its manifestations, and of the art of poetry, Mrs. Mandelstam helps us understand the inadequacy of the doctrine of sublimation.

"The one thing I cannot conceive of and have never observed in any form is "sublimation." What gloomy German brooding in his study ever thought of this one! The actual work of producing poetry does indeed disturb the humdrum rhythm of love's physiological expression, but, then, it upsets the pattern of everything else as well—eating, drinking, sleeping, movement and rest—subordinating them all to the inner music, thereby heightening and magnifying the need for them. What does this have to do with sublimation, that is, the conversion of the sexual urge into spiritual activity?"[11]

The ubiquity of anti-sublimitory media, of which television is the most powerful current example, demonstrates a technology of temptation that opposes the fiction of the refinement of taste called sublimation. The vulgarity of contemporary idolatry on the tube requires, in response from second culture symbolists, the development of a more, not less, ascetic morality. Reversals of the media effect have scarcely entered the preparation of traditional second culture elite guiding cadres. J. F. Powers caught perfectly in his story, "Prince of Darkness," the carapace of indifference that conceals the deepest indifference of characters developed according to principles dominant in third culture comedies of existence. The confessor in the great dialogue following cannot comprehend the confessant. Mandelstam did not carry far enough into the bottomless of third culture character. Her analysis of the Freudian fiction of sublimation, which is in its third culture dynamic a psychologically polite concealment of the dominant indifference that J.F. Powers portrayed with the nearest perfection I know in a work of art. I begin the excerpt at the point at which Father Burner does not know this kind of third culture character, but, in the defunct authority of his office, believes he knows.

"How long since your last confession?"
"I don't know . . ."
"Have you been away from the Church?"
"Yes."

"Are you married?"
"Yes."
"To a Catholic?"
"No."
"Protestant?"
"No."
"Jew?"
"No."
"Atheist?"
"No—nothing."
"Were you married by a priest?"
"Yes."
"How long ago was that?"
"Four years."
"Any children?"
"No."
"Practice birth control?"
"Yes, sometimes."
"Don't you know it's a crime against nature and the Church forbids it?"
"Yes."
...
"And you've been away from the Church ever since your marriage?"
"Yes."
...
"What else?"
"I don't know ..."
"Is that what you came to confess?"
"No. Yes. I'm sorry, I'm afraid that's all."
"Do you have a problem?"
"I think that's all, Father ... I don't have a problem."[12]

No Problem: there is one of the great battle cries of third culture therapeutics as they aestheticize morality. The aesthetic resolution that therapeutic doctrine depends upon the carving out of autonomous spheres of life as the foundation of the moral pluralism that has succeeded, in its hegemony, the claims to truth of second culture institutions in the traditions out of Jerusalem. In those traditions, sacred order doctrines, whether Jewish or Christian reject third culture realities of autonomous spheres as they do the Freudian doctrine of sublimation. There is a continuity between going astray—i.e., leaving the true way—and whoring after something impermissible. Impermissibility is scarcely a problem in consumer societies, which express imperatives of desire as the god-term of primordiality established in third culture. Third world social orders, therefore, teach a morality of radical remissiveness. By contrast, in second world teachings, the first prohibition of the Decalogue suggests at once the supremacy of commanding truths in the interdictory mode and the ineffable presence of the erotic in the most commonplace spaces and times. *You shall have no other gods beside me.* Absolute fidelity parallels the logic of absolute promiscuity. In first cultures, the couplings of the chief god or gods were notorious. It may be worth noting that trinitarian doctrine, however else it may multiply the unitary godhead, no more allows remissive implications in the god-term itself than the original Jewish insistence upon oneness. At the outer fringes of the feminist movement, proposals of a female godhead, with Science as her implicit consort, can be read as parodies of the first commanding truth.

Parodies are to commands as comedies are to tragedies: forms of release from moralities. In the exquisitely complex battles that have raged during the second historic form of world *kulturkampf*, that not between Sinai and Baal, but between abolitionist anti-cultures and mediating cultures of *sacred/social* order, the profundities and shallows of the more recent form of conflict constitute anything but laughing matters. Because both protagonists in this case of *se offendendo* are committed figures of our second world, defending their sacred selves and its truths by lies dignified in their necessity by the profane context in which they were trapped, both acquired the aura of inaccessibility about their selves that led to such typical expressions of vexation as Senator Heflin's repeated "quandaries." Auras of inaccessibility gather whenever inner truth, what Kierkegaard called the god-relation, carries the consequence of isolation from those who have no relation and, therefore, "No Problem." Cosseted by their indifference, to the absence of such a relation, the indifferent appear appalled and baffled at the sense of isolation evident in every self-defense by self-offense. But self-offense, in the case illustrated, supplied the one alternative available to suicidal confession in an utterly profane precinct. The consubstantiality that informs every identity, *imago Dei* in its true and ineffable individuality of meaning is isolating enough. There was a double isolation recognizable in both Judge Thomas and Professor Hill. Opposing each other, their self-defenses, which implied reciprocal self-offenses, left them both with more in common with each other than with any of their interrogators. Tellings at once both truthful and untruthful—that *un* standing always and everywhere for the function of repression—baffles the third culture mind for which there is nothing, no being, there to repress. Sacred drama, at once hard as truth-telling and easy as lying, becomes far too complicated for third culture minds to use for their own purposes. They can no more use Clarence Thomas or Anita Hill than they can use Hamlet or other Shakespearean characters of sacred drama. The uses of Shakespeare, like the uses of the bible by the Senators, during the hearings, pointed to their foolishness. Our second world definition of a fool is that in his (or her) heart they say, with a conviction that excludes inwardness entirely, there is no God.

To be baffled by protagonists for whom God is very much a presiding presence gave both the tension of an ineliminable antagonism, not only between themselves but, even more important for the drama, between each of them and the Senators. So the public purpose was well served. Public life levels the vertical in authority. Sacred order grows more and more irrelevant to social order. Shakespeare had his clowns, in *As You Like It*, pun on this leveling. In life, so far as it appears a comedy rather than tragedy of existence, everything is only "so-so." To be so-so is to achieve that distance from both sacred order and social by which every identity recognizes and defends its isolation from every Other. No more succinct expression of being in between what can be abbreviated as *so/so* has yet appeared in English logology. Being so-so is both repressive and expressive of the distance that prevents all mergings of identities. For one of the few times in the history of modern culture, if ever before on the tube, some absurd political proceeding took on a depth that the public watched for the best of reasons: namely, the shallowness with which depths are probed by the small souls who have political power in this riven time. But, then, the consolation of living in any time is to think it riven.

The public sensed that the interfusing of the political and the sexual made a decision between the inviolate inwardnesses of Judge Thomas and Professor Hill both impossible and necessary. In that necessity of decision, the preponderant vote went to Judge Thomas, and rightly so. A life cannot be destroyed by memories of words, more or less precisely remembered, which introduced archetypal images of a black male boasting his phallic power in a way that turned Judge Thomas into a caricature of the black male as black panther. The public understood that no flesh, not even that of Moses, can pretend that it is turned to the stone upon which the commanding truths were written. "Thou shalt not" does not eliminate, no more than sublimations eliminate sexuality, expressions of the flesh so offensive that they may touch the identity of an Anita Hill even ten years on. The promised and implicit punishment in every such Not, throughout the second world canon, became explicit in Judge Thomas' sufferings, undubitable on camera and off. The subtlest element of public judgment for him may have been that he had already suffered his punishment and would be the better Justice for it. He did, with patent accuracy, say that he was a changed man. Who would not be changed, utterly, by the experience of having one's sacred self so assaulted in such publicity? The publicity itself represented a punishment incarnate that paralleled Anita Hill's implicit portrayal of herself as purity incarnate.

Earlier efforts at punishing Clarence Thomas were animated by his independence of mind as someone more than a 'race man', given to the party line mania of racialist dogma as it prevails, nowadays, among the black elite and its white camp followers. The magnificence of Judge Thomas' denials, their inflexible dignity, and the denunciations by which that dignity was delivered, made it clear as can be that he had become qualified, through this ordeal, to become an independent canonist of the semi-sacred writ we call the Constitution. He is likely to be a deeply experienced adjudicator of constitutional cases pivoting upon the *kulturkampf*. Judge Thomas achieved a personal authority that more than overcame his coached evasiveness during the original Committee inquiry into his qualifications.

For and against Professor Hill, it may be said that her acceptable denial of any "personal vendetta" does not exclude the patent yet implicit affirmation of an impersonal vendetta. Whatever her intentions, their objective consequence almost drowned in the mythology of the black phallic swaggerer a man about to be vested with the supreme juridical black gown of lawful authority in America. Professor Hill's intentions, magnified by the mass media, objectified the entire historico-mythic sight and sound medley of the sexually supercharged predator black male, his phallus the racially given super weapon of sex and race war against which the retreating armies out of Jerusalem draw their easily erased lines in the sand. At her saying of a few words, Professor Hill appeared to show the secret of Judge Thomas. The secret black predator sends chills of fear and thrills of envy through adolescent male white suburban America, rap-marketed successors to the freedom-forging Huck Finns and Tom Sawyers of small-town late Puritan America. Lou Reed, that post-Jewish, ex-druggie, gay activist, singing elder statesman of our third culture god-term, the primacy of possibility, teased his nation of youth with the anthem of that nation: *I Wanna be Black*. The black underclass is the most influential culture class in America. The classical mode of authority transferred is from the top down. Those in the lower reaches of a social order identify up. In our transitional age, from second culture to third, the transfer of authority is from the bottom up. So far as a cultural revolution is taking place, that revolution is carried by the transgressive lifestyle of the underclass. To be accused of the secret exercise of that lifestyle cannot be thought less than an effort at total destruction. Professor Hill's accusation associated Judge Thomas with black primal power mythology, even as it is now profitable titillation of white youth consumers. Some exploration of this state of the art revolutionary image in its historicity may be useful to the reader.

The black primal power figure represents a vernacular version of *se offendendo,* successfully brought off, as it is found in the earlier art and myth of Don Juan. Leporello's "score" aria, with its astonishing and admirable total score of 2,165 at the time of bass singing celebration and the humiliation of Donna Elvira—surely a case of sexual harassment as masterpiece—is scarcely matched by the record suggested by Judge Thomas. But the mythological implication is there, destructively, in Professor Hill's accusation. The mythological appeals, however implicit, do not end at the predator stalking the world woman. The world woman herself is presented as yet another and invulnerably Christian mythic image: the virgin martyr. Massinger's play, *The Virgin Martyr,* who is named Dorothea, carries the point, remade as it was by George Eliot in her character of Dorothea throughout *Middlemarch,* of the attraction felt by the virgin martyr for the figure of Angelo, in his office the representative of divine power. In *Measure for Measure,* Shakespeare did not allow Isabella to express anything but loathing for her own and Vienna's moralizing Angelo. Isabella is reserved for the Duke of dark corners, sacred power in secular office, Vincentio. (So a character of his office is Vincentio that he is never called by name but always by his office.) Saint Dorothea, as she was to become in Church hagiography, had a clearer eye, in the Massinger play, for the phallic aspect of the divinity that shapes our ends. A Roman aristocrat asks, rhetorically:

Antoninus: .... what object
                  Is her eye fix'd on?

Macrinus:	I see nothing.
Antoninus:	Mark her.
Dorothea:	Thou glorious minister of the Power I serve (For thou art more than mortal), is't for me Poor sinner, thou art pleased awhile to leave Thy heavenly habitation, and vouchsafest, Though glorified, to take my servant's habit? For, put off thy divinity, so look'd My lovely Angelo.
Angelo:	Know, I am the same; And still the servant to your piety.[13]

To suggest the *psychomachia* that accompanies her inwardness Dorothea remarks:

I am largely paid
For all my torments: since I find such grace,
Grant that the love of this young man to me,
In which he languistheth to death, may be
Changed to the love of heaven.[14]

Here is sublimation at its simplest, the decisive element of sublimity removed, as it is from the Freudian doctrine as well. Against the doctrine of sublimity, there is the sanctity of the old Law, to which Massinger, subordinate to a better playwright, Middelton, devoted a comedy titled *The Old Law*. In act one, scene one, the opening lines of *The Old Law* state the structure of second world sacred orders. However the incarnation is read, the predominant Christian forms of our second worlds have never denied the structure of commanding truths put so succinctly as Middleton and Massinger put it in the play of which the earliest transcription, as from a prompter's book, was published in a quarto of 1656. The passage quoted below should be read with a remembrance of the opening scene quoted from act five of *Hamlet*.

Enter Simonides and two Lawyers

Simonides:	Is the law firm, sir?
1ˢᵗ Lawyer:	The law! what more firm, sir, More powerful, forcible, or more permanent.[15]

Now the sound of the old law, renewed in the offices of every sacred self as Remembrancer, is drowned in the phallic swagger-sound of Rap. (So ubiquitous is that third culture deconversionist propaganda, broadcast by its appointed priesthood, the mass media managers, that I have heard that sound, drowning out the old law, even on the streets of Madrid.) To his everlasting credit, Judge Thomas refused to be drowned in that sound as it reverberated, however unconsciously, from the words of Professor Hill's counter-remembrance. Here, the black underclass counter-culture was being put into play objectively, whatever the subjective intentions of Professor Hill.

In his public vestment—repressive, juridical black conservative, crypto-Catholic and offending the primacy of possibility in all of us, daring to have offered the phrase "natural law" (that agency of divine law)—Judge Thomas is not what he is: the Power. In his attributed phallic secret swaggering, in pursuit of the virgin martyr invulnerable in her spiritual whiteness, Judge Thomas was accused of being secretly the phallic fighter of the Power.[16] Against this mythological unification of opposites, of which the very capitalist and very communist Jew was the latest fatal variation on the *very God/very man* motif of our predominant second world, Judge Thomas counter-attacked courageously and brilliantly. He would not be a real sacrifice to the Moloch of abortion while being made a fictive sacrifice to the Moloch of racism. There is the brilliance and precision of his widely criticized denunciation of the hearing as a "high-tech lynching." Given the *kulturkampf* raging in America over the right to sovereign and individual existence of the sacred self, Judge Thomas' denunciation of the "process" as a "high-tech lynching" formula for race war rather than color-blind constitutional justice was courageous and nothing less than the truth.[17] As a secret swaggerer, of which there was no evidence, Judge Thomas was set up for sacrifice to the abortion Moloch. Both god-terms, the abortionist Moloch and the racist, were brought into play against him. Between these two Molochs, there appeared no way out of the second culture accusation against him launched by third: *se offendendo*. This is the offense that third culture elites, in their armory of recycled *juridical/spiritual* offenses, cannot claim. For third culture vanguards no self is sacred. Professor Hill did her dignified dirty work in vain. Third culture selves are self-invented. In future time, as this drama drags into books and lectures, we shall see a distance opening like an abyss between Professor Hill's sacred self and the invented selves that are demanded of every third culture *hero/heroine*. In the age of the world picture, the television camera functions as the greatest instrument of encouragement toward self-invention.

It would take a mystical aesthetic to argue that the feminist movement has taught the men of the world a lesson in how irresistible the movement toward equality in the work place has become. That equality can be ordered only in a world within which second culture membership grasps the offense to be not merely a violation of the woman's sensibility, her physical being inseparable from that sensibility, but even more important, that the offense has been against highest authority in its commanding truths. It does not augur well for the relations between the sexes that the question of violation has been transformed so radically into a question of status equality in the work place. Under such political stress modern reality experiences a decreation of the sacred order to which violations must refer if they are to be treated seriously and rightly. But that treatment, which must include the reassertion of sacred order as a sanctity given to both men and women in their most intimate relations, is precisely what the feminist vanguard cannot entertain.

"We assume not to ourselves to impose upon any a public relation of their experiences."[18]

Near the close of the seventeenth century, the Puritan guiding elite of Cambridge, Massachusetts, lost a certain consensus that drove the institution of the public relation. They were deeply divided on the question of continuing the primitive Christian discipline of a spiritual inquiry into conduct and expression in the *via* that required public confession. That public confession was abandoned by the ministers of the wealthiest Puritans as they organized themselves as the "undertakers of the New Church."[19] The abjuring of any public relation constituted article five of a manifesto of relatively literal modesty on the part of that elite. How ironic that five years short of three hundred years later, a third world culture political elite should undertake that institution on world television, in an effort to pluck the mystery out of two Christians' hearts, as part of a "process" of borking Clarence Thomas. The loss of that sense of sin, of sacred self-offense, did not deter a third culture elite from reviving the public relation as an instrument of the intense political warfare that always accompanies an intensification of cultural warfare.

The effort to stop judge Thomas was a great event in the current history of cultural warfare in America. The internal and historical logic of that event called for a public confession of his wrong sayings ten years before to Professor Hill. Here we can read a secular version of the tradition of public confession and repentance originating in the Jewish Day of Atonement. The predicative public confession in second world traditions, made in the presence of the God who has created, in the *imago Dei,* that element in all of us free of all faults, takes the following form:

> For the sin we have committed against Thee by profaning thy name.
> For the sin we have committed against Thee by disrespect for parents and teachers.
> For the sin we have committed against Thee for speaking slander.
> For the sin we have committed against thee by dishonesty in our work.
> For all these, O God of mercy, forgive us, pardon us, grant us atonement...
> *Wash away my guilt ... for I know my transgressions and my sin is always beforeme...*[20]

I have excerpted from the larger liturgy of repentance by which the public relation in Israel is constituted to this day even in the liturgy of the largest and most nearly third culture of all Jewish constituencies, the Reform.

With the development of Christianity out of Israel, as the New Israel, confession was made to the Bishop, on the church steps or at the portal. In Latin Christendom, public confession precedes auricular confession. Public confession had its most powerful American expression in the Methodist institution of the Class, in which everything about everyone's conduct was subject to scrutiny and correction by everyone else in the Class. The "public relation," as it was called in Puritan New England, is a method of inquiry by a guiding elite trained for the purpose; it is an institution of control and moralization, preliminary to some form of penitential discipline or another, not least excommunication. Of the Kennedys, Metzenbaums, Bidens, Simons and Heflins—or, indeed, of any member of the political class—it may be asked: were they entitled by exemplary character and training to conduct the public relation? After all, they themselves are engaged in an art that is the least moral the world knows, the art of politics. It is not at all clear to what, if any, commanding truths or sacred order the inquisitors are covenanted. Political inquisitions, however they may use moral matters, inevitably become political theater.

Hill v. Thomas was political theater seen in its rarest case: political theater which defeated its own purposes. Such a self-defeat never occurred in Stalinist Russia during the show trials of which this was to be a liberal reproduction. Inquisitorial pressure is the functional equivalent of physical torture. Typologically, all such processes, whether at the totalitarian or liberal end of the *spectrum practicum,* call for the subject to serve the largest purpose by recognizing as actual what was possible. We were shown a pure example of the

technique when Chairman Biden insisted on asking the splendid ladies who testified to Judge Thomas' rectitude: "Is it possible there is
life on another planet?" Each in turn was required to say yes to the
possibility. The implicit consequence was a possible metamorphosed
into the actual of Judge Thomas' occasional secret sexual maunder-
ing. Granted the symbolism implicit in the logic of the process, Senator Biden might have asked, more precisely, "Is it possible there is
death on another planet?" The mythic or commandingly true doctrine of a saving sacrifice had been brought into play by Chairman
Biden's demand that each of Thomas' character witnesses say 'Yes'
to possibility as a registration in this instance as in the case to be
given in its physical fatality, immediately below. Judge Thomas was
to be immolated by a firestorm of feminist response to a possibility.

The master of the technique of possibility in third cultural history
was the great Andrei Vyshinsky. Solzhenitsyn reconstructed the spirit
of the inquiry into Judge Thomas' mystery in the passage following.
The Thomas figure in the dialogue is the communist leader being
prepared for his ultimate sacrifice to the Revolution, Nikolai
Bukharin:

> [Vyshinsky] We are required to concretize the eventuality: in the interest of discrediting
> for the future any idea of opposition, we are required to accept as *having taken place*
> what could only theoretically have taken place. And after all, it could have, couldn't it?
>
> [Bukarin] It could have.
>
> [Vyshinsky] And so it is necessary to recognize as actual what was possible; that's all.
> It's a small philosophical transition.[21]

The convention of seeking a confession of the possible as tantamount to the actual appears and disappears in proportion to the intensity of the struggle for the production of world reality.

As an implicit requirement of televised proceedings, in which con-
fessors and confessants each have their required roles to play, confession makes for even greater political theater than ever before in
political-religious history. If the actors are consummately talented or
profoundly persuaded, the two conditions one and the same when
the actor plays his part artistically enough, the strain of the
psychomachia may not show in any way parallel to the battle itself.
The inner war for a mastered reality need not parallel, in its disclosures, the outer. At stake here is the degree of success achieved by
the repression, Freud's third culture term for second and first culture
psychomachia as it is represented in the greatest of all sacred dra-

mas in English, *Hamlet*. In Hamlet's reference to the fighting, himself literally at sea, he senses in his soul the fighting by which he has been divided, inwardly.[22] Beyond the question of his parents, there is the more profoundly divisive parent question of humanity: does he take his being as belonging in sacred order and to its Master or does he not? That question is answered, for good or ill, by Hamlet's descendants in third culture history as negations, of their second culture creation.

The absence of detectable fighting in the souls of either Clarence Thomas or Anita Hill has drawn repeated remark. Less often remarked was the baffled serenity of one of the inquisitors, Senator Heflin. But the one remark I have read, by George Will, regarding that serenity is worth an entire library of comment on the serenity of consummate liars and the ease with which the liar demonstrates his capability. In cultures of commanding truths, the liar has successfully repressed his sacred self by the agency of one or another of his social selves. Heflin had lied in the very reason of vote against Bork. The reason was highly moral. The history of Bork's "life and his present lifestyle indicated a fondness for the unusual, the unconventional and the strange."[23] Though there is not a shred of evidence to support Senator Helfin's lie, the lie has stuck to Bork as a commonplace of journalistic memory. Writing some days before Thomas' triumph in the Senate, Will wanted to make certain that there was a record of Senator Heflin, as judge and liar. Will made masterly paraphrastic use of an old quip by Adlai Stevenson as follows: "If Heflin will quit telling lies about good people, I will quit telling the truth about him."[24] If my hypothesis of the connection between an absent *psychomachia* and a present virtuosity of lying is correct, then Edward Cardinal Kennedy giving his proleptic lie on Robert Bork's America is worth citing as a second specimen of such virtuosity. Kennedy prophesied that if Robert Bork were appointed to the Supreme Court, America would become

> a land in which women would be forced into back-alley abortions, blacks would sit at segregated lunch counters, rogue police could break down citizens doors in midnight raids, schoolchildren could not be taught about evolution, writers and artists could be censored at the whim of the government, and the doors of the federal courts would be shut on the fingers of millions of citizens for whom the judiciary is—and is often the only—protector of the individual rights that are the heart of our democracy.[25]

There is a hidden connection between a diagnosable absence of ambivalence and virtuoso lying, on the one hand, and fictive public relations, on the other. The connection never remains hidden. The deathwork drive against Judge Thomas was palpable. He himself long expected the "October surprise." The last moment of truth, as a secular parody of the last judgment, is, after all, a standard technique of third culture warfare. The notion of saying "God is my judge" is purest and largest specimen bull to third culture minds. Eschatological judgment has become public relation tactics.

Yet another technique, the threat tremendous, of third culture warfare should be remarked before I conclude displaying variations on the theme of *se offendendo*. The technique is of an eschatological promise of blood in the streets if the appointed public confessant is not declared guilty. The exemplum of that technique can be read as it was delivered by Professor Derrick Bell, of the Harvard Law School. With broadest irony he stated his conviction that Thomas was really a radical revolutionary rather than a conservative and strict constructionist. So Professor Bell remarked that Thomas "plans to use right-wing dogma to spark racial revolt, a revolt he evidently sees as a dangerous but urgently necessary response to this society's growing hostility to African Americans."[26] However stimulated, Professor Bell promised blood in the streets, racial warfare, if Thomas was appointed. Cultural struggle includes the implicit alternative of physical force. Character assassination has as its logical conclusion, in case of failure, assassination. As a playing out of a truth inseparable from the doctrine of *se offendendo,* the Thomas hearings might well become the object of serious literary study.

Notes

A note on the text: The present text was last edited by Philip Rieff on 28 April 1992 and was written before that time. It has been subsequently edited by Jonathan B. Imber, with several citations added and augmented.—*Ed.*

1.   Friedrich Nietzsche, *The Gay Science,* trans. W. Kaufmann, (New York: Vintage, 1974) bk. 1, sect. 1, pp. 73-74.
2.   *New York Times,* Oct. 12, 1999, p. 11.
3.   Nietzsche, *Gay Science*, bk. 5, sect. 356, pp. 302-4; Nietzsche's italics.
4.   See the Spanish church father Prudentius, "Psychomachia (The Fight for Mansoul)" in *Prudentius,* I, trans. H. J. Thomson (Cambridge, MA: Harvard University Press, 1949), pp. 274-343.
5.   *Hamlet,* III.ii.94-96.
6.   *Poetical Works of Robert Browning* (Edinburgh, 1907), p. 621.
7.   *Hamlet,* I.ii.81.
8.   *Measure for Measure*, II.ii.201-17.

9. See Nadezhda Mandelstam's *Hope Abandoned*, trans. Max Hayward (New York: Atheneum, 1974), ch. 29, pp. 266-283. See, too, Teresa Toranska's *"Them"*: *Stalin's Polish Puppets*, trans. Agnieszka Kolakowska (New York: Harper-Collins, 1987).

10. For the first world predicate of third world infanticide to come, see Aristotle's *Politics*, VII.xiv.10: "As to exposing or rearing the children born, let there be a law that no deformed child should be reared." (H. Rackham, trans., [London: Heinemann, 1932], p. 631.)

11. Nadezhda Mandelstam, *Hope Abandoned*, pp. 243-4.

12. J. F. Powers, "The Prince of Darkness," in *The Prince of Darkness and Other Stories* (Garden City, NY: Doubleday, 1947), pp. 266-7.

13. Massinger, *The Virgin Martyr*, IV.iii, in *The Plays of Philip Massinger*, ed. William Gifford [1805] (London: John Templeton, 1840), p. 26.

14. Ibid.

15. Massinger, *The Old Law*, I.i., in Gifford, *Plays of Philip Massinger*, p. 495.

16. One of the thrusts of Rap is to celebrate—and cash in on—the white *fear/envy* of the black phallic swagger.

17. There is an analogous truth, a geopolitical as well as religious parallel, in the struggle over the right to sovereign national existence of Israel, also raging in America, with Israel losing that war of words and images.

18. Herbert W. Schneider, *The Puritan Mind* (London: Constable, 1931), p. 89.

19. Ibid.

20. *Gates of Repentance, The New Union Prayerbook for the Days of Awe* (New York: Central Conference of American Rabbis 1984), pp. 327-31.

21. Aleksandr Solzhenitsyn, *The Gulag Archipelago,* I-II, trans. Thomas P. Whitney (New York: Harper & Row, 1973), p. 418.

22. *Hamlet*, V.ii.5-30.

23. Quoted by George Will in *Philadelphia Inquirer,* Saturday October 12, 1991.

24. Ibid.

25. Quoted in *National Review,* October 7, 1991, p. 55.

26. *New York Times,* September 9, 1991, p. A15.

Name Index

Mitchell, Richard, 123-24
Moats, Louisa C., 127
Montesquieu,Charles-Louis,de
    Secondat, Baron de, 243
Moore, Joan, xiv,
Morgan, Patricia, 175
Moses, 267
Mowlam, Marjorie, 34
Muhammad, Elijah, 7

Needham, Rodney, 53
Newman, Graeme, 178
Niebuhr, Reinhold, 9
Nietzsche, Friedrich, xxiii, xxiv, 72, 83,
    85, 245, 249, 250
Nisbet, Robert, xxiii
Nolan, Jr., James L., 5, 13, 17, 71
Noonan, Jr., John T., 54

O'Hear, Anthony, 180
Olivier, Laurence, 248
Orbach, Susie, 35
Orwell, George, xv,

Palmer, Craig, xvi,
Palmer, Stephen, 23
Parker, Woodrow M., 16
Parks, Rosa, 9
Patterson, Cecil H., 119-20, 127
Patton, Jean, 203
Paul, xxiv
Philo, xxiii
Piaget, Jean, 221
Plato, 243
Polier, Justine Wise, 191
Pound, Roscoe, 94
Powers, J.F., 264
Putnam, Robert, x, 137, 138, 147

Raths, Louis E., 221, 225
Ratzinger, Joseph Cardinal, xxv
Rauschenbusch, Walter, 9
Raymond, Louise, 195
Reed, Lou, 268
Reich, Wilhelm, 82
Reno, Janet, 91
Rheingold, Howard, 137
Rice, John Steadman, 33, 34, 72, 82-83
Richards, Graham, 36-37
Rieff, Philip, ix, x, xi, xii, xiii, xvi, xxii,
    xxiii-xxxi, 3-4, 5, 17, 70, 75, 79-80,
    81, 82, 83, 84, 85, 138, 139-40

Rimbaud, Arthur, 70
Robinson, Roosevelt, 103
Rogers, Carl, 16, 72, 113-14, 116, 118,
    119, 122, 123, 124, 127, 131
Rose, Henrietta, 45
Rose, Nikolas, 25, 27, 37, 41, 42
Rosnik, Jeff, 92
Rousseau, Jean-Jacques, 72, 155
Ryan, Kevin, 221
Rychlak, Joseph F.,179

Sacks, Harvey, 173
Sade, Marquis de, 259, 260
Samuel, 243
Samuels, Andrew, 34
Satel, Sally, 102
Schma, Judge,108
Schumpeter, Joseph, 73
Schwartz, John, 99, 100, 105-106, 107
Scott, Stephen, 30
Sennett, Richard, 41
Serrano, Andres, 250
Shakespeare, William, 241, 251, 255,
    267, 269
Shattuck, Roger, 84
Siegel, John P., 66, 67
Simmel, Georg, 147
Simon, Paul, 273
Simon, Sidney, 225
Simpson, Alan K., 247
Smith, Frank,125, 126, 127
Solzhenitsyn, Aleksandr, 274
Sommers, Christina Hoff, 218, 219
Specter, Arlen, 253
Spencer, Herbert, xii, xix
Spock, Benjamin, 199
Stalin, Josef, 251
Stewart, Jill, 128
Straw, Jack, 31, 32
Strickland, Diane, 107
Sue, Derald Wing, 16
Summerfeld, Derek, 19
Swanson, Guy, 167
Swet, Judge,105
Szasz, Thomas, ix, 42

Tatum, Beverly Daniel, 16
Tauber, Jeffrey, 98, 100, 101, 107
Taylor, Charles, 35, 44, 76
Theis, Sophie van Senden,196
Thomas, Clarence, 63, 64, 242, 243,
    244-48, 251, 252, 253, 254, 256, 258,